A Model of Prevention

A Model of Prevention

Life Lessons

David A. Hamburg, MD

For Bob —
A great educator,
inspiring leader and
authentic humanitarian.
One of the last things I
ever did at Stanford was
to steal you from Yale.
You greatly enhanced the
quality of our medical
school. I cherish our
enduring friendship.
With deep respect and
gratitude
Dave

Paradigm Publishers

Boulder • London

Published in the United States by Paradigm Publishers, 5589 Arapahoe Avenue, Boulder, CO 80303 USA.

Paradigm Publishers is the trade name of Birkenkamp & Company, LLC, Dean Birkenkamp, President and Publisher.

Library of Congress Cataloging-in-Publication Data

Hamburg, David A., 1925–
 A model of prevention : life lessons / David A. Hamburg.
   pages cm
 ISBN 978-1-61205-926-6 (pbk. : alk. paper)—ISBN 978-1-61205-928-0 (consumer ebook)
  1. Hamburg, David A., 1925– 2. Physicians—United States—Biography. 3. Psychiatrists—United States—Biography. I. Title.
 R154.H237A3 2015
 610.92—dc23
  [B]   2015003003

Printed and bound in the United States of America on acid-free paper that meets the standards of the American National Standard for Permanence of Paper for Printed Library Materials.

Designed and typeset by Straight Creek Bookmakers

19 18 17 16 15   1 2 3 4 5

Contents

Prologue

Why this book? For some years, I have been encouraged by friends, family, and professional collaborators to tell the story of my unusual experiences, which have taken different, unexpected, surprising turns, hopefully leading to fruitful experiences. I have declined until now because I was concerned that such a book might be inherently self-serving and possibly inaccurate. But as I have tested the waters, I found much more extensive contemporary records that make possible accurate recollections—the net effect being a set of very unusual opportunities, many totally unexpected and altogether reflecting the American spirit at its best. These materials include oral histories from several points in my career, conference summaries, interviews with key people, and personal experiences in highly stressful situations.

From childhood on, the central theme of my life has been the relief and above all the *prevention of human suffering* to the extent possible in light of best scientific evidence. This theme has been present in my adventures in an immigrant family in the early twentieth century, my attempts to find ways to help individual patients and then small groups, and in my efforts to prevent mass violence. The main organizing principle for such prevention has been learning from others: friends, family, scientists, scholars, practitioners of various kinds. Throughout these twists and turns of opportunity, there are basic themes, values, and approaches. I hope to make them clear in this book.

The issue is the extent to which the account of my adventures becomes self-serving beyond my actual desire. That is what held me back from writing this book for several years. But then I got feedback from people I respect highly who essentially urged me to include material showing that the work I had done is taken seriously by serious people, has been useful in difficult situations, and has been recognized and used by institutions of high caliber. There is an optimal range for this kind of material. The dilemma is that one needs to show that all this work done, and all these strange twists of fate, can provide useful lessons for others, can be built upon in future years for useful purposes—and yet not claim too much. As a professor at heart, I particularly think about gifted, dedicated young people in this context, hoping that my experiences may give them encouragement to pursue a *prevention agenda* of one sort or another and improve on what I have done.

I became aware of the increasing dangers, not only from diseases related to my early interest in medicine but also those related to the pervasive use of lethal weapons, the ultimate destructive power of weapons of mass destruction, terrorism, the risks of drastic climate change, and the dark side of information technology. Facing these dangers, I found myself searching for ways to help in coping with them, more and more looking toward *early* prevention of damage and the benefits of *sharing capacities* out of necessity for well-being. I have come to an emphasis on ways in which *prosocial orientations* could be developed on a universal basis *throughout the lifespan* and *across the world*—no easy task but an essential one and probably feasible, some steps being possible now or soon, others measured in decades and generations.

I have tried to make friends whose knowledge, experience, and skills could illuminate very difficult questions, and I made every effort to bring out the best in those who could make constructive contributions and see to it that they have opportunities and recognition for wisdom and accomplishments. We would have to face dangerous problems if we were going to make any contribution to Cold War issues. The board and staff had the courage to stick with me in this improbable exercise for fifteen years. And so have other institutions with which I was associated.

From an early notion of practicing medicine on an individual basis, and thus relieve suffering, I came to the stunning question of whether we can really learn better ways of living from the horrible casualties of World War I, World War II, the Holocaust, the Cold War, and recurrent terrorism. I make no claim that my experiences and reflections in this book have done a lot to answer these terribly difficult questions, but they have developed a point of view based on the best available evidence the world can provide, with emphasis on *prevention—earlier the better* and *sustained over time.*

This book is not a novel and not a textbook. I tried to select interesting stories from my voluminous experience and tell them accurately in a way that highlights the useful lessons I have learned. My fervent wish is that such lessons will be useful to others as well. Above all, I hope my adventures and recommendations will stimulate serious consideration and *generate better ideas.*

My work on human stress responses early in my career led gradually to my study of the particularly severe stresses of mass violence and my formulation of the *pillars of prevention of mass violence*: education for human survival; proactive help, including early preventive diplomacy; fostering indigenous democracy; building equitable socioeconomic development; promoting and protecting human rights; and major restraints on highly lethal weapons. There is great potential for preventing mass violence if such pillars are built early and applied to the *tensions* of human adaptations, especially *intergroup and international* differences.

Modern humanity is a single, interdependent, crowded, worldwide, weaponized species, vulnerable to pervasive stress from severe poverty, from harsh disparities, drastic climate events, destructive ideologies, and much more. So we must *cooperate in our own self-interest.* This should be *crucial in modern education, research, and public policy.* There is no illusion here that weapons and their use will soon go away. The inherent right of self-defense remains. But there are perspectives that open the way to cooperative efforts that diminish the various risks that are so apparent in 2015.

We must clarify *superordinate goals* and show how highly desired aims (e.g., avoidance of nuclear war or very lethal terrorism) can be achieved only by cooperation. This becomes feasible if we can mobilize the intellectual, technical, and moral strength over sufficient time to bring it about. We must formulate well-analyzed attitudes, norms, and patterns of behavior that bring us together in our *common humanity.* There is need for global understanding of the *paradox* that *advances in technology* are both beneficial through education and innovation but also exceedingly dangerous by fostering hatred, striving for the deadliest weapons, and promoting unbridled egocentric, ethnocentric behavior. We must clarify the *pillars of prevention*, make them *widely understood*, and strengthen institutional policies and practice paths to their *implementation*. My own *unexpected experiences* and *improbable opportunities* suggest ways in which we can at last *learn to live together amicably and fruitfully*.

CHAPTER 1

Early Influences

THE TWENTIETH CENTURY: A DIFFERENT WORLD

My father was born in 1900 and my mother a year or two later. They both lived in the twentieth century—a different world. They came from severely prejudiced Europe and landed in Evansville, Indiana—also a different world. My father's father came to this country within a year or two of my father's birth. My paternal grandfather came on his own, basically because of anti-Semitism in Russia, then controlling Latvia (they lived near Riga). He came from the culture of the shtetl—the small Jewish villages, holding together in the face of nasty pressure—to New York, a drastic and courageous change. He was very impatient, frustrated that a man with a pushcart couldn't make a living in New York quickly because there were too many others trying to do the same, so he went to Cincinnati where I think he had a cousin. He hoped to get established more quickly in Cincinnati and bring his family over. That also wasn't quick enough for him; he was a very dynamic, impatient man, not formally educated but very brilliant and adaptable. In fact, I find it mind-boggling to think of his adaptation, coming to this country, not knowing the language, all by himself, in New York, Cincinnati, and then downriver a couple hundred miles to Evansville, Indiana, where there was an ecological niche for him—no other pushcart peddlers, so he could start his business very quickly. And then he brought his wife and my father over, and he largely devoted the rest of his life to bringing relatives from Europe.

He brought my father and my father's mother within a year and then they stayed in Evansville and he kept on bringing people; he'd make a few bucks and he'd bring another relative. He brought fifty-some relatives over a period of years, stopped only by World War II. He lost everything in the Depression and had a brief hiatus, and then as soon as he began to make some money he again was bringing more. That and the synagogue were his two investments, family and synagogue, and so that was the context. We ended up with a large, cohesive family in Evansville because of his efforts.

He had a strong sense at that time of the necessary cohesion of the family. My grandfather's devotion to bringing all kinds of relatives, their devotion in turn to him, and this kind of support system of the family with open doors and easy accessibility in this relatively small community—all that was inspiring.

It was a very warm family with a great *sense of humor* and a *strong mutual-aid ethic*—all of which had lasting effects on me in both the content and process of my professional life. The Hamburg home was religious, but the emphasis was more on the historical and ethical aspects of Judaism than in the rituals. Although my grandfather helped to build the first synagogue in town and they attended regularly and observed all the holidays, they were not deeply Orthodox, and they were oriented to the human side of Judaism with strong emphasis on the ethical traditions. This became my outlook, too. This shows how early orientation, under favorable conditions, can have enduring effects.

My parents, when they were first married, set up housekeeping in Evansville, in a house near my grandparents' house. We lived at 304 East Virginia Street in a fairly tough industrial, working-class neighborhood. Evansville was a heavy industrial town at that time, and still is to some extent. We had around the corner from us my mother's sister, who had married a cousin of my father's—the two families, the Becker and Hamburg families, were quite intertwined—and so in that industrial neighborhood there was the immediate and vivid sense of family support and mutual aid—powerful influences. I was an only child. On the other hand, my mother's sister had wanted a son but had three daughters instead, so we became very close. It was almost as if there were four of us, the three daughters (Neecy, Shirley, and Debbie) and me, as functional siblings. So in a way I was an only child; in a way I wasn't. But that was the immediate family cohesion on the scene, and it was only a ten- or fifteen-minute drive to my grandparents' house. The early years were pleasant. These relationships linked us forever and the cluster of this family now lives in Los Angeles where they have been very close to our son Eric. I feel very close to them still and grateful for their kindness, encouragement, and tangible help wherever possible.

On the whole, I look back fondly on the *primary and secondary school years*. First of all, it was on a human scale; you really could know a lot of people and you could feel at home, you could know what was where and how to cope with a city of that size. Within the city there was the Jewish community, which wasn't physically delineated—we were spread through the city—but it was socially demarcated and we were close among ourselves. But both the scale of the Jewish community and the city as a whole were manageable and there was a sense of belonging. You would see people again and again and you had a sort of *mutual responsibility*; that was on the whole very positive. Moreover, there were dependable social support networks, mainly the family and, beyond the family, mainly the Jewish community, but also the surrounding school and neighborhood, and this was now not just Jewish community, it was more mixed, but people were mutually helpful, indeed felt an obligation to each other. So that kind of social support network was really very important. A town like that participated still in the traditional virtues (probably of millennia) of the small community with a mutual-aid ethic in which, if you behave according to reasonably well-defined ground rules, you'll be accepted and you'll have a chance to do well, moving toward peace and prosperity—but not easily. This orientation probably influenced my whole career. We perceived this orientation as an inherent asset of American society.

The overwhelming bulk of my experiences in Evansville was, as far as I could tell, free of overt anti-Semitism. I was conscious of it, I was alert to it, I'd been brought up not to be surprised by bias but not to have negative expectations—no chip on the shoulder.

We had a sense that you do have to adapt to the majority culture, we're few and they're many, we have to be sensitive to their outlook. But with that caveat, I would say that it was quite a remarkable experience of being taken as a person in my own right and being treated well and getting on well with others. I worked at the process of getting on well, there's no question about that.

Overall, I have very fond memories of the high school years and these have persisted to the present day. The students were generally friendly, considerate, and helpful. The day-to-day atmosphere was pleasant and there was a real sense of growing up together. The attachments formed in those years were reflected in the fact that class reunions were carried on for about half a century. I have persisting regret that I was only able to get to a few, but they were certainly rewarding. Charlie Haag, our great basketball player, was a strong unifying influence all the way through until his death a couple of years ago.

In 2000, I was given an honorary degree from the University of Southern Indiana, which did not even exist in my youth. I was lucky enough to get many honorary degrees, but this is one of three that stand out most vividly because it was my hometown and they made arrangements for the members of my high school class to sit together and to join me in a warm reunion. A few stand out in memory: Bob Oswald, who was one of my roommates throughout medical school and who practiced obstetrics in Evansville until his retirement, taking care of my relatives; another was Sam Clifford, who was a leader in the business and civic community of the city—and the first to call Wendall Wilkie to my attention, who turned out to be a very constructive internationalist working with FDR after losing a presidential election to him; and Janie Lou Harris, a person of warmth and enthusiasm. It was, however, very sad that some of my best friends from high school had died by the time of this very special occasion—for example, Pat Harding, a thoughtful relative of President Warren Harding. I have always felt warmly about my peers in high school and learned a lot about human relations from them.

Incidentally, my very first honorary degree came from my alma mater Indiana University, and it turned out my inspiring mentor Tracy Sonneborn was the instigator of it. How very gratifying that was. A third honorary degree of special significance was from Duke University in the final year of the presidency of Keith Brodie, who had been one of my bright young men at Stanford and who had moved very rapidly up the academic ladder from Stanford to Duke with a decade as president, succeeding the great Terry Sanford, who had been both governor of North Carolina and senator. In the course of my career I had a great deal of contact with Sanford and his positive feelings about Brodie meant a lot to me.

Now, back to high school, one of the most significant experiences of the high school years was the opportunity to write a weekly column for the high school paper. The scope of my interests must indeed have been broad since I gave it the title *Yesterday, Today and Tomorrow*. In the final column, I made some suggestions about future strengthening of the curriculum, particularly in the sciences and especially in behavioral science. Over many years, I kept in touch with the teacher John Boyd, an earnest, dedicated man who saw the newspaper as an important intellectual growth opportunity for the participants and a widely stimulating influence for the school.

Another highlight of the high school years was the debate team. In those days, there was a national debate competition and the team would drive together to whatever city was hosting the debate. This drew us closely together, and there was a great deal of intellectual stimulation in figuring out what positions we wanted to take, what we really believed, and how we could best present our arguments. We were also indebted to our debate coach, Betty Carlson, whose brother had been in high school with my father, and that was another bond.

COPING IN THE DEPRESSION

In the depth of the Depression, a high school friendship of my father's adolescence led him to getting a job in the courthouse. Jobs of all kinds were scarce. It didn't involve much money, but it was respectable, it was interesting, and it was public service, and my father always had a strong public service ethic. That in turn got him involved a bit in politics, which was novel for us, and he was an alternate delegate for the Democratic convention in 1932 that nominated Franklin Roosevelt in the depth of the Great Depression—and I remember that quite vividly. From then on, there was a certain interest in policy, politics, and public service in the family that influenced me. When some opportunities arose, I got involved later on, as we shall see.

There were lots of people out of work altogether—at least a third of the population. Moreover, my father's courthouse job was interesting and worthwhile, and it had led him into this political involvement, which he and I found quite fascinating. Our orientation, and that of our extended family, was to make the best of a bad situation. This outlook was helpful later, and contributed to my formulation of a stress and coping paradigm.

OVERVIEW: EXPANSION OF INTELLECTUAL CURIOSITY AND PROSPECTS FOR PREVENTION

Certainly my father and his side of the family had very strong intellectual curiosity. My father had lots of books. Even during the Depression, when he had minimal income, he would always add to his book collection. I've been the same way, only more so, throughout my life. My wife says that I don't understand that there are libraries. After the Andrew Carnegie connection, I understand there are libraries. But I think if a book is worth reading, it's worth having and underlining and writing in the margin and so on. Anyway, I'm sure I got that from my father. And in general, the impetus for higher education came from him. I recall how meaningful was the fact that he was the first member of his immigrant family to attend college, and he believed that knowledge could diminish human suffering.

The part of it that was totally unexpected was my turning on to science, and that came in college, with a busman's holiday. I was in college during World War II, headed toward becoming a doctor. The government wanted as many doctors as rapidly as possible. There was a speed-up program, and the army and the navy each had a program. I was in the army program, where they would pay for your education and, in turn, you would be available to be called up as a medical technician or, if necessary, called into active duty as a doctor as soon as possible. In that wartime speed-up program, I felt I was to some extent missing the richness of the university education, because I had to concentrate on the pre-med courses so strictly—good as they were—and I wanted very much to branch out. I did so when I could and will never forget the impact of my course in genetics with Tracy Sonneborn, who was one of the pioneers in modern genetics. It's become such a preeminent field now, but it wasn't then. Sonneborn was one of the people who made the transformation. In sensing the enthusiasm as well as the content of his work, I got turned on to science. It shows at a higher level, a more advanced level, what teaching can do. It changed my whole life.

It certainly influenced me, probably much more than I realized at the time. There was a great perplexity to it, because I perceived Germany as one of the most advanced and civilized countries in the world. If you wanted to do advanced work in medicine or in many of the sciences, you went to Germany. There was a great tradition in music and in many fields. So there was this enormous perplexity: How could a country that was in some ways so advanced be so incredibly barbaric in other ways? It's been a conundrum for me throughout my life. I studied some of the leading historians of Germany (e.g., Gordon Craig of Stanford and Fritz Stern of Columbia), in order to ask, could World War II and the Holocaust have been prevented? Much later, this became the spirit of our Carnegie mission on preventing deadly conflict. It led me to explore more deeply what did happen in Germany and some of the factors that were conducive to that awful turn of events. I wondered, if it could happen in Germany, could it happen anywhere? I simply couldn't believe that Germany was unique. It somehow was part of a human propensity that certain conditions would bring out, could bring to the surface. But it strongly influenced my interest in aggression, conflict, and conflict resolution, and heightened my awareness of the dangers of the historic paths of humanity, where I felt there had been so much slaughter that in the future we were going to have to find ways to deal with these tendencies. As a practical matter, the killing power would increase, and we'd simply destroy each other unless we could find better ways to deal with ubiquitous tendencies to human conflict.

How did this relate to basic mechanisms of stress responses? I had been turned on to science by genetics and I wanted to hold on to that if I could. I had gone through a transition of interest during the medical school years, from genetics—this was single-cell genetics—to cellular physiology, to general mammalian physiology, and then to behavior; from the then new molecular and cellular biology to the organismic biology of human adaptation. And as I got into the field, I was looking for some way to connect those, and eventually did. For whatever reason, I've always had a kind of broadly integrative turn of mind, wanting to draw together ideas and information from different sources, from different disciplines, and see if I could try to make a coherent picture.

Hans Selye's lecture at Yale in 1948 intrigued me very much because it proposed the question of whether psychological stress could have an impact on the adrenal gland. There was already a fair amount known about that with respect to one part of the adrenal gland—the adrenal medulla, which secretes adrenaline and another adrenaline-like hormone—but there was essentially nothing known about the other part of the adrenal gland—the adrenal cortex, which secretes corticosteroids such as cortisone, the cortisol type of hormone—which seemed biochemically quite independent. So we set out to investigate that, to see whether psychological stress in humans could stimulate both the adrenal cortex and medulla. I spent some years working on that sort of problem. It turned out, to my surprise, that there were not precise, reliable biochemical methods for measuring those hormones at the time. There were bioassays, which, although highly sensitive, were not so specific. So we spent years trying to get better methods on both the biochemical side and the psychological side to measure quantitatively different reactions to stress, first doing it in naturally occurring circumstances and then in experimental situations, and eventually demonstrating beyond a shadow of a doubt that the adrenal gland in both of its parts, the medulla and the cortex, responds strongly to psychological stress in humans.

Along the way, we made what was one of the most striking discoveries I was ever associated with in my career: the adrenal cortex also responded very powerfully when people were *depressed*, even if they were sitting, huddled, not moving (in psychomotor retardation as the jargon went at the time), where you'd think it's almost like hibernation. But the alarm systems of the body were clearly responding physiologically, biochemically, under those conditions. It was counterintuitive. We actually repeated it in a different way before we published any of it, because we didn't trust our own findings. The prevailing conventional wisdom at the time was that, if anything, the alarm responses were dampened in that kind of depression. But it turned out that regardless of whether the person was overtly agitated, the depressive emotion was associated with the powerful stimulation of the adrenal cortex. In all of this work we were greatly energized by a young first-year psychiatry chairman at Yale, Fritz Redlich, a refugee from the Holocaust. He became a close, permanent friend, indeed an inspiration forever.

A lot of very good people have worked over several decades in elaborating and tracking down the implications of that advanced discovery. The technical capacity to evaluate these systems has improved enormously since we made the discovery in the 1950s. Basically, it wouldn't be too much to say it's now just a matter of filling in details—very important details, but the fundamental fact of the alarm systems being mobilized in depression, as well as other conditions of emotional distress, was something that we were able to establish. It was an exciting time, and I did some of that work in several different places over a couple of decades, with a variety of colleagues. It was all interdisciplinary collaborative work, but I perhaps provided a certain intellectual spark and cohesiveness. One of the things that I've always enjoyed doing was to elicit cooperation from people who bring different skills to the table, and getting a good collaborative enterprise going where people work together to get around the contours of a complex problem in a way that no individual could do alone.

What were the psychological mechanisms by which people could come to terms with life-threatening situations or otherwise highly stressful situations? I became engaged in answering that question over several decades, and I think it had some interest for people in the psychoanalytic field, particularly those concerned with what was called ego psychology, but it had broad significance not only for psychiatry but also for pediatrics, various other parts of medicine, and eventually in public health.

The series of coping studies on really life-threatening situations dealt with powerful human experiences—indeed, many of the patients died—including severely burned patients in the Korean War; and then later patients with severe polio before the vaccine; and then later studies of the families of children with leukemia at a time when leukemia was a uniformly fatal disease. Ironically, Jonas Salk's polio vaccine became available when we were providing care and doing coping studies on polio patients in iron lungs. It was a poignant circumstance that illustrated the power of prevention in the ensuing years.

CHAPTER 2

The Wider World and Wartime Experiences

INDIANA UNIVERSITY: MOVING INTO THE WIDER WORLD, UNDERGRADUATE AND MEDICAL SCHOOL

Indiana University was a lovely, traditional campus, very attractive aesthetically. I had a sense of wonderment about all of the scholars and the scientists and the laboratories and the opportunities. I also felt absolutely inadequate. I remember being extremely apprehensive as to whether I could really make it and they all seemed like geniuses to me. Bear in mind, they were older and I was coming from a small town, not a very cultured place, and my image was that these people all came from much stronger backgrounds and they were knowledgeable. Also, I had goofed off a lot in high school. My father used to be very troubled that I was able to get through and do well in high school without doing much work. And so I was terribly apprehensive that I didn't have the right work habits, didn't have the right background, I was in with all these geniuses, and could I really get through? So I really buckled down and worked very, very hard, and John Mason was considerably helpful. He had more confidence about such things, and he had more aptitude in laboratory work than I did. On the other hand, I was helpful to him in some other ways, such as friendship patterns and social life. So we had a real *mutual-aid ethic* between us, and at the end of that first year I realized I had done well and that I could function, and then I could enjoy the rest of it more. Although it was a wartime speed-up program and it was very heavily concentrated on pre-medical courses, at least I had the sense that I could do it, that I could master it and could take advantage of the very rich intellectual fare that the university offered. I went directly into the pre-med program in keeping with wartime requirements.

There were some opportunities to explore, and an extremely important, formative experience occurred, in the semester after I had completed the pre-med requirements. They were packed into a couple of years, and it was like almost four years packed into two. But I finished the pre-med requirements and I could take one semester of other courses, and one of those was a seminar in creative writing that I enjoyed. I'd written some short stories, which was great fun, and it helped me in all subsequent writing. I had a very helpful creative writing professor, Ralph Collins, who later had a building named for him. He encouraged me to read and write beyond prior experience. That gave me a chance to read modern American novels, Dos Passos, Wolfe, Steinbeck, Faulkner, Farrell, and others, which I found extremely interesting.

But the big thing, a sort of busman's holiday, was that I took a science course. After all that science for the pre-med requirements, during which I'd sort of held my nose and gone under for two years, day and night with pre-med and army drills. But I had heard about a truly great professor named Tracy Sonneborn, and taking his course was one of the most formative experiences in my whole life. All I knew was that Sonneborn was a good teacher who was teaching the science of heredity, which was not highly developed as a science at that time. But it seemed fascinating; there was something weird about how a son could look a lot like a father or have characteristics like a father. How was it that these characteristics could be transmitted so faithfully from one generation to the next and how could the complexity of the human organism come about from generation to generation? So there was a great curiosity about that and I took his course and little did I know the effect it would have. I have recently learned to my delight that Indiana University has established an endowment in his name.

Sonneborn was a tremendous teacher, a very charismatic person, and he taught in terms of open-minded inquiry, a lot of it around his own research and related research. So it was asking questions, formulating problems, trying to think about an approach to the problem, how you could get at it and how the data would unfold, and false leads and paths you could go down that were blind alleys. So, the way he taught the course was like an unfolding mystery story, and you got caught up in the mode of inquiry that character-izes the sciences: not a rigid style of inquiry, but open-minded problem solving, and from that day to this it's been a kind of central organizing principle for my life.

I had a vaguely formulated image of my future—perhaps I would go into medicine and probably go back to Evansville to practice or maybe stay in Indianapolis to practice or conceivably even go to Chicago, I wasn't clear, but I would practice medicine, and maybe some kind of connection with a university if possible. Sonneborn really turned me on to science, and everything was different after that.

There were a couple of odd experiences in that period that are just amusing but are worth telling. One was that Sonneborn's course was very difficult; in addition to other things, it had a good deal of mathematics in dealing with population genetics, and I worked very hard and thought I was doing well. The custom was they'd send out postcards on progress at midterm. Also, we were seated alphabetically in the classrooms; everything was very old-fashioned. But I had gotten straight As through college up to that point, to my surprise and delight and certainly to my parents' delight, and had in fact made Phi Beta Kappa in my junior year, which was one of my parents' dreams fulfilled. Now a shock: the midterm card in genetics was a "smoke up"—that is, I was failing genetics. Here was the course I loved and a man I was so devoted to, though I didn't really know him as an individual, and I was stunned. On the next class day, there was a big football player sitting next to me. And he had always been complaining it was too hard for him, he didn't know what he was doing, he shouldn't have got into the course, and he said to me he was absolutely amazed and delighted he'd gotten an A, couldn't believe he'd gotten an A. Then the light went on in my head, there must have been a clerical error, I'd gotten his F and he'd gotten my A. Now I was also a football fan, I didn't want to get him flunked out; I didn't want him to beat me up either, as he was a powerful fellow. For twenty-four hours or so, I tried to figure out what should I do about it, and then finally this brilliant insight occurred to me: I didn't have to involve him at all. I simply could go to Sonneborn and say I thought I was doing pretty well, I was very surprised to get this F, could he check the records and see if it might have been a clerical error and, if it wasn't an error, could he give me guidance because I loved the course. So it turned out, he was covered with shame. He saw that I should have had an A instead of an F, and then took me under his wing. *The personal relationship was formed out of this clerical error.* That was halfway through the course.

At the end of the course, another bizarre thing occurred. A friend of mine named Ed Berman, whose father was a professor of surgery in Indianapolis at the medical school, was frightened to death. He'd gone to the library to get the previous year's examination. He came to my house the night before the exam in a panic, said it was a terribly difficult exam; I looked it over, and it was terribly difficult. So I offered to study with him, all night if necessary. But he was so anxious that he did as anxious people often do: he had to attach to a concrete symbol of the problem and it was the previous year's exam; he insisted that we work the problems from it, and I simply couldn't talk him out of this. I was distressed because I was very doubtful that the same exam would be given again. We ended up spending all night working those extremely difficult problems together, had about an hour's nap, and went into the exam. I felt just terrible. To my utter astonishment, the problems were the same, it was the same exam, and I did spectacularly well on it. So well that Sonneborn called me in to congratulate me and say nobody had ever done so well on this exam, and I felt I must explain to him what happened, I had to be honest about it. So again I reinforced our relationship. Funny, the twists of fate that made for a close relationship with Sonneborn that continued until he died. He had done a great deal to advance the emerging field of genetics, particularly for Indiana University. Some years later, he provided the impetus for me to get an honorary degree from Indiana University.

My good wife Betty, who is a very wise person, says it's good to be smart and it's good to be nice and honest and resourceful; it's also good to be lucky. Very good to be lucky.

On the social side of the university experience, I had an objection in principle to fraternities, although there were some Jewish ones on campus. But I felt that they basically were beer-guzzling, time-wasting enterprises.

John Mason and I felt the whole arrangement was a kind of institutionalized prejudice—beneath the dignity of a great university. Mason, who was not Jewish, didn't join a fraternity. He was courted by the high-prestige ones but didn't join, so we stayed together happily, with long-term mutual aid.

As for social life, I sort of went underwater that first year and didn't come up again until I knew that I could do all right academically. I remember I was very intrigued that a girl I'd known in Evansville in high school, somewhat older than I was, somewhat more mature and very attractive to me, asked me what I was doing in the middle of the first year and I told her and she said, "Well, when you decide to come up from underwater, please call me." So I did at the end of the first year, and then I became pretty active socially from there on. I had a little problem about it because I had grown up younger than everybody else (skipping grades) and I felt less socially mature than the others and I had to feel my way around that, but my social life was okay after that fright of the first year.

Extracurricular activities were fewer than I would have wished. One of the odd jobs that was most delightful was ushering for concerts, because I got into the concerts free. But I didn't do much outside work or extracurricular activity; I really did concentrate on the studies, as it was a very intensive program with this speed-up because of the wartime. When I got into medical school, I was taken straightaway into the army. We all were in uniform and we drilled, we'd get up at five o'clock in the morning and we'd have drills before classes. The idea was that we'd be available on short notice should we be needed as medical technicians or whatever. The army wanted us to complete medical school and come into service as doctors, but we knew that we were available to be called sooner if it came to that. So again it intensified the academic speed-up to get through as soon as possible; everything was compressed. We lived in a dormitory, a kind of barracks, and there was a lot of camaraderie. But it also meant that there was extremely little time for extracurricular activities. So the army played a prominent role in my college education.

At IU, the first part of my studies took place in Bloomington for basic sciences, and then I moved to Indianapolis for the clinical years. These were intense, stimulating, exhausting years. Then came the end of the war and that incredible jubilation. I person-ally had a sense always of great risk and vulnerability about the war as to whether Hitler would win in the end; the early setbacks in the first part of the war were very painful. It was hard to grasp the culmination of it—to actually know the war was over was, to me, almost beyond imagination, and I do remember the vividness of that joy, first with V-E Day and then with V-J Day, and it did bring a sense of immense hope and possibility. I guess we shared a lot of illusions about how perfect the world could become with Hitler defeated, with the United States out in the world now, creating possibilities for democracy spreading throughout the world and the end of the colonial era and all that. There was a sense of very, very high hopes. I shared the joy with a dear, kind, compassionate friend, Mita Petcoff (later Markland), who served in the women's part of the navy and gave me great encouragement in those difficult years.

There had been some transitional points in my development that are worth noting briefly. I had been very excited about the then newly emerging science of genetics through Sonneborn, and I think that, had it not been for the war, it's very likely I would have gone into genetics, probably shifted to a PhD program in genetics and stayed with that. But it wasn't a feasible proposition because of the war, and in any event I was strongly oriented to medicine and so I don't know how it would have come out. But that was a transition. When I got to the medical school there was a very good professor teaching cellular physiology, which was related to the biology of single-cell organisms that I'd studied with Sonneborn. Then that cellular physiology led to the physiology of the whole organism, the functioning of mammals, and of course particularly humans. So I went from genetics to cell biology to mammalian physiology and I thought that I would probably go into endocrinology and study the way the hormones are involved in coordinating the cells of the body.

I wrote in my high school newspaper column about certain gaps in the high school curriculum, one of which was psychology. I relate that insight back to aspects of my family and perhaps to certain aspects of the Jewish experience. I had vivid curiosity about how such terrible things could happen, like the Holocaust, or, even before the Holocaust, the pervasiveness of anti-Semitism. Issues of blame and scapegoating in human behavior— how was it that people could so easily be roused to hatred and violence? It didn't make sense to me how to square the good side of human nature with the bad side of human nature.

There was one important episode in the family that came somewhat later when I was in college. An aunt of mine in Chicago committed suicide, and I even wrote a short story or a piece of a novel about it that was sort of a roman à clef. It was an attempt on a fictional basis to make a plausible explanation of how she might have come to suicide, and that was an effort from a writer's standpoint, an amateur writer's standpoint, to think about human motivation and emotions and human relationships, and it may be that that experience was a significant precursor to the impact of Freud on me. In retrospect, I guess that my aunt had bipolar disease (manic-depressive), since the symptoms now seem clear in that context. My lost aunt was a person of high intellect, strong energy, and deep compassion, and she gave me much encouragement as well as kindness. It was a shock for the family. Why? Freud was trying to understand motivations and emotions and human relationships and to put them all in the context of development during childhood and adolescence. Freud's work on formative influences was very congenial to me from the family standpoint and culturally.

I was always looking for ways to connect various streams of interest—from cellular to psychosocial—and to a certain extent was able to do so over the years. The way it came about was the following. I decided that I would go into psychiatry and, now with the impetus from Sonneborn and consistent certainly with my father's values, that I would try to help develop the scientific side of the field, and I thought that in some way or another the psychoanalytic ideas ought to be related to what was going on within the body. Of course Freud had thought that, too, with a nineteenth-century biology scheme.

FROM IU TO MICHAEL REESE TO YALE

When I learned of President Roosevelt's death in 1945, my parents were visiting with me in Indianapolis, I was in medical school at wartime, and we had that same experience that the nation had of being stunned and shocked, in a state of disbelief. This man was an institution, he was almost a religion, and it was impossible to grasp that he was gone. It was a great sense of loss, of bereavement. So, too, our love for his extraordinary wife, Eleanor. My wife Betty had gotten to know Eleanor in college, when the first lady was on the Vassar Board and took a liking to Betty—who years later passed to her granddaughter Rachel an invitation to tea from Eleanor.

In general we felt extremely fortunate that Roosevelt seemed to be aware early of the danger of the Nazis and in general friendly to Jews in his administration, in the country at large as well as in Europe—reinforced strongly by Eleanor Roosevelt. So we really had a sense of his being a benefactor on a large scale. When the questions arose about possible anti-Semitism, my father's reaction was that Roosevelt probably made as reasonable a political calculation as he could given the difficulty of the circumstance, that he was trying to bring the United States into the war if necessary, or at least be ready to come into the war, to somehow find a way to cope with Hitler, which was an extremely difficult thing to do in a fundamentally isolationist country. There was certainly a sense with the Roosevelt administration of the pride that Jews were playing an active and constructive role in the government and that he seemed to have respect for ability across the board including Jews—for example, Secretary of the Treasury Morgenthau.

One particularly traumatic experience I had was with a friend of mine named Jerome Ennis from New York, who died in 2014 while still practicing in New York. Ennis came from New York to Bloomington and we were in school together, we became friends; a very bright student, he made Phi Beta Kappa, and it was clear this was a person of outstanding ability. He applied in his junior year to fifty-some medical schools and was turned down by all, though he was obviously superbly qualified. Lots of people less qualified, non-Jewish, were being accepted to the same schools, and in some places they told him quite candidly, "Look, we'd like to take you, but we have a Jewish quota, and you're from New York. We have so many applications from Jews from New York who are outstanding, even more outstanding than you; we just can't take you, we're very sorry." I did everything in my power to help with encouragement, sustain morale, and consider strategies to improve his chances. And he made a second round with determination and finally, after another some fifty applications, was admitted to Indiana University for medical school as kind of a native son—not a native of Indiana but having gone to the school—and ultimately did go through medical school there. But that experience was vivid. Many schools had Jewish quotas.

Once the barriers were down in the postwar years, Jews came flooding into the field, and not only in medicine but in much of science you see a transformation. In a later stage of my career, I was on the faculty at Stanford University. Stanford had had a reputation for being anti-Semitic for a long time. When Wally Sterling became president of Stanford he was determined to build it into a world-class university and to do that on the basis of merit, and when he did that, the faculty changed in a matter of a decade, from having very few Jews to having a high percentage, and they made major contributions in science especially. Once you started going on merit and accomplishment alone, Jews did excel, and to that extent it confirmed the apprehensions that some biased people had had about what would happen if you let the barriers down.

I think it's enormously important to have the full diversity of the nation represented in every field of activity, not by precise quotas but with a serious and systematic program to see to it that people do get qualified and to provide the conditions under which they can develop the ability and can earn their way into the school and beyond. That may take some special facilitation at certain points, but the facilitation has got to be on real, solid accomplishment, and you can do that, but you have to compensate in certain cases for deficiencies in early experience.

Jews have done so well because of the very high premium placed on *learning* as part of Jewish culture. However that may have arisen, it was certainly quite manifest in my own family. There was strong encouragement and positive social reinforcement for working hard at the process of learning and scholarship. Implicit in that is the coherence of the family and its commitment to the value of education. You hang in there through the tedious parts and the aggravating parts because, in the long run, to be an educated person is of inestimable value. So all of that was beneficial with respect to the progress of Jews in education generally and science in particular. But when it comes to medicine, I think there was also a special premium on health. The doctor was an immensely esteemed figure in any Jewish community that I'm familiar with. Again, I don't know the history of how that came about, but there was a pragmatic belief that if you made the best use of the available talent in medicine it would be a good thing for the Jews, and so you had the extra value placed on health that certainly steered a number of us toward medicine who might possibly have gone into other fields.

There are individual talents, for example in mathematics, athletics, music, whatever, that must be influenced by genetic factors. But even if the genetic capability is there, it certainly helps if there are favorable environmental conditions to recognize the talent, foster it, and bring it out, and I think in a number of areas we Jews had that going for us, once we were able to move past the high barriers. I think that is one value I have pursued in my career and one reason there are so many friends who still remain appreciative—look for talent, recognize it, encourage it, bring out the best in others. On the other hand, if that talent is being expressed in a direction that isn't constructive from a historical point of view or is seen as very impractical in terms of current conditions, then you may get into conflicts about it. My own experience was that one of the strong values is to recognize talent early and foster it, to view individual excellence over a wide range of fields as intrinsically worthwhile. Do what you can to bring out the best in people with clear potential—intellectually, emotionally, interpersonally.

I think there was always a pragmatic tendency to take into account where there might be openings, what the culture would permit. There was a show at the Jewish Museum of New York a few years ago about the history of the Jews in Russia over the past several centuries, and you got a very clear sense that the Jews recognized that certain pathways were simply not open and they would have to concentrate pretty heavily on the few pathways that were open.

In the civil rights period of the 1960s, our wonderful Rabbi Axelrad of the Stanford community went to the South with other clergymen to work for equal opportunities. My son Eric and I were identified with him, as were many Stanford students. I had the privilege of speaking at the first lecture given in his honor.

AN IMPROBABLE MARRIAGE:
CREATIVE AND PRODUCTIVE

An important person in my life from medical school onward was Roy Grinker, who had been a professor of neurology at the University of Chicago and then the chief of air force psychiatry during World War II. He did ingenious work and together with John Spiegel wrote a classic book, *Men Under Stress*. This was an inspiration to me and so I went to Michael Reese Hospital in Chicago for my internship upon graduating from medical school in 1947. I had a very stimulating experience with Grinker during 1947–1948. The following year, because Grinker's slots for eligibility were filled, I went to start a residency in psychiatry at Yale. Grinker helped me get into a new program there that was very exciting, headed by a man named Fritz Redlich, who later became dean of Yale Medical School and a very important mentor for me. Betty and I often referred to him as our matchmaker. And I went there, but with the understanding that I would come back with Grinker in a year, and that's what I did. I went to Yale, had a marvelous, stimulating year, including meeting Betty, my wife-to-be, who was also in training in psychiatry. She had just graduated from Yale Medical School a short while before, and then we got really torn about whether to stay at Yale. Redlich very much wanted us to stay there, and we liked Yale, but I had fundamentally made a commitment to Grinker that I would come back at the first opportunity. I then persuaded

Betty to follow me out to the Midwest, and so, after a wonderful year at Yale, one that influenced the whole rest of my career, I came back to Chicago and continued my graduate work in psychiatry.

My wife's father had been a surgeon who actually died while operating when she was very young, and she had only a very vague memory of him, though he was an important family legend because he was apparently a brilliant man and a very successful and respected surgeon. Her mother was a schoolteacher and also a very gifted person; she was a cellist and later in life she studied law. She was always studying something else, she had an insatiable curiosity, and enjoyed getting new skills and new hobbies and what have you. So both of Betty's parents were very gifted, but the father was kind of the family legend and I think that had a lot of bearing on Betty's decision to go into medicine and her mother encouraged her to do that. She was a very good student. She grew up in the New York area, went to Vassar as an undergraduate, and then to Yale Medical School, which she had just finished. She had already decided that she wanted to do child psychiatry, pediatrics, and general child health and development, so she was taking her groundwork in general psychiatry, as was I, but her intention was to then specialize in the child mission, which she did. So we had from the beginning a high degree of complementarity in our interests and we were able to share a lot, which we have to this day.

I didn't have a lot of knowledge of my family history, but a pertinent part of it for my own family was that she wasn't Jewish and so we had to work that through with my parents. I had always vaguely expected, as had my parents, that my wife would be Jewish, and it was difficult for them, particularly my mother. They were very devoted to Betty, had enormous respect for her, and in time they worked it through, but it was a difficult thing. And Betty, I think to her great credit, agreed to convert to Judaism. She wasn't a religious person in any event, but she knew it meant so much to my parents that she did convert and we were married by a rabbi and were moderately observant Jews—not as much as my mother would have wished, but enough for all normal purposes.

Betty had been widely respected and honored as a pioneer, personally and professionally. Her family background was Irish and African. In those days, a few African genes posed a formidable barrier. She was the first with such a background to attend Vassar College (where she was "adopted" by Eleanor Roosevelt) and the first woman to graduate from Yale Medical School. Later, she was a pioneer in helping to create the field of adolescent health and within that to create peer-mediated interventions, which have since spread over much of the world.

After a second year in psychiatry, during which Betty was in Cincinnati at the Children's Hospital there—a superb place with people like Albert Sabin (a pioneer in the polio vaccine) and Katherine Dodd on the faculty—and we were seeing each other as often as we could, suddenly the Korean War broke out. As a matter of fact, I had gone down to Cincinnati to collect Betty and bring her to Chicago, where she was going to join me at the end of the year and continue her professional work in Chicago so that we'd be together. We were driving back and heard the news of the invasion of South Korea by North Korea. I was still in the army post–World War II and got called up promptly. So the next thing I knew, I was sent down to San Antonio, Texas, as an army doctor in the Brooke Army Hospital, and Betty had a contract in Chicago and she had to remain there for a year. I was on alert to go to Korea at any time and she was prepared, if need be, to meet me in

San Francisco or Las Vegas or wherever to get married so that she could come at least as far as Japan; the army would bring my wife as far as Japan if I got sent to Korea. As it turned out, I made myself "indispensable" and I didn't get sent to Korea, but the medical experiences of the war in San Antonio and later in Washington, DC, were unforgettable and invaluable. Betty finally completed that year in Chicago and then came and joined me in San Antonio, where we were married.

The San Antonio experience was very fascinating, difficult, and creative. I was upset to be ripped out of my training before it was complete and to be separated from Betty at a time when we'd just had a reunion and were planning our marriage. Roy Grinker said to me that his own experience in World War II had been professionally valuable: you could learn a great deal if you took a constructive attitude, you could turn it to advantage, you could do some good things for a lot of people, and you could deepen your capabilities in your professional work. "Don't feel sorry for yourself," he said. I took that very seriously and found that he was right.

Several things happened in San Antonio. One was that I had gotten increasingly interested in human stress responses, partly from reading Grinker and others, their work during World War II, and partly from observations I made in my internship and residency years, and particularly while at Yale I saw an opportunity to make this connection I wanted to make between psychology and biology.

Hans Selye's brilliant 1948 lecture had a strong effect on Betty and me. His research was essentially on the biology of stress and the effect of stress on the adrenal gland. I began to think of ways in which we could study that, not in rats but in people. And I was actually planning to do that. I began the planning in New Haven, continued it in Chicago with Grinker and his colleagues there, and had an approach. I had written a paper already at Yale in 1948, which was a seminal paper because it influenced not only me but several of my colleagues in the future to pursue this line of inquiry, to relate psychological stress to the functioning of the adrenal gland and other glands, and later to relate psychological stress to the functioning of the cardiovascular system as well. In San Antonio I began to see ways to do that.

We were getting soldiers flown back from Korea, in very large hospital planes that were used to transport casualties, who had been through terrifically stressful experiences, sort of explosive experiences, psychiatric casualties. It was deeply moving for me. And so I started to find ways to set up a research project in which we could study the correlation of their emotional distress with their endocrine function. And to do that, I got a colleague interested, a pathologist interested in making the biological measurements while I made the psychological measurements. And then, by a great piece of luck, my closest friend throughout high school, college, and medical school, John Mason, was assigned to the same Brooke Army Hospital, and so then I drew him in. He had earlier been planning to go into cancer research, but partly through our friendship and partly through the intellectual challenge of this psychobiology of stress, he changed fields and made important contributions. He was a professor at Yale for many years. Perhaps one of the best things I ever did was to stimulate his interest and draw him into this field, quite different from his prior expectations. So we started a collaboration that persisted for many years after that, looking at the correlations of endocrine and psychological factors in stress responses. That was one very important outcome.

Also, this situation permitted me to more or less open up a new field: coping and adaptive behavior under highly stressful conditions. The way this came about was that, in the officers' club in San Antonio, I met a surgeon named Curtis Artz and an internist named Eric Reiss. They were in charge of the superb Army Burn Center and they had heard something about me, so they asked me to come and have a look at their severely burned patients. The army's burn unit is still to this day one of the premier burn treatment units in the world. Badly burned soldiers were brought in from all over the world for the most advanced care. And it happened that, to try to minimize the risks of infection and fluid loss, they were pioneering in "open" treatment, where they would minimize the bandaging, which was conducive to infection. But in order to keep the burned surface open to the air, they had to have the cooperation of patients, and it was very difficult to get that cooperation. They were deeply concerned about people who were depressed, people who were angry, people who were otherwise uncooperative, and wanted my help to sort that out. So I used evenings and weekends to help. I was astonished by the severity of these burns; I'd never seen anything like it. I must say I was depressed by it. Some of these patients were charred remnants of their youth. But I also noticed that, of the total of forty patients they had, at any given time it was only five or six who were highly uncooperative, and the thing that struck me was how remarkable it was that most of the patients not only were cooperative but were somehow coping. I went to the literature to see what was known about coping with severe burns or other severe injuries and I found there was essentially no such literature; I was on my own. So it was a very important watershed in my career. It led to a series of studies on stress and coping over many years that did much to open this field.

LEARNING FROM THE CHILDREN
AND GRANDCHILDREN AS THEY GROW UP

As I have been working on this book, I have been increasingly impressed with the fundamental family values and relationships that have shaped my life and made it possible for me to do anything useful I have done. Let us have a glance at the early years of our two children. Eric was born in 1953 and was an exceedingly appealing child, not only for us but for our relatives, friends, and neighbors. Betty often said that he was such an agreeable infant and toddler that he made motherhood look easy. He was affectionate, responsive, and intellectually curious. In preschool, he made friends who have done good things with their lives and stayed in close touch with them, for example, Joshua Goldstein, a distinguished scholar of international relations, and Daniel Drell, a respected member of the scientific community on problems of energy. So Eric did very well academically and interpersonally.

But he had the bad luck of coming to adolescence just when the world seemed to be falling in on young people with the advent of the extremely unwelcome Vietnam War and the quasi-religious efforts of some clever people to make the most of illicit drugs and to undermine the confidence of adolescents not only in their parents but in adults generally. One popular slogan used by the drug pushers was, "Don't trust anyone over 30." Many of Eric's peers had extremely difficult and even some tragic experiences. The intensity of this dangerous subculture was especially early in onset in the San Francisco Bay area. This is what led Betty to suggest in her ingenious way that I undertake research on chimpanzees and baboons in Africa as my friends in that field had been urging me to do for some years. I turned them down earlier because I felt the children were too young either to come with me or to have me away for an extended time. Betty's insight on the value of getting out of this toxic environment led me to take Eric with me for a summer in Africa. He learned a lot, getting to know very interesting people such as the great ethologist Robert Hinde and steering clear of the noxious atmosphere back home. There is more to this story, most of it heartening, but we will come back to some of the derivatives later. The immediate result was the finest existing photograph collection of aggression and conflict resolution in chimpanzees and baboons, published in such places as the cover of *Nature* and Hilgard's distinguished psychology textbook.

Peggy is two-plus years younger than Eric and was remarkable from the start, as she continues to be in 2015. She has a warm personality, intellectual curiosity, and high initiative. We used to enjoy her saying "Me do self" as a little girl, and she acquired a variety of skills at an early age. Mother and daughter had continuing interactions day to day that I observed with respect bordering on awe. Peggy soaked up the wisdom of her mother, thoughtfully tried out new ideas on her, and steadily made progress in her academic work. She observed very keenly the mistakes her peers were making in the unpleasant and dangerous atmosphere I have just sketched. She was very astute in learning what to do—she had many constructive ideas and activities—and equally astute in what not to do. In a low-key, professional way, she steered clear of the troublemakers and avoided the tragedies that befell some other girls in her peer group. During the "war on campus," I can't claim to understand just how she built these strengths but she did, and she was very well liked by her peers as well as adults. From that day to this, she has had a remarkable capacity to organize and accomplish in a humane and compassionate way, especially in public health and public service.

A vivid example occurred when I made the initial plan to take Eric to Africa to participate in primate research at age fifteen. Peggy was unhappy because she had always been more interested in animals than he was and felt she should be involved too. Betty's response tells us something significant about both of them. Betty called her four-year roommate from Vassar and lifelong closest friend, Martha Solnit. She understood they were seriously considering a European trip that summer, particularly so that the father Al Solnit, director of the Yale Child Study Center, could get the most up-to-date information about that field in the European countries. Of course, this work was of great interest to Betty as well, being, like Al, a child psychiatrist and pediatrician. They had a daughter about Peggy's age. Betty barely finished her sentence inquiring about the trip when the deal was closed: she and Peggy were invited with great warmth to join the Solnit family in Europe. They did so and had an excellent summer. Peggy was not deprived after all, and did her African stint later. The experience tells you something about our relationships, not only within the family but beyond.

When it came time for higher education, Peggy went to Harvard, where she did well as an undergraduate, working on the *Harvard Crimson* and for a while even considering journalism as a career. But she had made up her mind in childhood to study medicine and was firm in her convictions, though some influential friends urged her to consider other possibilities, not just following her parents' footsteps. She decided in her open-minded way that she should consider their outlook and sought a way to get a broad view of medicine and public health so as to make a more informed decision. I arranged for her to spend about half a year at the World Health Organization in Geneva and this did indeed give her a worldwide view of the field. In the final month of that year, she and Betty hit upon the notion of traveling together across southern France so they could have plenty of time to consider the options, see a beautiful part of the world, and, curiously, to eat an identical dessert in each city they visited. From my vantage point in Washington, DC, where I was establishing the Institute of Medicine and a townhouse to go with it, I thought this exemplified a wonderful relationship.

Peggy went on to Harvard Medical School, did well again, and then decided it was time to move away from Boston, though she was later elected with the maximum votes to be a Harvard Overseer and was very constructive in that role. During her medical residency at Cornell, she was very good at clinical medicine and particularly took an interest in infectious diseases. This was the mysterious and alarming onset period of what turned out to be AIDS. She dealt with it wisely and courageously.

Then she came to Washington for a while to learn disease prevention and health promotion, which had not been a prominent part of her earlier education. This led her to work with Anthony Fauci, one of the great leaders in infectious diseases and a powerful contributor in leadership tackling the AIDS problem. He appointed her assistant director of the National Institute of Allergy and Infectious Diseases. The next thing we knew, she was the youngest commissioner of health New York City ever had, and she made some contributions that took on worldwide significance, particularly through the World Health Organization. One important example is the development of a technique for directly observed therapy. To deal with the terrible outbreak of tuberculosis in New York City, she and her deputy Thomas Frieden found that many of the very sick people, especially in poor communities, were simply not taking the medication they were given in the city clinics. They therefore kindly persuaded most of these people to allow themselves to be observed in the process of taking the medication in order to get well. As word spread in the city that this technique was working well, it became a valuable part of the public health repertoire. Since Peggy was aware that other cities in the world were having similar tuberculosis outbreaks, she recommended that the World Health Organization take up this technique, educate people about it, and demonstrate its efficacy. Tom Frieden played an important role in this work and later, with Peggy's strong backing, was made the director of the US Centers for Disease Control and Prevention in Atlanta (CDC). Peggy went on to a major health position in the Clinton administration and when that term was over she joined the remarkable ex-senator Sam Nunn in creating a biological (biopreparedness) program in his new Nuclear Threat Initiative. So her career has been a remarkable one in public health and public service. She is now a highly respected commissioner of the US Food and Drug Administration and has had major accomplishments.

Two of these accomplishments are ingenious dedicated efforts to internationalize the FDA beyond its prior experience. She went all over the world to strive for mutual understanding of the way countries in the globalized world depend on each other for the safety of their food and medicines. Many countries responded positively to a greater or lesser degree, and a movement is well under way to cooperate in laboratories, standards, and monitoring procedures for mutual benefit. Another important accomplishment of her years at the FDA was the advancement of personalized medicine. Cooperating with leaders of the National Institutes of Health, such as its director Francis Collins and her old mentor, the great infectious disease scientist Anthony Fauci, she strongly fostered the newer knowledge of genetics and applied it to specific disease processes. In other words, future medical practice would increasingly include specific knowledge of which genes predispose to which diseases. There is reason to believe that this may well be a major advance in medicine, perhaps even a transformation, in the next decade or two.

Now back to Eric. I recently asked Eric to give me some reflections on his early experiences and I quote here what his response was.

"My interest in American history, government, and politics began when we lived in Washington, DC. At a young age I was exposed to American history by going with you to visit the monuments to Abraham Lincoln, Thomas Jefferson, George Washington, and others, and by reading about their lives. I also developed an interest in politics starting with the election of John F. Kennedy in 1960, due to your interest in the campaign and support for him.

"I was able to memorize the names of the presidents, the state capitals, and also the flags of many countries. I remember we used to go to the International House of Pancakes in Chevy Chase that had the flags of all the countries and I learned all the flags there and could recite them.

"Later, when we lived at Stanford, I remember events such as the assassination of President Kennedy, the elections of Johnson and Nixon, and the escalation of the Vietnam War, which became a big issue on campus in the 1960s. Of course you were involved in these things with the campaign of Bobby Kennedy in 1968, and later the Bruce Franklin hearings at Stanford and the 'war on campus.' I also remember watching the Watergate hearings together on TV every night, which later led to my making of the *Nixon* film.

"I also remember our trips to Africa starting in 1968, which exposed me to poverty in the Third World as well as animal behavior in the wild. This made a strong impression on me. I also recall our trip to Israel in 1968, shortly after the 6-Day War. This of course was a historic occasion in which we were able to visit the Wailing Wall with our relatives, as well as occupied territories in the West Bank.

"All of this contributed to my growing knowledge about politics and world affairs, which has continued to this day. We made trips together to Moscow, Prague, Budapest, and other places, as well as the Aspen Institute meetings in Jamaica, which furthered my interest in and knowledge about the events leading to the end of the Cold War. Later of course we worked together on the *Preventing Genocide* documentary, and then on the book *Give Peace a Chance*. All of these shared interests have had a strong and continuing influence on me and the work I have done, both in Washington and in the film world."

Eric spent most of a decade working for two of our finest members of Congress, John Kerry (now secretary of state) and later Lee Hamilton (co-chair of the 9/11 Commission and former head of the Woodrow Wilson Center for International Scholars). Through them, he encountered the Academy Award–winning movie director Oliver Stone and led the way to two prominent movies, *Nixon* and *Any Given Sunday*.

During most of a decade in the '80s and '90s, Eric had fascinating accomplishments in Congress, taking a year off in the middle for a fellowship at Stanford in arms control. While working with John Kerry, he became alert to the possibility that Agent Orange may be doing much damage to Americans as well as Koreans while opening pathways through forest and jungle. Although influential members of Congress objected, assuming that there could be no harm, Eric explored with the National Academy of Sciences the question of whether a research program was needed to clarify the issue. With Kerry's backing, along with the Academy, they set in motion a process that led to years of research in various institutions, sponsored and guided by the Academy. The findings were devastating, so Eric's impression at the outset certainly proved to be correct.

Another rewarding experience was in working with other staff members in the Senate, especially Senator Lugar, to build support for sanctions that could put pressure on the dictatorial apartheid regime in South Africa. In due course this group of young men had sufficient influence with members of Congress that sanctions were indeed imposed. When Eric returned from his year of fellowship at Stanford, working particularly with Sidney Drell, he took up a position with Congressman Lee Hamilton, one of the most respected members of Congress. Hamilton was concerned with the excessive secrecy in American government, having chaired the intelligence committee as well as foreign affairs. They managed to overcome many difficulties in establishing a presidential commission that opened up a large amount of valuable information on the Kennedy years while at the same time protecting the Kennedy family from injury and preserving national security.

Through Eric, I quickly got to know John Kerry and we hit it off very well. I became a perennial adviser to him during his years in the Senate and in October 2014 he paid tribute to me at a State Department gathering for all the help I had given to him in his years in the Senate and the help I had given several secretaries of state that preceded him in office.

So we learned a lot from our children and as we aged their kindness to us was extraordinary. We now live with Peggy and her wonderful family, which enables us to be useful still.

I conclude this section with the wonderful experiences of the relationships Betty and I have had with our grandchildren. The first one, Rachel, has just completed her junior year at Yale and was elected to Phi Beta Kappa for honorary achievement. When the family lived in New York, we spent a great deal of time with her and developed a deep attachment that will last forever. From the beginning, she showed much affection, intellectual curiosity, and sense of humor. The second grandchild, born about two years later, is Evan, who is now in his freshman year at Harvard with high-tech inclinations. Their characteristics as young children were very similar and altogether attractive. As we interacted with them in the early years, there was a kind of renewal of our lives. During that time, their mother Peggy was very busy as the youngest commissioner of health New York City ever had. Their father Peter was commuting to the research campus of IBM in Armonk, New York. He is a creative computer scientist/statistician. He conducted brilliant basic research that turned out to have powerful implications for the financial system and he became a highly successful pioneer in techniques that permit huge numbers of transactions per day with minimal risk. This opened unique possibilities. He is today the chief executive officer of the Renaissance Technologies corporation, a highly regarded leader in his field.

The time came during their New York period when Peggy was offered a major position in Washington, DC, and her husband Peter had a great opportunity at Stonybrook, so they were poised to leave us behind in New York. It was especially touching for me to see Betty's courage and integrity, since she was so close to the grandchildren, to encourage their parents to take these positions, bearing in mind that we would get to Washington as often as possible. Some years later, they very generously built a house that included within it an apartment for us so we could be close to them again and that's where we have been during the past few years. It is now very gratifying to see not only how gifted our grandchildren are, as their parents have been, but also what good, honest, decent, compassionate, and democratic people they are.

The same can certainly be said about the youngest of our grandchildren, Eric's son, also named David, who from the beginning of his life was outgoing, friendly, affectionate, and full of intellectual curiosity. Now, at age twelve, he has become a truly good person, an excellent musician, made good friends, and done very well in school. We are sorry that he has to be in Los Angeles but we greatly enjoy his periodic visits and frequent telephone calls. As with the other two grandchildren, we believe he has a very good future, provided that the world can become genuinely civilized.

BACK TO MICHAEL REESE HOSPITAL, CHICAGO

In my final year of medical school, I came to psychiatry and was fascinated with it, particularly the readings. I read the introductory works of Freud. The wartime work by Roy Grinker, head of air force psychiatry, on men under stress was just coming into view and highlighted some of the ideas about which Freud wrote. The lectures were fascinating in that senior year. On the other hand, the practice of psychiatry in Indianapolis then was with deeply disturbed people in locked wards in the city hospital with no treatment. It was just one cut above a jail, and I couldn't see at all how you could relate this to the fascinating view of human behavior that I was reading in Freud. I decided to see if I could, to get an internship where one could find out about the then newly emerging modern psychiatry. So I applied to Michael Reese Hospital in Chicago, where Grinker had just come back from doing his pioneering work on men under stress during the war. The idea was to see whether one could connect these interesting ideas with some kind of decent, promising practice of psychiatry; in the back of my mind was also the question of whether one could connect that with the science of biology, so I was groping for ways to link several different strands of intellectual interest.

When I graduated from medical school, the next thing was to do an internship and it was an important consideration for me; I took nothing for granted. I had lived through the time of the Jewish quotas in medical school. It affected me to some extent but affected some of my friends quite stringently, and it wasn't clear at all how that would be a factor in getting into internship and beyond internship into further graduate training. I recall a visit that I made in connection with possible internship applications. I went to Johns Hopkins and saw letters posted outside the dean's office from graduates of the medical school inquiring about younger colleagues. They wanted to recruit new graduates to come and work with them in their practices, and a number of the letters said, "Jews excluded," and I was horrified that the dean would post those letters quite casually—there was nothing special about it, evidently. So I crossed Hopkins off, assuming it was out of the question. It left me with a sense of apprehension.

In any event, I was particularly intrigued with the possibility of going to Michael Reese in Chicago. There the issue of anti-Semitism didn't arise. The hospital was supported by the Jewish community, but more than that, I was interested specifically because of Roy Grinker, who had done pioneering wartime work with John Spiegel, particularly culminating in the book, *Men Under Stress*, which I found absolutely fascinating. I thought if I could get in there and work with Grinker, it would give me a chance to find out whether modern psychiatry really had anything to offer. Freud's ideas were intriguing, and so the question for me was whether I could get an internship where I could find out what this emerging field can really do.

It was my good fortune to get into Michael Reese in 1947 and to hook up with Roy Grinker. Indeed, as a matter of chance, I drew the psychiatry service for the first month, because I was in some conflict about what to do. I wanted to do something that would have a research orientation. I saw one pathway to internal medicine, perhaps with a special emphasis on endocrinology, the study of hormones. There was a very gifted and inspiring endocrinologist named Rachmiel Levine at Michael Reese, and he was an attractive model as well as Roy Grinker. It did turn out that the actual practice as well as the concepts of psychiatry—as exemplified by Grinker and his colleagues, particularly his deputy John Spiegel—made it very appealing to me as a field worth pursuing, and I began to see some ways in which I might connect the interest in biology with the interest in psychology, and Grinker encouraged that very strongly. His wartime experience had led him to believe, for example, that psychological influences of great stress have an impact on a number of biological systems throughout the body and that we ought to do research to learn more about that. In wartime it wasn't possible to pursue in depth what those links might be. So the upshot of the internship year was a very broad experience rotating month to month in different specialties of medicine, surgery, and much else. I decided on a career that was at least going to explore very seriously the possibility of going into psychiatry and to find ways to link it with modern biology.

So many people were beneficially influential in the internship that I could go on with a long list but it is feasible only to mention a few: Arno Motulsky, who barely escaped the Holocaust in adolescence and went on to be a great scientist, one of the authentic pioneers in specifically human genetics; Earle Silber, a gifted psychiatrist who later joined me in research at the National Institute of Mental Health Intramural Research Program, and who subsequently wrote a very touching autobiography; Janet Pfeiffer, who taught me the value of first-rate social work in connection with all aspects of psychiatry; and my cousin Jerry Becker.

At the end of the Korean War, I once again went back to work with Roy Grinker at Michael Reese. We had kept in close touch. By this time he was not only a professional mentor but a good friend, and our friendship continued to the end of his life. He was very anxious to have me back and, to my utter astonishment, now wanted me to be his right-hand person, his associate director of the then brand new institute that he'd gotten built, particularly with a generous gift from Albert Lasker. And so it was a tremendous opportunity and I couldn't believe my good fortune. My recollection is I was still in my twenties when I went back to work with the great man in the best facility in the field at the time.

In the position I took up as associate director of this Psychiatric and Psychosomatic Institute of Michael Reese, one responsibility was to carry on with the stress research. Grinker very much wanted me to do it, as it was consistent with his pioneering wartime work, but I had enriched it and made it more complex in ways that he hadn't anticipated but which he valued greatly for its interdisciplinary power. He helped me put together a diverse team with a very good biochemist, Harold Persky; excellent psychologists Sheldon Korchin, Seymour Levine, and Harold Basowitz; neurophysiologist Jim Toman; and research psychiatrist Melvin Sabshin, who later became medical director of the American Psychiatric Association. We set up both animal and human studies on the psychology and biology of stress. I got more deeply into the hormonal side of it as techniques became available for doing the work better, particularly biochemical techniques that gave more precise and reliable measurements than had been possible earlier. I also got more deeply into the psychological side of it, both in terms of quantifying the measures so they would be more reliable from one piece of research to another, and in pursuing the coping studies and getting other people interested in working on them.

There was another major part: he asked me to head the training program in psychiatry, and I was really awfully young for it, but I was also very challenged by it. The people who came in for residency were about my age, but I had this opportunity and I took it. What intrigued me about it was that Grinker and I shared an outlook that, although psychoanalysis was very important and stimulating, human behavior was too complex to be understood at that stage by any single approach or theory or way of collecting evidence; we needed to cultivate a variety of sources of evidence and ideas, in the biological domain, the psychological domain, and the social domain. So it meant we had to look for people from different fields, we had to try to bring in ideas from many different sources, and that was the spirit in which I tried to infuse the residency program: this was going to be a residency program that broadened the scientific base for psychiatry. It might lead to some perplexity, but would be very stimulating.

In those days, psychiatric residencies were typically tied to structured psychoanalytic institutions and the Chicago Institute for Psychoanalysis seemed to me the most progressive, open-minded, and research oriented of these. I was influenced by senior analysts such as Thomas French, Franz Alexander, Therese Benedek, and Joan Fleming. Among my peers, I made long-standing friendships with people such as Jim and Virginia Saft, Morris Sklansky, Arthur Miller, Samuel Weiss, Joseph Kepecs, and Roy Grinker Jr. This young group was stimulating, kind, and encouraging. I miss them now.

STRESS AND COPING IN THE KOREAN WAR

The Korean War took me from Chicago to San Antonio (Brooke Army Hospital) to Washington, DC (Walter Reed Army Medical Center). It gave me insight into coping behavior and emphasized human problem solving in the direction of adaptive change. It brought into focus transactions of individuals or groups that are effective in meeting the requirements or utilizing the opportunities of specific environments. It highlighted possibilities for enhancing the competence of individuals through developmental attainments, including ways of learning from exceptionally difficult circumstances. It also suggested ways in which such stressful circumstances may be modified to diminish human suffering.

The study of adaptation links biological sciences, social sciences, and the clinical professions. The findings and implications of these studies are useful in psychotherapy, counseling, rehabilitation, preventive intervention, and in the practice of physicians, nurses, social workers, and teachers. Much, however, remains to be done in providing dependable information within the framework that has been constructed by workers in this field.

New information about coping patterns under specified conditions could benefit both individuals and institutions challenged by crises of social change. Such information, respecting the nature of human biology and the nature of social systems, could both help individuals acquire coping skills and assist institutions in anticipating typical or recurring coping exigencies.

I have touched on a variety of stressful circumstances, especially major transitions of the life cycle, that occur in a fairly predictable way. Unfortunately, only a few of these have so far been the subject of multiple studies that provide reasonably dependable information in some depth. For most stressful situations, we must do the best we can, as a practical matter, with fragments of information about the tasks embedded in the situation and the ways in which these tasks can be met effectively. I have tried to provide a useful framework for analysis of stressful situations and hope that it will stimulate a new wave of coping studies. In due course, it should be possible to construct (1) a roster of stressful situations; (2) the tasks embedded in each of these situations; (3) the range of strategies employed in the general population in meeting these tasks; (4) the distribution of these strategies by pertinent biological and social criteria—for example, age, sex, ethnic group; and (5) the risks, costs, opportunities, and benefits associated with each strategy in each situation, taking into account relevant factors such as cultural and subcultural settings. It is not difficult to imagine the utility of such knowledge for physicians, educators, and psychotherapists.

I asked permission of the leaders of the army's burn unit at Fort Sam Houston during the Korean War to take my time in seeing all their patients and interviewing their staff, in order to get to know the setting and try to figure out how it was that people came to cope with such a devastating injury. I thought if I understood something about the setting and especially the social context, I could help them with that fraction of patients who were uncooperative or were very depressed or otherwise suffering. And so it led to a systematic study of strategies for coping with severe injury. Several publications grew out of that study and other studies followed; over a period of roughly two decades, I was engaged partly in studies of coping with life-threatening injuries and then later with major life transitions that were not life threatening but nevertheless involved big changes that were difficult. And so I came to be seen as a pioneer in the study of human coping responses. It was an important part of my career, totally unexpected, that grew out of the San Antonio experience.

As for the psychiatric patients, they would have been called shell shocked in the First World War, but we just called them psychiatric casualties. They, too, were deeply stressed and coping. They were people who had become very anxious or very depressed or very angry or otherwise emotionally distressed during wartime combat experiences. When I arrived in San Antonio, I was quite stunned because in the residency we did very intensive work with a small set of patients; at any given time, under the psychoanalytic influence, we would have six, seven, or eight patients we saw every day and worked with very intensively in the hospital in Chicago or in New Haven. But when I arrived in Texas, I had 206 patients in the army, and a high turnover rate. It was unbelievable. For instance, the first night I was there I got a call from the emergency room, woke me up at two in the morning and said, "Doctor, you've got twenty-seven new patients," and I thought I had misheard; it was unbelievable to me. Well, a big hospital plane had flown in from Korea with twenty-seven psychiatric casualties, and so it went. It was a totally new experience and I had to adapt myself. In the long run it was very good for me, to wake me up to the wider range of casualties out there and the fact that the more traditional psychoanalytic approaches, whatever their merits, simply could not come anywhere near meeting the vast needs in the population at large.

One particular aspect made a deep impression on me: a subset of these patients who felt they had failed other people in combat. That is, they were attached to a small primary group at the squad level and had a sense of mutual interdependence: my life depends on him, his life depends on me. So one common problem was the sense, "I've survived, he didn't; I let him down, I made some mistake, I failed in that crucial human relationship." The anguish for these patients was intense.

There were many patients who had made a marginal adjustment prior to their experiences in the war, episodes of depression, episodes of anxiety, dropping out with fear of failure, and there was a kind of continuity into the combat situation. On the other hand, there were a lot of patients where nothing like that was apparent, patients who'd been good copers in the past, who had not experienced great emotional distress, for whom this seemed to be unexpectedly overwhelming. But that kind of experience in World War II led some of the leading psychiatrists to use phrases like "every man has his breaking point." You could push beyond the tolerance limits of any person, no matter how strong, if the exposure to hardship conditions was severe enough and long enough.

I stayed in the army for the entire duration of the Korean War, which was about three and a half years. I was in Texas for roughly the first half of that. I ran the psychiatric unit there with several hundred patients, and on the side I did this continuing consultation and research work with the burn unit. I was incredibly busy. But along the way Betty and I did get married, she came to San Antonio, and she helped me with the burn study. She didn't have an official capacity, but she was well trained and very smart and so we would go over my notes together and try to figure out what was happening and she was very helpful in concepts, techniques, and morale.

About halfway through the Korean War I got transferred to Walter Reed. The way that happened was odd. A very distinguished neurologist and psychiatrist named David Rioch came to visit Brooke Army Hospital. I had heard of him, an unusual person. We started out with an argument. He was a person given to very provocative statements, very intellectually challenging. He was a civilian consultant to the Walter Reed Medical Center, the great army medical center in Washington, DC. I didn't know it then but it turned out he was developing an entirely new division on neurology and psychiatry in the Walter Reed Institute of Research. And so after the initial case conference, in which we had an argument, he asked me to come to breakfast the next day and we had several talks and he told me what he was doing, and we were obviously drawn to each other, a very high level of mutual respect, and after a while he got me invited to Washington, transferred to Walter Reed to help him establish this new division of neuropsychiatric research. This provided great opportunities for stress research: because it was the army, we had access to all kinds of stress problems that would be difficult to come by otherwise. But it had the advantage over San Antonio in that it was a research institute, there were excellent facilities, there were resources to really develop research on a systematic basis.

The contact with David Rioch had another side benefit that proved to have long-term significance. He learned that Betty and I were planning to take our honeymoon in Santa Fe and on his own initiative wrote to the eminent Frieda Fromm-Reichmann to introduce us, since she had a house where she spent her summers in Santa Fe and he thought we would have a lot in common. She was a tiny woman of great wisdom and courage who had managed to escape the Holocaust and undertook clinical exploration of the treatment of schizophrenia. This was in the days before there was any relevant pharmacology and Freud himself had been pessimistic about the possibility of treating schizophrenics by psychoanalytic means. He was reported to have said, "psychoanalysis is a wonderful therapy—especially for well people."

In any event, Frieda was noted for taking on big, strong, overtly disturbed men and working with them over extended periods of time if there was any sign of improvement. She was one of the creative people who believed that psychoanalysis should keep moving forward on new frontiers.

We got to know her well on our honeymoon, and when we came to Walter Reed during the second half of the Korean War, we spent a lot of time with her and found her an inspiring figure. When the Center for Advanced Study in Behavioral Sciences opened in 1954, she was one of the first people invited and, unknown to me, she strongly nominated me and I was lucky enough to spend 1957 there, as discussed elsewhere in this memoir. It was a profoundly stimulating experience with lasting effects.

It took me a while, actually about a year, to persuade Rioch to transfer my colleague John Mason to Walter Reed. After he did, he had some mixed feelings about it, but eventually he came to share my respect for Mason, and Mason stayed there for years, long after I left, and was a bulwark in developing a part of that institute. I also had the chance to bring some other people who became leaders in the field, including a later chairman of psychiatry at Yale named Morton Reiser and senior people at Columbia and other excellent institutions. Rioch gave me considerable latitude in working with him to persuade outstanding young people to come to Walter Reed, and we had a wonderful group of people, including one person who later won a Nobel Prize, not in psychiatry but in neurophysiology, David Hubel; and one of the world's greatest neuroanatomists, Walle Nauta from Holland. We had excellent scientists in various specialties of the neurosciences at a basic level as well as in clinical investigation, work with animals (Seymour Levine), work with people, and worldwide work, particularly on stress problems. So that second half of the Korean War, roughly two years, was a very formative period. When I left Walter Reed, I continued as a consultant there for some years and continued to be involved with David Rioch, John Mason, and others.

In the work on stress and coping, one surprise was the importance of social support. Among the burn patients, some of them had friends and relatives nearby and some didn't. Those who were isolated, without friends and relatives nearby, were really more vulnerable than the rest. That was an important insight for me because I had cut my professional teeth on a very individualistic formulation of psychology in which family was often hazy and beyond the family there was nothing that was thought to be consequential; social and cultural factors beyond the family were very obscure. And that experience in the army taught me the immense importance of current social supports, for concrete help of various kinds, for encouragement, for the deep meaning of human attachment that never stops. It doesn't just end with the mother-child relationship; it goes through the lifespan. I should have known that from my own family experiences, but I had to rediscover it in a professional context.

We could do wonderful things with some of those people, partly by arranging to bring in good friends or relatives who could offer the ongoing, day-to-day social support that they so badly needed. This approach had turned out to have much practical significance in many fields of medicine and today has worldwide application in stressful circumstances. In such conditions, we strive to maintain a sense of worth as a person, rebuild close interpersonal relations, and meet the tasks required by the situation with the help of mentors and additional information—no small undertaking. In subsequent years, I tried to stimulate interest in the health professions and social sciences to strengthen coping capacities in a variety of situations.

A PERSPECTIVE: COPING AND ADAPTATION

We tried to work on both biological (earlier) and psychological aspects (later). How is it that people could maintain a sense of worth as a person, maintain significant human relationships, and mobilize some hope for the future and come to terms with the immediate requirements of the situation, and think about some ways of getting out of this terrible box they were in and move ahead? So we tried to delineate cognitive, emotional, and interpersonal strategies by which people cope with very severe life-threatening situations.

Then I got to a point on a personal basis where I didn't want to do that anymore. It was just too draining emotionally. It occurred to me that we were dealing with major life transitions, and there were major life transitions that were not inherently life threatening, but they nevertheless were difficult and required some new adaptive patterns. So, then, in later years, I spent considerable time with a variety of excellent collaborators (e.g., Betty Hamburg, Earle Silber, Stan Friedman, John Adams, Fred Solomon, George Coelho, Bettye Murphy, and Bob Cohen) studying those situations; and every so many years I would try to do a synthesis that would draw together the strands of research on coping and adaption.

We put out one multiauthor book on that, which had about a twenty-five-year life in graduate studies. It was called *Coping and Adaptation*. We had some very distinguished contributors, including Erik Erikson, Robert White, and Walter Goldschmidt. That was an important part of my life, which was totally unexpected. But it seemed to me you couldn't really study biological responses to stress, important as they were, without also getting interested in psychological responses. And to the extent that we could link the two, we tried to do so. We drew mainly on the instrumental resources of the US Army, the then new intramural program of the National Institutes of Health and Stanford University.

The different strands of my research interests were interrelated. Certainly the thing that struck me about the coping observations, against the background of the field, was that, understandably, medicine was very pathology oriented, and psychiatry inherited that tradition of pathology. You see symptoms, you see disease, and you try to understand how the disease came about. It is largely in recent decades that medicine has come to pay more serious attention to the body's own responses for adaptation. Take the enormous development of the field of immunology in medicine. There was really very little immunology when I went to medical school. And we've learned something about the very rich, complex capacities of the human body to deal with foreign agents and threatening influences at the microbial level.

So, too, I think that when I came into psychiatry, at first what we were really taught was to focus on breakdown of function, maladaptive behavior. Then, as we began to make the coping observations, I started one of my papers with a sentence something like this: "Why doesn't everyone break down?" I listed many of the ubiquitous stresses of life, and argued that, if you went by the earlier tradition that emphasized the pathology and the vulnerability and the breakdown, you would think there would be no way to escape it; sooner or later we'd all disintegrate. But we don't. We suffer, but by and large, we cope, we adapt, we solve problems, make the best of situations, transcend difficulties.

But both aspects, two sides of the coin, are real and significant. I did feel that I was able to add something to the outlook of the field by pursuing the coping and adaptation in a serious way. Now, I may have been influenced in that by the early exposure to biology, including evolution. You have to bear in mind that adaptation is perhaps the central concept in evolution. I had been exposed to that kind of thinking as an undergraduate at Indiana University. One of the teachers of evolution in my day in Bloomington was Alfred Kinsey, who is known for the sex studies later, but was a fine teacher of evolution. Kinsey, Breneman, Sonneborn, and other professors were very stimulating on the evolutionary perspective—later Sherwood Washburn and Joshua Lederberg.

The evolutionary perspective came into my own life again in the stress work, because as we went along in that with a variety of collaborators and followed the general research literature, it became very clear that the stress responses were a kind of mobilization for action, mostly without action in contemporary circumstances. The energy metabolism of stress, cardiovascular responses of stress, and the role of these hormones in stress all pointed in the direction of the body's preparation for some intensive exertion. Years earlier, Walter Cannon, the great Harvard physiologist, had characterized that as the "fight or flight" response.

I got really perplexed about that. It seems to me that those responses must have served adaptive functions over a very long period of time, under the conditions in which we evolved; there were millions of years during which the human organism and its predecessors must have been able to take the actions they had to take, and there would be a real value to *anticipatory mobilization*—getting revved up and ready to go in the face of danger so that you could do whatever you had to do to survive—but that did not apply in the same way or to the same extent in contemporary circumstances.

The people we were studying were in more or less sedentary situations and, for that matter, many lived fully sedentary lives. However, all the drastic transformations since the Industrial Revolution that made such sedentary lives possible were really just a moment of evolutionary history—a hundred or two hundred years of historical time in which these modern improvements have taken place—compared with the millions of years during which we've evolved, so it seemed to me that we probably carried over these responses from an earlier time, and they might no longer be adaptive. In fact, that became a general orientation of mine, certainly about *aggressive behavior*, that much of what was adaptive earlier was no longer adaptive in contemporary circumstances. That led me into some evolutionary studies, which I never in my wildest dreams thought I would do. That's what took me to Africa. We will see shortly how my evolutionary interests led to extraordinary adventures, insights, and collaboration.

CIVILIAN CONTROL OF THE MILITARY AND NEW OPPORTUNITIES

There was an amusing and informative aspect to my departure from the army. I had served my term and then some, and was eager to be released from service. Fortunately, Grinker was highly motivated to get me back as soon as possible. He wrote to his former colleague, Paul Douglas at the University of Chicago, who in the meantime had become a well-respected senator with emphasis on economics. In response, Douglas was sympathetic to our plight but did not feel it would be proper for him to make a forceful intervention. Then, Grinker turned to the Pritzker family, who were very influential in Chicago and over the intervening years have become highly respected throughout the country in business, philanthropy, science, and public service. The senior Mr. Pritzker, a well-known lawyer, had been helpful to the powerful Senator Dirksen. He asked the senator to intervene in my dilemma, since I already spent more time in the army than was required, and Grinker needed my help in trying to adapt some of our lessons from World War II and the Korean War to the advancement of knowledge and skill in psychiatry. This contact began a half-century relationship with key members of the Pritzker family. For example, I had the privilege of advising them in some of their philanthropic interests and took the initiative in creating a Pritzker Consortium on neurobiology and mental illness, with special attention to adolescent depression. Later, Jack Barchas played a leading role, working closely with me and several key members of the Pritzker family to create psychiatry as a behavioral science. To this day, decades later, Barchas speaks cogently and publicly of this work as a turning point toward the new psychiatry, emphasizing neurobiology and major mental illness. I have more to say on this elsewhere in this memoir.

Dirksen responded in a forceful way, telling me that I should be released within six weeks and if not, I should contact him for direct and dynamic help. Six weeks passed and Dirksen invited me to come to his office, from which he called "Charlie" at the Pentagon. He gave "Charlie" stringent orders to have me honorably discharged within twenty-four hours and to meet with me as soon as possible. With more than a little apprehension, I went to the Pentagon, and "Charlie" turned out to be a three-star general, a well-respected leader in the army. He responded in an orderly way to Dirksen's instructions and walked me from office to office as papers were signed that moved me toward my release. In a kindly way, he saw to it that Dirksen's requirements were promptly met. I was embarrassed, feeling reluctant to put such a prominent man in an awkward position; yet on reflection I realized that, whatever else it was, it was a clear demonstration of civilian control of the military and a good deed had been done. So we see again, there is something to be said for civilian control of the military.

The wartime experiences turned my attention to prevention. I was deeply moved by the immense amount of human suffering associated with psychiatric problems, the emotional distress and the personality disintegration of the more severe disorders, and I thought that we were at an early stage in the field and we had to try to utilize the strengths of modern science from every angle. I was certainly thinking about treatment and then later even about prevention, particularly about early detection and aid, because lives were ruined in adolescence and young adulthood.

When there were early warning signals of emotional distress or some personality disintegration, we had to find ways to intervene, to relieve the distress. When the distress was at least at a moderate level of intensity, then people could use their coping capacities and develop them further. And that led me to an interest in whether there might be medications. There weren't any very useful ones at the time, but the rationale was that if we learn more about the hormones and then later about neurotransmitters in the brain, if we learned about the chemistry of the brain and the associated organs, we could have a rational basis for understanding how the body mediates experiences of anxiety, depression, anger, and despair, and if we understood the biology of those emotions, we would have a rational basis for developing drugs and preventive interventions. And that is, in fact, what's been happening in the intervening decades. We always felt that the psychological aspect was important in its own right, the learning and problem solving and coping; that the biology would probably mainly come in at the level of relieving excessive distress, but you'd still have to use those great human learning and problem-solving capacities to adapt to changing environments.

I became immensely interested in individual differences, consistent individual differences. Partly I came to look toward genetic sources—remember my inspiration from Sonneborn—of consistent individual differences that would make some people more vulnerable than others. I also looked for early experiences, in the family, in the community, that might make some people more vulnerable than others, for example, losing a parent early in childhood. I became increasingly interested in how it was that people learned in the course of growing up to cope with the inevitable stresses of life.

The brain is such a fantastically complex instrument, even at birth, and then it is subject to so many enriching, modifying, but also damaging experiences in the course of the years of growth and development, that you have to keep an open mind in this field to the many different sources of vulnerability and many different potential ways of offsetting vulnerability, and that's why much of my career came to be characterized by building into departments of psychiatry a very broad base of the sciences. When I went to the National Institutes of Health (NIH) in Bethesda in the late fifties and early sixties, and then in the roughly fifteen years at Stanford, I built departments in each place that have lasted to the present time, in an exceptionally broad way, with scientists from biological, psychological, and social fields, to try to map the contours of the many different sources of vulnerability, strength, coping, and resiliency.

If we knew enough to be very efficient in our interventions, then in principle some kind of psychiatric help would be beneficial to everyone. But I don't think we know enough, and I think we have made, with the best of intentions, some serious mistakes. One of those, and only one, is characteristic of the period of the heyday of psychoanalysis—when I entered the field—in which we tended to assume that it would be good for virtually everybody to be analyzed. And that's a very intensive, long-term undertaking with a lot of murkiness about it, and I think a lot of people were drawn into a much bigger enterprise than they needed to be. It wasn't by any means helpful to everybody. I was very lucky (again via Grinker) to be able to get a wonderful psychoanalyst, Gerhart Piers, and he was surely helpful in therapy and in friendship. Like Redlich at Yale, he had escaped from Vienna during the Holocaust, and they were friends. Psychoanalysis concentrated very heavily on a small percentage of those who needed help. As the drugs came on the scene, we were very naïve about the side effects that might come with long-term use of the drugs. These are potentially powerful tools and we have to learn much more about how to use them judiciously, like all of technology.

My career was evolving and I don't think that I had a very clear concept about the whole population. I was in favor of working to deepen research. We had very few researchers in the field when I came into it. I was one of the hardy band of people who tried to strengthen the research base of the field. I just felt that we needed to learn so much more before we could really intervene judiciously. But I must say I did come to be concerned, largely out of the army experience, about how we might address a large population in need over the long term. Up until then, I'd simply taken the patients who'd come to me; then I got to thinking about the field. The situation in the field was that we were mainly getting either rather affluent and highly educated people drawn by the model of psychoanalysis in small numbers, or else very poor, more or less down-and-outers who were going to state mental hospitals of the day, many of which were snake pits, and there was a very large population in between that was largely untouched. One aspect of what the army taught me was that there were always ways to communicate across cultural barriers. I had patients who came from very poor backgrounds. The field was opening up. We brought some ingenuity to bear in the army situation out of sheer compassion, even necessity—for example, the development of group therapy, which we later pursued at Stanford, especially via Irvin Yalom, who became a world leader in the field.

CHAPTER 3

Institution Building

BUILDING THE NATIONAL INSTITUTE OF MENTAL HEALTH (NIMH) INTRAMURAL RESEARCH PROGRAM

We had some unusual opportunities at NIMH in the 1950s and 1960s, as we had new and excellent facilities. Moreover, the planners wisely arranged for *proximity* between basic and clinical investigations, thereby stimulating an exchange of information and ideas leading to useful advances in basic science, clinical medicine, and public health.

In stress research, we could also make unusual arrangements, for example we cooperated with Bennington College so that students' summer work period could be spent at the NIMH. We provided them with essentially college dorm facilities and explained that we wanted to try to understand the day-to-day variations in stress hormones and emotional fluctuations. We were trying to see whether there were group effects, in addition to emotional stress-hormone fluctuations for each individual. In effect, it was a clinical unit for healthy people and facilitated the idea throughout the country of similar units for other biomedical problems.

The findings were not dramatic but the finish was. The students presented us with a large multicolored rug they had made privately with the title, "Save all urine." That was because every day we were measuring their excretion of steroid hormones and comparing these with diary observations that reflected their day-to-day emotional responses. The experience became known throughout the country and encouraged the participation of college undergraduates in serious scientific research. We learned a lot about individual differences and also common patterns of stress response.

Another part of the NIMH looked at the question of the relationship between coping strategies among high school students and coping strategies after students went off to college. It gave us a sense of the variety of individual, personally improvised strategies as well as social support influences, especially friendship clusters. We encountered some remarkable people, such as Martha Angle, who had developed extraordinary capacities to deal with a wide range of people from different backgrounds as well as stressful situations. In this study, we arranged to have a follow-up visit to the students' college in the first year and made direct observations of the extent to which their high school strategies were carried over and ways in which new ones were formulated. Martha Angle later became a highly respected journalist.

Both the Bennington group and the special study of high copers aimed to clarify a range of possibilities, ways of taking advantage of opportunities, coping assertively with new situations while at the same time avoiding hatred and violence.

One of the people I recruited to NIMH was Dr. Herant Katchadourian, who came from the American University in Beirut by way of Rochester and Dr. John Romano. He exemplified very well the value of cultural diversity and later I brought him to Stanford as well, where he stayed for many years. He began with clinical psychiatry, and considered adding psychoanalysis, which was at the peak of popularity, but decided with my encouragement to range widely to make the most of his unusual background and rich experience. In his excellent memoir *The Way It Turned Out* (2012), he is generous in giving me credit for broadening his horizons. The observations on Stanford in this chapter show how he became a genuine statesman in higher education and philanthropy.

One of the outstanding people I recruited from his residency at Yale to NIMH was William E. (Biff) Bunney, who has made superb contributions over more than half a century. Bunney is one of the pioneers of the biological approach to understanding mood disorders and schizophrenia. His research findings—published in several hundred papers—have provided extensive evidence on the nature of these illnesses.

Early in his career, Bunney published a seminal paper on the neurotransmitter norepinephrine's pivotal role in depression. This stimulated a great deal of work on the biological basis of major depressive disorder and potential therapies. He received the 2011 Rhoda and Bernard Sarnat International Prize in Mental Health for his groundbreaking research in depression and schizophrenia. Betty and I received the award a few years earlier and Jack Barchas was in this rewarding lineup too.

In 2013, the Bunneys published a groundbreaking paper titled "Mechanisms of Rapid Antidepressant Effects of Sleep Deprivation Therapy: Clock Genes and Circadian Rhythms." So his contributions continue.

At NIMH, Biff and I confirmed my earlier finding that the corticosteroid stress hormone, cortisol, was markedly elevated in connection with psychologically stressful experiences—and this applied even in so-called retarded depression, when the person showed no overt signs of distress or agitation. This finding was a major surprise and stimulated a great variety of research on the role of stress hormones in psychotic disorders. We also formulated a behavioral measuring technique that was systematic, quantitative, and reproducible in respect to behavior patterns such as anxiety, depression, and anger. This method spread widely. The unique component of the behavioral measuring technique for anxiety, depression, and psychosis was that we collected nurses' ratings on the Bunney-Hamburg Behavior Scale every hour, 365 days per year, and twenty-four-hour urine samples on every patient on our depression ward for severely depressed individuals. We were able to correlate the behavioral data with alterations in 17-hydroxycorticosteroids and breakdown products of serotonin, dopamine, and norepinephrine. Our research unit set a new international standard. Later, with Helena Kraemer, we adapted this system of behavioral assessment to chimps, both at Stanford and in Africa.

A few years ago, the NIH Historical Society held a fascinating meeting to review and understand reasons for the success of those early years that helped to establish a great research program for the long term. This included our program but was of course not limited to it. Altogether, over the years, the NIH Intramural Program has become one of the world's greatest scientific institutions.

I would have stayed longer than a few years, but the Stanford faculty kept coming back again and again. They would not take no for an answer. Stanford, as we shall see, was in a dynamic, creative period of development, linking the new medical school with the rest of the great university and responsibly fostering what became the unique Silicon Valley. Moreover, they were ideally suited to provide the unique facilities I wanted for studying our closest relatives, chimpanzees. Stanford cooperated fully in an on-campus semi-natural laboratory, so that groups could live together and we could develop methods for systematic quantitative measures of behavior and hormones. Moreover, they encouraged me to pursue my interest in the natural habitat in Africa.

The NIMH was well established in a few years, with outstanding young leaders such as Biff Bunney, Herant Katchadourian (intercultural psychiatry), Lyman Wynne (family therapy), Jim Maas (psychobiology of stress), Fred Snyder (in the new field of sleep research), and Bob Cohen, a mature overall leader of great wisdom and skill in institution strengthening. So I felt, albeit with regret, that I could leave a strong unit with much promise both scientifically and clinically.

One legacy of this program was a collaborative linkage with my old stress research unit at the Walter Reed Army Institute of Research. John Mason, my long-time friend from high school onward, played a dynamic role in stress-hormone studies involving such outstanding young people as Ed Sachar and Bob Rose. David Rioch facilitated these efforts in conjunction with Bob Cohen as a wise manager.

I left with great reluctance and maintained both official and informal contact for years to come. This unit became one of the pivotal entities in creating a new psychiatry, both in my initial launch period and for years thereafter.

STANFORD UNIVERSITY

University-Wide Cooperation: Psychiatry and the Sciences

It was a wonderful group of people building Stanford in the 1960s, starting with President Sterling. Sterling decided that although it was a good school, it was missing opportunities of the kind originally devised by the Stanfords. He wanted it to be a great university. He said the only way you can do that is to make it a meritocracy—just take the best people you can get. I noticed that he had on his desk an emblem that said, "J. E. W. S." After I knew him well enough, I said, "Does that stand for Jews?" He laughed and he said, "Well, it is true that almost every Nobel Prize we've gotten since I came here was by somebody who was Jewish. But it's J. E. Wallace Sterling."

That's the kind of guy he was. Completely informal and set for a meritocracy. Going after the best people you can get and undertaking bold measures if you have to. A strong example is provided by the two-mile linear accelerator. In today's money it would be about a billion dollars. They convinced Sterling—he didn't know physics—that it would create a unique possibility for discoveries. I don't know how many Nobel Prizes were won on that machine. But getting it done wasn't all pleasant. It was not *Pollyanna*.

I was a failed mediator in that situation—not a task I sought but a sense of responsibility I felt. Two brilliant people, both Nobelists in the Physics Department, invented the concept of the two-mile linear accelerator. One was our close friend, Bob Hofstadter (and his wonderful family—Nancy, Doug, and Laurie). The other, Felix Bloch, helped develop the MRI, today's ubiquitous medical device. They had made separate discoveries and came together. The work on magnetic resonance imaging had many ramifications over many years. Bloch and Hofstadter had been crucial in inventing the two-mile linear accelerator and they sort of took it for granted that they would have control over it.

But for funding on this extraordinary scale, it had to be passed by an act of Congress and signed by President Eisenhower, and the legislation had in it that it was a national resource to be available to the scientists of the country. It even had some loose language that permitted scientists from other countries. That turned out to be lucky because we got some of the best in the world. The two leading people in building the accelerator were Wolfgang Panofsky and Sidney Drell, both great physicists and arms control experts. They figured out how to make it work. They took the concept in abstract physics and mathematical language and made it into something you could actually build and use. They were physicists with strong engineering capabilities, and they were genuinely modest. I've never known scientists with less ego. So they decided, with permission, of course, that somebody had to do it, to go ahead and plan the machine and work out the engineering of it, and make it available for the physicists of our country, and, to some extent, those of the world.

But one day Leonard Schiff, the chairman of the Physics Department—a lovely man—came to me and said there was a total divide between Panofsky and Drell on the one hand, who understood correctly that it was in the legislation that it had to be available at least as a national, if not international, resource, and Hofstadter and Bloch on the other hand. Hofstadter and Bloch had conceived of this great innovation, and therefore they felt they should have control over it—or at any rate the Physics Department should. And all four were friends of mine. Therefore, Schiff hoped that perhaps I could help.

I spent a summer trying to mediate. I had some reputation already as a conflict resolution person, though I was nowhere as deeply into it then as I later became. I told Schiff at the beginning, I don't think I can do this. He said, "You're the only person we know on campus who is really good friends with all four of these people and you have the requisite skills. All four of them speak very highly of you." I tried but I couldn't do it.

President Sterling was stuck and, for that matter, so was Senator Cranston of California, who had taken a great interest in the project. The matter had to be decided in keeping with the law. They did everything possible to give Bloch and Hofstadter very good access to it. It was, like the NIH committees, composed of great scientists who made priorities and considered approval. How much time on the machine will you need with this experiment? It eventually worked out but there was a continuing strain. I was very happy to see a few years ago there was a Hofstadter memorial lecture given by Panofsky, with a beautiful introduction, so they came to terms in the end. Thus, scientists can have bitter internal disputes and yet cooperate to get very important work done. I never had known a university that was so open minded, so cooperative, so ready for innovation. Faculty would help you get a grant when they didn't need to spend time on it. They were generous with ideas and opportunities.

Stanford and the Center for Advanced Study

I met Stanford faculty in 1957 when I was a fellow at the Center for Advanced Study in the Behavioral Sciences, which was located at Stanford, but an independent institution. This remarkable institution was established by the Ford Foundation in 1954 and greatly strengthened these sciences over the next half century. Scholars from about a dozen fields and many countries were invited out of the blue to spend a year at the Center doing anything they felt would advance their knowledge and enhance their ability to contribute in the future. So this was inherently an interdisciplinary international organization with remarkable scope and latitude. Although it was formulated primarily as a completely individual enterprise, it struck me immediately as an unprecedented opportunity to benefit from the sharing of knowledge among subgroups and indeed the group as a whole. For me, it was an incredible opportunity since I was one of the youngest people there and I could sit at the feet of masters. I took the initiative to make informal contacts with people who might like to have joint sessions in order to help each other become informed on related interests. So, for instance, I joined with the great pioneer in modern biological anthropology, Sherwood Washburn, and an excellent geneticist, Ernst Caspari, to have an informal seminar on biology and behavior. To our surprise and delight, this drew people from a variety of fields including Nobel economists. Later in the year, I did the same for research on early child development, centering on my newfound friend from England, John Bowlby, who did such pioneering work on the formation of early attachment and the consequences of loss. Altogether, this was a great learning experience for me and the relationships we formed tended to last for a long time, for example, Alex George in political science, Fritz Stern in history, and Bob Solow and Kenneth Arrow in economics. A decade later, I was lucky enough to be invited for a second year at the Center, and Betty was able to join me, so we had a great education.

On the evolutionary side of that, the way it was manifest was in trying to understand how human stress responses evolved. In 1955, I got a letter out of the blue that invited me to spend a year at the Center for Advanced Study in Behavioral Sciences. I felt almost like it was a mistake when the letter came—how could they be inviting me to come there? But it turned out they wanted some young scholars of promise, and I was very lucky to be in one of the early groups. And doubly lucky because, due to my hospital and clinical responsibilities, I had to go for a chronological year rather than a standard academic year. That meant I spanned two groups. Most of them came in September and left in September, but I came in January and left in January. So I, therefore, got to know almost a hundred distinguished people in a dozen fields spanning the biological and the behavioral sciences, from all over the world. Many friendships and professional relationships were formed that continued for many years.

On the informational sheet that came from the Center, about my interests I wrote, "I'd like to learn something about human evolution." I knew very little about evolution, about *human* evolution specifically. But I wanted to learn something about that in order to try to understand the evolution of human stress responses. The first or second day I was there, a wiry fellow appeared at the door and introduced himself. His name was Sherwood Washburn, and he was one of the great pioneers in the modern study of human evolution. Years later, I was one of the coeditors for a volume in tribute to Washburn called *The New*

Physical Anthropology; we should have done it years before. A dedicated former graduate student of his, Shirley C. Strum, was the driving force behind it, and that volume shows the intellectual history of Washburn's work and his stimulating effect on his students and others, and certainly on me.

So there began a collaboration with Washburn on many facets of human evolution bearing on stress and aggression and attachment and child development. This eventually led me to go to Africa and establish a research and education unit there. Washburn had begun the new wave of primate studies in natural habitats, just in the early fifties, and it really caught on.

We also took the initiative to propose to Ralph Tyler, the Center's first director, a modification of the Center's basic individualistic plan. Washburn and I proposed that a group of outstanding young scholars developing a new field might be invited jointly and would conclude their year with a book. Tyler agreed. Washburn and I invited young Irvin DeVore (later a professor of biological anthropology at Harvard) to be coordinator of a group of primate field researchers who were enriching our understanding of human evolution. Twenty years later, I repeated this pattern of organization, this time with my former graduate student Barbara Smuts as the coordinator, now a professor at the University of Michigan. These groups did much to solidify an emerging field.

When I joined the Stanford faculty, the presence of the Center was a great asset to my new department of psychiatry, since we could enlist the involvement of outstanding scholars. For most of its history, the Center was an independent institution, though geographically located at Stanford, but a few years ago, it became incorporated into Stanford, which was essential to keeping it intact financially. And so the work continues.

Stanford Won't Say No

During 1957 at the Center, we were forming friendships and intellectual exchanges. Initially, the Stanford faculty was not inquiring about my coming to head a department of psychiatry at Stanford; we were just getting acquainted and we found we had much in common. Most of them in that era were very puzzled about psychiatry—with good reason—and they asked me, among other things, to clarify how I saw psychiatry. If I were going to build a department of psychiatry anywhere how would I do it? I had already signed up to come to the National Institutes of Health to start psychiatry in the intramural program in Bethesda—not throughout the country, not a grant-making program, but a research program. I told them what my thoughts were and that's what got them fired up.

Key people were Avram Goldstein (pharmacology), Joshua Lederberg (genetics), Henry Kaplan (radiology), Ernest Hilgard (psychology), Donald Kennedy (biology), and Lowell Rantz (medicine). We all admired Wally Sterling's courage in moving the school from San Francisco to the main campus in Palo Alto. To my delight, he took an interest in my recruitment. I had very good offers from Harvard and NIH. I chose the NIH largely because it meant I could virtually do full-time research and would not be bound by some of the rigid traditions of Harvard, as much as I respected Harvard as an institution and much later spent a few years on the faculty. In essence, my approach was a precursor to the human biology program because I thought that biology and behavioral science in general, and psychiatry in particular, were at a very early stage of development, and there were very promising advances pertinent to the understanding of human behavior in a variety of fields.

Thus, such a department could contribute substantially to the understanding of human behavior, however complex. That appealed to the Stanford faculty. I also pointed out to them the advantages they had in having a department of psychiatry on campus. My view was that there were great frontiers in biology that were pertinent to the psychiatry of the future, ten, twenty, thirty years down the road, whatever it might be. In neurobiology, neurophysiology, neurochemistry, neurogenetics—the whole nervous system, which was just emerging—we were getting past the phase of thinking that the brain is too complex ever to understand. We ought to explore promising avenues and see where we could go. Then I thought that there was a need for a variety of behavioral sciences, especially psychology (not only clinical but developmental and social), as well as anthropology, since it was pertinent to human evolution. This mix of disciplines proved to be valuable. Major options in biology and behavioral science were interfaced and could teach us much about human learning capacities. We were beginning to see the emergence of a crop of new medications that might take the sharp edge off some of the worst human suffering, depression, anxiety, and anger. We weren't there yet, but there were indications of progress.

I wanted a strong interdisciplinary department and, indeed, to the extent feasible, international as well, for two reasons. One is that some of the best people were from other countries. I appointed a couple of Indian psychologists at a time when people thought of India as a very backward country, not knowing they had some brilliant people in their academics. George Coelho was a key example. He got a PhD in psychology from Harvard. He and I worked on stress and coping from a social perspective. Of course intellectual resources from the United Kingdom and other places as well offered great talent, and the Japanese were very advanced in primate work, which came in later. Some of the best people in the world were from other countries and I believed that as Stanford was on the Pacific Rim, it was inherently international. Let's get the best people we can get from abroad. Some of the approaches taken to problems in other countries were different from ours and I thought we ought to find out what they were. Interdisciplinary first and foremost, international second. That's the kind of department I wanted. There was no such department at that time. I wanted to hire people from other disciplines directly into our own department so that we could have the proximity of day-to-day contact, and set up special meetings in order to teach each other. You could do that at NIH, but it would take a long time. After three years of such discussions and this bombardment from Stanford urging me to come, when I went out to look with my wife's strong recommendation, I found that at Stanford you could simply do it, if you could convince your peers that the people you were talking to were extremely able people. Bureaucratic hurdles didn't matter.

So in 1961, we moved to Stanford to build that kind of department. We were very careful about whom we selected. Psychiatry had a special place because it was at the intersection of a number of different fields, and several of my colleagues inside and outside psychiatry recognized that, and they wanted to take advantage of it. They also knew we had to take care of patients. We had a responsibility to suffering people. We had responsibility for the VA hospital as well as the Stanford Hospital. It took me four years of going back and forth to Washington, DC, and I finally got President Johnson to modify the building they had built so that we could put research laboratories and special therapeutic facilities in it, and it came to pass. We had everyone from veterans to students. We helped develop the Student Health Service. We didn't take it over, but we put a strong psychiatric influence in the Student Health Service.

It's odd now because I was the youngest psychiatry chairman in the country. I never thought of myself as ever getting old, but I thought that, just looking at the demography, someday you were going to have to have geriatric psychiatry and I went to the chairman of Medicine to see about a joint psychiatric-medical arrangement. I even took with me the chairman of Pediatrics, who understood the concept, although he wasn't expecting to have elderly patients any time soon. But, we failed. At that time, departments of medicine in most schools were fearful of filling up with "crocks."

We set up a geriatric psychiatry unit on our own, which got wonderful results. After a while, I asked the man I had appointed to run it, Dr. George Gulevich, "How come these people who have been in trouble for two, three, four years are getting out in good shape?" He said, "Mostly because we stopped the medicines they were on." What was happening was that one doctor would give them medication, and then maybe the same doctor would give them a second medication, and some other doctor would give them two other medications, and then they would take over-the-counter medications, so a lot of our patients were ultimately getting eight or nine medications. Gulevich had the wisdom to inquire, "What are you on?" He wouldn't take them off all at once because sometimes that can be dangerous, but he gradually eased them off. Their brain was muddled from the stuff that they were taking. So, there was a relatively simple policy that was therapeutically effective. I wanted, on the one hand, to get the cutting edge of the new psychopharmacology and brought a number of people from NIH and Yale who were among the best young investigators and clinicians. At the same time, I wanted to pay attention to the demography of an aging society. Elderly patients would become increasingly important throughout medicine.

Attracting the Finest People—e.g., William Dement

Recruitment was not difficult. One of the most satisfying and worthwhile aspects of professional leadership and institution building is the opportunity once in a lifetime (or rarely), to attract an extremely creative, dedicated person of the highest ability and integrity. I have had that opportunity even more than most people in our great research and educational institutions. An excellent example was the "father" of the sleep field, William Dement, who was honored all over the world in due course. Early in my career, I had the opportunity for a leadership position in the new Michael Reese Institute in Chicago. I heard about a graduate student at the nearby University of Chicago who was making important discoveries early in his career on the nature of sleep. We humans spend about one-third of our time sleeping and yet it had not until the 1950s been anywhere near a major subject for research in the biological sciences. Dement played a large role in a set of transforming discoveries that over the ensuing years stimulated profound research interest as well as advances in clinical medicine and public health.

I immediately tried to recruit Dement to move across town in Chicago and join our interdisciplinary research crew, but we ran into an unexpected snag caused by a senior and respected psychiatrist at Michael Reese who earlier in his career had earned a PhD in neurophysiology in the University of Chicago and then took up psychoanalysis. He was a fine man, but he became enchanted with psychoanalysis, and when he met Dement at my request, he instead recommended that Dement put aside his current research for some years and take a purely psychoanalytic approach to sleep and dreams. This was too narrow for Dement and for me, so it fell through.

Then Dement took a position in New York, where he was continuing his research fruitfully, and I moved to the National Institutes of Health, helping to build a strong program in biobehavioral sciences. I promptly made a second run at Dement, pointing out all the vivid advantages of NIH, a great institution in a phase of growth and progress. Although we hit it off once again, he was apprehensive about the multiple complications of the move and, in this case, the particular complications of bureaucratic affairs in a new governmental institution. So I lost him for the second time.

But a few years later, I moved to Stanford and recruited him without difficulty. Getting Dement was a turning point. He had played a crucial role in the discovery of rapid-eye-movement sleep and basic elements of neurophysiology in sleep. I also encouraged him to explore options in the genetics of sleep disorders and he did so fruitfully. I knew we would need lots of first-rate help to fulfill our dreams. He spent the remaining decades of his career at Stanford in exceedingly valuable ways and came to be known by many around the world as the father of the sleep field: basic science, clinical sleep disorders, and the role of sleep problems in public health. Leaders in the sleep field from all over the world have come to pay tribute to him for his truly unique leadership.

In addition, as if what I have said already were not enough, he is an exceedingly good human being, characterized by kindness, compassion, generosity, and integrity. By common consent, he has turned out to be one of the most highly respected members of the Stanford faculty. Indeed, I believe he has had more students than anyone else in the history of the university. The student demand for his courses has been extraordinary. I have attended some and even filmed one for a documentary on human biology. He deals brilliantly not only with sleep and dreaming but with crucial aspects of brain function, biological rhythms, and the uses of adequate sleep in human adaptation.

So in 1963, Dement joined the Psychiatry Department of Stanford, where for the past half century he has continued his studies on the neurochemistry of sleep and the functional significance of the different sleep states. In 1964, Dement initiated a special narcolepsy clinic through which he demonstrated that the syndrome of narcolepsy involves disordered REM sleep processes. In 1970, he started the world's first sleep disorders clinic, which introduced all-night examination of patients with sleep-related complaints, and emphasized the clinic's medical responsibility for and management of the patient, as well as the objective assessment of the relationship between nighttime sleep and daytime function. For the latter, Dement developed the Multiple Sleep Latency Test, which remains the standard diagnostic measure of daytime sleepiness. Dement and his colleagues were the first to understand the clinical implications and high prevalence of sleep apnea syndromes, periodic leg movement, narcolepsy, delayed sleep phase syndrome, psychophysiological insomnia, drug dependency insomnia, and other disorders.

In 1973, Dement discovered narcolepsy in dogs and developed the world's only research colony of animals with this disease. This colony represented one of a handful of animal models of a neurological disease in the world. Dement's basic research team has discovered and described neurochemical abnormalities associated with narcolepsy in dogs. Later, the research focused on the biological clock—the overseer of all the body's many rhythmic processes—which is located in a single brain structure and can be kept alive in a dish, or transplanted from animal to animal. Dement's human research program elucidated sleep apnea and developed effective treatment strategies. He has conducted numerous studies on insomnia, circadian rhythms, sudden infant death syndrome (SIDS), jet lag, sleep loss, and sleep hygiene. Finally, he has helped develop a thorough understanding of the determinants of daytime sleepiness, including the demonstration that partial sleep loss is cumulative, that the circadian curve of sleepiness is biphasic, and that sleep needs must be defined in terms of daytime alertness. Overall, he broadened his contribution from basic science to clinical medicine to public health.

With this widening of interest and knowledge, a number of us concerned with these issues decided there was a need for a national commission for sleep. I took Bill Dement to meet my friends, senators Jeff Bingaman and Hillary Clinton, who were on a committee relevant to support such a commission, and they responded positively, following through to make it happen. This commission greatly enhanced public interest in the subject and led to a variety of useful initiatives.

In late 2014, the National Safety Transportation Board held a major hearing on sleep deprivation and serious injuries, especially among adolescents. They called upon leading sleep researchers and sleep organizations to synthesize the data of recent years on this problem. The results were alarming and called for major public health efforts. Virtually all the participants, individuals and organizations, had been strongly influenced by Dement over many years—for example, Dr. Mary Carskadon and the Sleep Foundation. The research findings converged powerfully on a major public health problem that could be helped in many locations, for example by starting school at a reasonable hour rather than unnecessarily early in the morning. This hearing also had a large public education function since it was broadcast nationally by CSPAN. Thus, Dement's work goes on with great significance far beyond his early breakthroughs in fundamental research.

Fostering the Development of Scientific and Professional Careers: Stanford and Elsewhere

Huda Akil and Stan Watson

In 2014, the Society for Neuroscience released the eighth volume of its history of neurosciences, in which the focus is on people of great accomplishments in a partially autobiographical framework—how they came to be scientists and the opportunities they seized to make major contributions. In sending me their copy of this extraordinary publication, Akil and Watson say, "We wanted to take this opportunity to thank you for everything you have done for us over the decades. It is incredibly lucky, and humbling, to be on the receiving end of such generosity and wisdom. The only way we can think to pay back is to take the lessons we have learned from watching you—about caring deeply about others and the importance of exerting whatever influence one can for the greater good. Thank you for everything!"

Their work is particularly interesting scientifically but also illustrates beautifully my emphasis over the years on international and interdisciplinary cooperation. They came from very different backgrounds. Huda was born in Damascus, Syria, and Stan in Louisiana. When they came to Stanford, for graduate research and clinical experience, I could immediately see their potential even though they were completely unpretentious and started from different scientific vantage points. Huda was inclined toward neurochemistry that might in due course contribute to the understanding and treatment of behavior disorders. Stan was inclined toward clinical problems and the possibility that understanding of the cells and circuits organized in the anatomy of the brain might also contribute to this end. So there was a high degree of complementarity in their joint efforts. Huda was particularly interested in exploring the body's own opiates (endorphins) and among others relied heavily on the work and encouragement of Avram Goldstein, who had done so much to recruit me to Stanford years earlier. Huda and Stan entered this field in an exciting time with great potential for clarifying a problem area of neurobiology pertinent to psychiatric disorders. When they were at Stanford from 1974 to 1978, I hooked them up with Jack Barchas, who conducted a unique laboratory with the most extraordinary scientific and personal mentorship as well as collaboration with talented and dedicated young people like these two. They flourished with his guidance and remain close to him and to me to the present day. Of special interest to me was their discovery of a new function of endogenous opiates—coping during stressful experiences.

Some years later, they accepted an excellent offer to head an established institute at the University of Michigan on molecular and behavioral neuroscience. They have been there ever since. They have continued to pursue the interplay of stress and opioids that they initiated at Stanford, now able to pursue it in greater depth as techniques have evolved. They have also played a crucial role in the Pritzker Neuropsychiatric Research Consortium. The Pritzker family has become a great leader in philanthropy. I was lucky enough to play an initiating role in this enterprise. It had great potential since it brought together outstanding people at Cornell, Stanford, and the University of California. It was greatly facilitated by the fact that Barchas, Akil, Watson, and Biff Bunney had all worked with me and each other early in their careers, so the usual obstacles to interinstitutional cooperation were very well overcome. They conclude their essay for the Society of Neuroscience with the following profound remark: "During this journey, we have learned the importance of relying on each other—not just each other as a couple, but on our research group, our students, our mentors, our collaborators and colleagues, and our scientific community including those who have come before us. We have come to understand the critical need for different kinds of minds working together to try to solve the ultimate mystery: how the mind works."

Richard Wrangham

Richard Wrangham's work is discussed in Chapter 4, where I detail our field experiences with chimpanzees in Africa. He is today one of the most respected primatologists in the world. He has recently published an extremely important paper in the distinguished journal *Nature* that reflects a magisterial effort to draw together many studies from different places by different investigators who have cooperated over the years to understand the causes of chimpanzee violence. It turns out that the findings of these many investigators are consistent with our original discovery at Gombe in Tanzania in the 1960s, which I will sketch shortly. They compiled information from eighteen chimpanzee communities and bonobo communities studied over five decades. It included 152 killings among the animals, most of which were male-oriented and involved intercommunity attacks. Variation in killing rates was unrelated to measures of human impacts, so the results coincide with the earlier adaptive explanations for killing by chimpanzees in terms of fitness benefits through access to resources such as food or mates. Thus, our early hypothesis has held up well in the face of much more adequate data, and Wrangham deserves great credit not only for making a two-decade study of chimpanzee behavior in Uganda but also for eliciting cooperation from a variety of scientists from different countries working from different locations. Once again, the interdisciplinary international focus proves to be rewarding.

Other Career-Promoting Examples

Now let's turn to young psychiatrists who grew up professionally in the Stanford department and went on to achieve even more through interinstitutional research collaboration across the country. A fruitful example is the Pritzker Consortium on neurobiology and mental health in which Jack Barchas and I played the key role initially and now have passed the leadership baton to Huda Akil. William Bunney's group at University of California Irvine also plays a crucial role now. He was with me in the early days at NIH, described earlier in this chapter. Thus, a multi-institutional network has grown over the decades into a powerful collaborative research entity of interdisciplinary nature and made exceptional accomplishments. I feel very gratified that the key players all got their start with me and have kept me in the loop as an adviser.

Another example of the outstanding development of a young psychiatrist I brought to Stanford was Irvin Yalom, now an expert in group therapy. His appointment grew out of my Korean War experiences. My mentor, Roy Grinker, for all his great work in World War II, thought group therapy was no therapy at all. I didn't know anything about group therapy, except I thought, "How in the world are you going to do anything for so many patients unless you have people help each other?" Grinker had also said, "Don't be reluctant to try innovations to increase treatment opportunities and don't feel sorry for yourself. With all its tragedies, war offers opportunities for learning and improvement." So, for one example, I tried out group therapy. I got some people in and we improvised at the Brooke Army Hospital in San Antonio. When I came to Stanford years later, I made a national search and got the best young man in the field, Irvin Yalom, and he became a world leader in group therapy. He's now a fine novelist. His novel on Spinoza is especially interesting.

My interest in group therapy was related to social support systems in tragedy. I had learned something of this from my wife, who had worked in the White House as the Director of Studies for President Carter's Commission on Mental Health. Mrs. Carter was very interested in it. Betty got a colleague from Johns Hopkins, Marie Killilea, and they looked into the question of social support systems, which was marginal then but has since become very important. Out of that grew not only a lot of group therapy in a psychiatric sense, but also social support systems. For example, you won't go into a clinical cancer unit without finding a notice stating, "Social Support Group meets at eight o'clock tonight," or even announcing a more specialized group, "Breast Cancer Group meets tonight." Social support systems, people helping each other with some guidance.

We had a lot to do with facilitating and developing the concept and converting it into something useful for psychiatry. Here was a psychiatrist working with social scientists to help people in groups. It wasn't so desperately urgent as it was in the army, but it has been helpful over the years since the need for help is so great.

We had plenty of patients and once the word got out that it was a very good department at Stanford, the demand was great, but we had very few facilities. In putting together this department, an important part of my philosophy was to get good young people who were research minded, some clinicians, some not. In fact, at the end of the first year the dean said, "When are you going to appoint a psychiatrist?" I appointed a number of excellent young biologists and behavioral scientists who had good research training, good methodology, and were intellectually curious, and I thought if I put young research-minded psychiatrists into that environment, it would be very stimulating for them, and so it was. They didn't have much opportunity in psychiatry at that time for such exposure. Psychiatry was not a research field particularly. I won't go into all the ins and outs of it, but it was a very contentious and largely nonresearch field.

The following year, I traveled a lot to find the best young psychiatrists I could find. The *New York Times* had one article that described people like me as faculty raiders. Why? Because I made it my business to come in the middle of winter to New York and Boston when the weather was lousy, and I'd already identified some promising people and I would invite them out to Stanford and they would love it—the temperature and the natural beauty and the people. I put a large amount of faith into these young people, so they were somebody at Stanford and they had opportunities to learn what they found very interesting. I also spent a lot of time recruiting residents. A medical resident is like a postdoc or PhD. You've done an internship, you may have done a year after that, a couple of years after internship, but it was typically in those days a three-year or sometimes a four-year residency. I treated the residents like young professors.

As I went around the country, I tried to identify who was the best resident at Vanderbilt, for example, which had a strong medical school. I admired the dean very much. He said, "I hate to tell you this, but a fellow named John Adams is terrific. I hope you can't get him, but to be honest if you can get him, he'll be a professor before long," and he was. I had a very young department—bright, intellectually curious, and knowing that they would have opportunities.

I recruited one of today's leading psychiatrists, Jack Barchas—now the chairman of a large, excellent department at Cornell—from NIH to Stanford when he was a terrific young neurobiologist. He and another neurobiologist discovered functions of adrenaline in the brain. It was thought at the time that adrenaline was not in the brain, only back over the kidney in the adrenal medulla gland. He is today one of the world leaders in medicine altogether. He spent many years at Stanford and he continued the progress we had made after I left. He is now not only chairman of Psychiatry at Cornell in New York, but one of the country's leading medical statesmen. When we were young at Stanford, he was intellectually curious, fascinated by the subject matter, wanting to learn more about it.

His wife Patricia at that time was a very promising young sociologist who worked creatively to link social and biological variables. Very few people in her field had the vision she had of linking these bodies of knowledge—and doing so experimentally. I had the privilege of doing some teaching with her. She and Jack did research together on a distinctive kind of sociobiology. Tragically, she developed a brain tumor, which recurred after several removals. Jack did everything humanly possible to care for her over a period of years. They also raised a fine son. But the time came when her illness was simply too much and we lost her. I will always remember his kindness and compassion during her ordeal.

Barchas is now the Barklie McKee Henry Professor and chairman of the Department of Psychiatry at Weill Cornell Medical College and Psychiatrist-in-Chief of Weill Cornell Medical Center of the New York Presbyterian Hospital, including the Payne Whitney Clinic in Manhattan and Westchester. At Stanford, he held the Nancy Friend Pritzker Professorship and was the Director of the Pritzker Laboratory at Stanford, an interdisciplinary program centered on fundamental aspects of behavioral neurobiology.

Apart from his departmental administrative activities, Barchas has been deeply involved in public policy issues. For twelve years he chaired the Board on Biobehavioral Science and Mental Disorders of the Institute of Medicine of the National Academy of Sciences. The board produced evaluations for the federal government dealing with health needs and research opportunities. He served for four years as chair of the Board of Trustees of the New York Academy of Medicine and currently chairs the Board of the Association for Research on Nervous and Mental Disorders. He is president of the Pasarow Foundation, which provides awards for extraordinary scientific achievement in the fields of neuropsychiatry, cardiovascular disease, and cancer. He also edited the *Archives of General Psychiatry* for about a decade, succeeding Grinker.

So Jack Barchas has become a superb leader in psychiatry and medicine altogether. This is Barchas's statement at Stanford's Human Biology fortieth anniversary. (It is aspirational in nature, utterly sincere, but more credit than I deserve. Bear in mind that I recruited him from NIH over half a century ago and we have been close friends ever since.)

CELEBRATING THE PROGRAM IN HUMAN BIOLOGY

Stanford University—October 18, 2011

David Hamburg has been and is a transforming force who crosses disciplines with ease. He can cross multiple fields, multiple dimensions, and complex situations; transforming for ideas, individuals, institutions, and nations. A physician, psychiatrist, psychoanalyst, biologist, he deals with the interdisciplinary world; early recognized for remarkable gifts: clinician, researcher, teacher and administrator; extraordinary researcher and scholar. With his wife, Betty, did pioneering studies on patterns of coping in stressful experiences. He provided first evidence of adrenal steroid changes in depression; a profound discovery now leading to new approaches to treatment. He developed the first modern clinical research center for mental illness. His work has ranged from nonhuman primates to the human condition. Multiple studies on stress, coping, aggression, violence, conflict resolution.

At a young age he became chair of psychiatry at Stanford, he set up the first department that could harmoniously span all aspects of the field; characterized by an open minded, thoughtful, collegial approach; he led the preparation of a report that provided a new scientific plan for psychiatry. *Psychiatry as a Behavioral Science*—pathbreaking, integrative, transforming—on behalf of the National Research Council.

Early on at Stanford, with colleagues, he had the dream of a human biology program. A true joining of Medical School and Arts and Sciences faculties; made possible by the open spirit of faculty and the magical talents of Stanford students; few believed it could be as important as it came to be—widely copied, never equaled.

Learning from others was important. The Psychiatry Department had a Monday night seminar that we called the *Scientific American* Seminar. What did that mean? That each one would take an evening to explain his interests, activities, research if he was doing any yet, the research he wanted to do, at the level of the *Scientific American*. In other words, not a beginner's level, but not an advanced level either. An intermediate level so that we could understand each other, but we could also be sophisticated about the knowledge that was involved. That continued for five or six years. The national organization that assessed programs posted online the rankings by interns or residents of what residencies they wanted or what faculty places they would like to go to—Stanford was first in about our second or third year. People were astonished. What was Stanford, this nonentity, doing first? It was very encouraging.

Once or twice a year, we'd go to a place called Asilomar, which is on the Pacific Ocean, a lovely place owned by the state, very cheap, and we'd spend a few days there. It was like the Monday night *Scientific American* seminars. It was more extensive sharing of information about different fields and different lines of research. The whole thing was, I think, very gratifying to most of the people in it.

From then on, Stanford was special because of the youth, vigor, curiosity, and risk taking, and the power of cooperation, both within the department and beyond. That was the kind of department we built. It was very special and I remain very proud of it. I am told that Stanford has more members of the Institute of Medicine, National Academy of Sciences, than any other psychiatry department, and one of the winners of the 2013 Nobel Prize in medicine has a joint appointment in psychiatry along with another department. So the trajectory of the department's early years has gotten even higher.

On the university citizenship, President Sterling sort of adopted me. He asked me for advice from time to time and formed a small "kitchen cabinet." One funny thing is that he knew I wasn't crazy about raising money. He said to me, more than once, "Someday you will make a great university president." But when wonderful opportunities arose, I promptly declined because I wanted to stay deeply involved in the substantive work.

I want to mention some other *remarkable people whose careers I tried to foster* and who have expressed gratitude. In fact, there are too many for me to cover adequately. All of these relationships were two-way streets. I helped them and they helped me. In working with undergraduate students, medical students, psychiatric residents, research fellows, and faculty colleagues, the mutual benefit was always clear. Over the years, I have come to feel deeply about the value of friendship at all levels of interaction. Our friendships make it possible to learn so much more than would otherwise be the case.

Let me mention a few remarkable people whose careers flourished at Stanford and beyond—from all of whom I learned a great deal and all of whom I fostered at crucial steps in their career.

I recruited Keith Brodie from NIH as a young innovator and worked with him in building a department at Stanford. He was extremely good at organizational matters, clinical psychiatry, and research in psychopharmacology. I was approached by Terry Sanford, president of Duke University, who had been both governor and senator, about outstanding people in psychiatry and medicine. I highly recommended Keith, who was an assistant professor, and they gave him a double-jump to associate and full professor; he soon became chairman of the psychiatry department at Duke and then president of the university. In his tenth and final year as president, I had the memorable experience of getting an honorary degree and learning from people at Duke how much they appreciated Keith's contributions. He served for ten years as a valuable member of the Carnegie Council on Adolescent Development.

John Adams was another double-jumper, going from assistant to associate to full professor and chairman of the Department of Psychiatry at the University of Florida. He built an excellent department in a short time and then tragically developed a severe melanoma and died much too young.

Roland Ciaranello was an outstanding person who also died much too young. He was a superb medical student and psychiatric resident at Stanford who did groundbreaking research with Jack Barchas on genetic factors in stress responses in keeping with my early formulation. He quickly earned national recognition and was about to be appointed director of the National Institute of Mental Health when he died of a cardiovascular problem while jogging in Puerto Rico, where he was visiting for a research meeting.

Anne Pusey was a graduate student who came to me from England. We did field work together in Africa in which she made important discoveries, particularly about the behavior of adolescent female chimps. Later, she was entrusted with the entire set of chimpanzee research records from Gombe, first as a professor at the University of Minnesota and then at Duke.

Nancy Merrick combined her interests in medicine with her interests in primates. She has been an excellent physician and at the same time a leader in primate conservation. In 2014, she published an important book, *Among Chimpanzees: Field Notes from the Race to Save Our Endangered Relatives.*

Barbara Smuts was one of the best graduate students I have ever had and one of the finest people I have ever known. Her exemplary behavior during the hostage episode is described later in this chapter. For some years, she has been a professor at the University of Michigan and has made valuable research and teaching contributions with several species: chimpanzees, rhesus monkeys, dolphins, and now dogs. She also assembled a definitive book with outstanding coauthors on an overview of primate societies.

Carrie Hunter is also discussed later in this chapter for her courageous role in the hostage episode. Subsequently, she closely monitored developments in the Congo, did graduate work at MIT, and became a leader in the environmental movement as well as a superb advocate for ways of improving medical care. In our later years, Betty and I had the good luck of having her in Washington, DC, and so we benefited greatly from her wisdom and enthusiasm. She helped Betty greatly in writing an integrative overview of her work on adolescent development and health.

Rudy Moos is a distinguished psychologist who spent most of his career in our department at Stanford and was very helpful to students, faculty, and behavioral science, especially in research methods.

When I came to the task of organizing a new department of psychiatry at Stanford, I sought out a statistician who could help the whole department in research methods. I went to Lincoln Moses, then chairman of the Statistics Department at Stanford, and he identified an outstanding young woman named Helena Kraemer. She stayed in the department for many years and became a leader in her field.

Jim Mark is a remarkable surgeon and international physician who responded positively to my request that he help the University of Dar es Salaam develop its medical school, and he kept in touch with Tanzanian medical leaders for years after spending one year full time in that developing country. Always helpful in a crunch.

Bill McKinney was one of the few psychiatrists who combined primate research with broad knowledge of psychiatry.

Peter Rosenbaum was an extraordinary psychotherapist who worked with me in the NIMH in the 1960s and came along with me to Stanford where he was a strong clinician and a unifying influence in the department.

Frank Ochberg was an excellent resident who developed a long-range interest in mental health policy, was a leader in the National Institute of Mental Health, and developed a network of people in psychiatry and related fields concerned with violence and special attention to helping victims.

David Daniels was another astute clinician who also took a particular interest in violence and made a valuable contribution in helping psychiatric patients to acquire occupational skills suited to the then emerging Silicon Valley.

Alfred Weisz was an outstanding resident and junior faculty member who was making contributions in the stress and coping field when he died very prematurely of cancer. We dedicated a lecture in his honor.

Kenneth Davis was a research fellow in our department at Stanford upon graduating from the first class at the Mount Sinai Medical School. From the start he showed great talent, and, although he could have gone anywhere, he chose to go back to Mount Sinai and help build a new school. He and his wife Bonnie became pioneers in research on Alzheimer's disease and in due course he built a first-rate department of psychiatry. In recent years, he has been the president and CEO of the Mount Sinai Medical Center, which is discussed in Chapter 5. Suffice it to say, he has become one of the truly outstanding leaders in academic medicine.

Ernest Noble was a distinguished young psychobiologist and clinical psychiatrist who later became one of the leaders of the National Institutes of Health, particularly heading up the institute concerned with alcohol abuse and addiction.

Human Biology

Human biology emerged from the then new molecular and cellular biology, spearheaded by such people as my dear friends Joshua Lederberg and Tracy Sonneborn. The human organism is not just a bag of molecules. The molecules and cells are organized into functional systems and constitute integrative biology. They are also highly pertinent to behavior and disease. Human biology was an extension of basic values from an early part of my career—that it's absolutely vital to have the interdisciplinary, and, if possible, international composition of groups that are going to do complex research and teaching.

I was talking about this with Joshua Lederberg, who was a giant of an intellect, one of the greatest scientists of the twentieth century, a Nobelist at a very young age, with an exceedingly wide range of scientific interests and knowledge. He proved to be a close friend, collaborator, and mentor.

Don Kennedy, the chairman of the Biology Department at Stanford, was about the same. They were two extraordinary human beings; luckily, both very good friends of mine. So I was talking to both of them about this concept, and would it work, could we put it into action in some way, this interdisciplinary, international kind of pooling strengths, all the intellectual and technical resources we could. Lederberg said we should teach a course on the human organism, building on the newly emerging molecular and cellular biology to which he had contributed so much. These insights could be extended to *each functional system of the body in health and disease.*

I urged him to teach the course himself. I was building a big, complex department that had basic and clinical components, and we were all over town, and in addition to that, I had become very much a university citizen, though he was, too. So I might not be able to do justice to this innovation. I just felt he was better qualified. To start it off, to try it with a Nobelist teaching it, with perhaps the youngest Nobelist in history, was not a bad idea. But after he got about halfway through, he said he would drop the course unless I came with him. So I joined him, and we finished it up with satisfaction and we thought the enterprise was over. We were going to do it once and try it out, and take it up with some faculty members we highly respected. One of the things I always said about the Human Biology program was that it was a group of faculty who liked each other and were looking for an excuse to work together.

This is related to a story that illustrates the point about Stanford's cooperative mode in relation to support from the Ford Foundation. Larry Hinkle, a professor of medicine at Cornell and a good friend, was a major consultant of the Ford Foundation, and he heard about the course, and called me and asked if it was true that Josh and I taught this course. Yes. How'd it go? We told him what we thought, and why. He said, well, do you think some of your colleagues would be interested in joining with you and making this a larger program? I said they might. He asked if we could get them together in a couple of months. I said, why a couple of months? Why not next week, or in two weeks? I anticipated enthusiasm in the faculty. So we did meet and we had a terrific session. We began to plot out one more course, a larger course like this one. We didn't think about a major. The major came from the students' enthusiasm. That was a central theme. Stanford students were themselves not only extremely bright, but also highly innovative, and they loved the idea of this novel plan.

We approached the Ford Foundation—the president was McGeorge Bundy, who later spent the last six years of his life as a visiting scholar at Carnegie with me. He'd been in government, of course, and he'd been a dean at Harvard before that, and then he was president of the Ford Foundation. Hinkle went to Bundy, who said to encourage Stanford but make it clear to them that the foundation can't support the whole thing. In the end, they did support almost the whole enterprise for the first several years.

But then Bundy said we ought to have another university. If you have only one, it looks like something peculiar that is not reproducible. Let's get another highly regarded university. Hinkle said to him, well, you were a dean at Harvard, let's try Harvard. So they tried Harvard. The long and short of it is, the people on one side of the Charles River, that is, the Medical School and School of Public Health, said we'll do it, but we won't do it with the Arts and Sciences on the other side of the river. The Arts and Sciences people said we'll do it, but not with the Medical and Public Health people across the Charles River. So Harvard wouldn't do it. I tell you this story not to knock Harvard. It's a great institution, and I loved my years there. But the experience does illustrate the difficulty of achieving the high level of faculty cooperation necessary for such programs.

But Stanford had this remarkable openness. One other example. There were seven very distinguished biologists at Oxford in England who wanted to do a course like ours. Not a major, but one course. Oxford, of course, is not historically the prominent biological school in England; that is Cambridge. But still it's very, very good today in science. It took them several years to get approval at Oxford. In contrast, it took us twenty minutes in the Faculty Senate. We sent the members a concise summary. Then two of us made presentations and the faculty responded very well. Go with it and report back to us in a year, or if you want to make it two years, it's all right. Give it enough time, whatever you think you need, and give us an evaluation. That was Stanford.

When I came back to Stanford from the National Institute of Mental Health, one of the main institutes of the great National Institutes of Health, I had to raise funds for the new programs of our department, which was something I did not have to do with the government at that time in the creation of the NIH Intramural Research Program. But nevertheless we did what had to be done. In the first place, the money was more generally available in the field. In the second place, the people knew me at NIMH, and they really liked the new Stanford department. They even called it NIMH West since we got much support from the extramural grants program.

Lederberg and Kennedy helped with an application for a site visit, arranging for six distinguished people to come out and look over this program—it's a big grant, several million dollars, so would you come in for an hour? They would come in all day if necessary. That's the kind of cooperation we got. That was great for fundraising and for morale.

The medical school dean at Stanford, a lovely pediatrician, Bob Alway, was helpful. The second dean I got to pick myself, Bob Glaser (I was chairman of the search committee), so that was easy. Dick Lyman was provost (later president) with me again as chairman of the search committee and was very cooperative. The Human Biology program was kind of strange to him, but he was very smart, he could see the logic of it, and he went along with us just fine. We had other valuable deans—for example, Jim Gibbs and Al Hastorf. Not only were they cooperative, they said they would like to participate. Such dynamic encouragement helped in putting together the Department of Psychiatry even before we began Human Biology.

In that era, I recall only one intense dispute. When we brought in Bob Glaser as dean of the medical school, he wanted the dean to have control (some or all) of the money made in the clinical departments, as is true in a number of places. And Henry Kaplan, the distinguished radiologist, was second only to surgery in the money made by the department. He objected strongly. So Glaser and Kaplan had a big duel.

People ask why academic battles are so fierce, and the answer usually is that the stakes are so small. But in that case, they weren't so small—they were a few million dollars a year. So we did not have a panacea, but in general, we were very cooperative. We knew we had to cooperate to succeed.

They were in the process at that time of moving the medical school, or working on it—it was a big work in progress—from San Francisco to Palo Alto. The situation in San Francisco had been that the clinicians, and very good clinicians they were, remained preoccupied with their practices. They didn't have much time for teaching and hardly any time for research. So it was a very good school of its kind, but it was not what I was looking for. I was looking for a place that put a lot of emphasis on research and where there were rich interdisciplinary possibilities in the broadest context of human knowledge. I was tremendously impressed with President Sterling, with whom I became a close friend over the years. He had the courage to make the move. Most of his trustees had their doctors in San Francisco and the doctors were pressing the trustees hard, "Don't move." But Wally Sterling saw the huge possibility of having the medical school together with the rest of the university.

Kaplan and Bob Hofstadter provided one clear and encouraging example of the wisdom of Sterling's decision to move the medical school to the general campus: with their newfound prosperity and their joint activity, the Departments of Radiology and Physics collaborated to convert leukemia from a uniformly fatal disease to a treatable one (at least in some forms of the disease). I had the deep satisfaction of arranging for the treatment of a very sick friend, a scientist at NIMH, Dick Wyatt, to come to Stanford for the new treatment, and he had several decades of good health as a result.

There were very few universities that had a close connection between the medical school and the rest of the university. Now, a lot of that was geographic. Ithaca is several hundred miles away from New York, so Cornell is no possibility. But even in other big cities, they were separate. In Boston they're across the river, and they have very little contact—there is even animosity, actually. I know that because I was on the faculty there for a few years. Sterling saw that opportunity and had the courage to work it through, including raising the money. It was a very difficult proposition. Nobody expected it from him. He had not been a scientist. He was head of the Huntington Library in Pasadena, which is an important institution. He had a vision. So he was in the process of bringing the school together.

Kaplan provided an illustration of the soundness of Sterling's concept in his work with Bob Hofstadter, who had gotten a Nobel Prize in physics. Mrs. Nancy Hofstadter was my wife's closest friend, and Bob and I were good friends as well. Hofstadter, as I have discussed, had the concept for what became the two-mile linear accelerator. He had devised a smaller, mini accelerator, and he and Kaplan used it to provide a certain kind of acceleration to a certain kind of cancer cell, which made those cells much more vulnerable to the chemotherapy that existed at the time. Certain kinds of leukemia that were totally incurable then became curable.

The innovators realized that I had in mind a different kind of psychiatry department. Such psychiatry departments as existed, and there were a few, were very rigid and narrow, of two basic kinds. One was the old Germanic kind, which was essentially diagnostic. You made diagnoses, but there was very little you could do. And the diagnoses weren't very meaningful to begin with. The other kind came in after the war, and it was psychoanalytic. Freud was an inspiring figure, and a lot of people got interested in psychoanalysis. He was interested in fundamental issues: the relation between emotions and motivation, relations between early experience and later behavior. As a very progressive psychoanalyst, Gerhart Piers, later said to me, "I always view these like trying on a coat in a store and if it fits, that's fine. If it doesn't fit, we look for something else." But we were enchanted by psychoanalysis in this country. We're a very enthusiastic country. And the new departments of psychiatry across the United States were almost all psychoanalytic. That was okay up to a point. They were studying important problems, and they were seriously looking for ways to help people. There were implications for therapy that grew out of these basic issues, so that was attractive, but at the same time, I began to have my doubts. I thought this was somewhat in the Germanic tradition, too rigid, too dogmatic, and it wasn't sufficiently research oriented. Freud himself was research oriented but most of his colleagues were not. They were more in the European tradition, where you sit at the feet of the great professor and memorize what he tells you.

The same principle of interdisciplinary cooperation was illustrated by my inspiration earlier about genetics and that opened me to the realization that there were other fields opening up—neurophysiology and neurochemistry; the biological study of the brain was emerging. It was crude at the time but highly promising. Genetics was expanding into new arenas. If you could have a department that incorporated within it people who were interested in the biological, psychological, and social aspects of mental illness and therapy of mental illness, that was really worth exploring.

All this influenced our decision to move to Stanford. Betty said, well, maybe you ought to consider it. It's three years, and you've got people at NIMH that you've trained who could replace you. We loved it when we were at the Center for Advanced Study. It's such a beautiful place. We know a lot of people at the university. We didn't know much about the medical school. They had a search committee headed by Lowell Rantz, professor of medicine, an infectious disease person. Then he came to visit. He was a lovely man and he saw the potential. This approach to this subject matter was new to him, but he saw the value, and on behalf of the committee, he offered me the position. Ernest Hilgard was a member. He was a very distinguished psychologist. He, too, I had known before. So they just said, look, you've been at NIH long enough. It's quite decent, three years. You've trained a successor and there's a lot of talent there. You've set up your laboratories. You've got your basic experiments under way. And Stanford needs you. We've looked everywhere, all over the world.

They promised autonomy and cooperation, but little money. I never got to 10 percent of Stanford hard money in all the years I was there. I raised essentially everything we needed to implement this vision. In 2011, former students were determined to honor me on the occasion of the fortieth anniversary of the Human Biology program—wow! I was deeply moved and yet reluctant to have all the focus on me. So I urged the students to survey widely and see who would come. Answer: almost everyone. I insisted that we also honor Don Kennedy and Josh Lederberg, and that former students and former faculty describe their activities, regardless of field, over these forty years. Carrie Hunter, a brilliant, compassionate, imaginative student, and Jack Barchas were the spearheads.

Stanford as an International University

One of the many ways in which I tried to help Stanford develop maximum strength in international matters was by backing the development of an institute on international studies (now called Freeman-Spogli Institute). After the faculty years, I used my position on the board of trustees and my friendship with then president Donald Kennedy to broaden and strengthen the international activities in research, education, and international relations for faculty and students across boundaries. I served actively on the advisory board for this center for some years after my time ran out on the board of trustees. In 2014, the Center on Democracy, Development and the Rule of Law was a highlight. Current research programs include the following: American Democracy in Comparative Perspective, Arab Reform and Democracy, the Governance Project Comparing China and the United States, the Program on Human Rights, the Program on Liberation and Technology, and the Program on Poverty and Governance. A variety of distinguished and dynamic Stanford faculty as well as visiting scholars, headed by the extraordinary political scholar of democracy Larry Diamond and the former president and eminent legal scholar Gerhard Casper, have now developed an exceptional program.

Herant Katchadourian: International Enrichment

At Stanford, Herant Katchadourian's remarkably engaging personality and wide range of cultural experiences put him in a good position to strengthen ties between the medical school and the rest of the university. With my encouragement he took a strong interest in undergraduate education. Being a person of great intellectual curiosity and flexibility, he not only helped me build the new kind of department but also entered into various committees and organized activities to strengthen opportunities for graduates. This logically led him into the human biology program, particularly because he was able to offer a very high-quality historical and international perspective on human sexuality. I felt we should take up such matters because they were extremely salient to the students and were not dealt with at an academic level. He then wrote an excellent textbook, the first of its kind, which subsequently had five editions and was published in a variety of languages and very widely read. It became in due course remodeled for other enterprises of this sort, which had been largely lacking in university life. He was a very gifted teacher and some statistics say that more Stanford students in aggregate took this course than any other. The same has been said about Dement's course on sleep, dreaming, and biological rhythms, but I do not know which one is actually in first place. I do know that they brought into the curriculum material of great practical importance relative to health and disease, and largely lacking in academic life throughout the world.

Katchadourian gradually became a university statesman, the first ombudsman, dean of undergraduate students, and other positions. In the course of this work, he became acquainted with the Hewlett family, founders of the great Hewlett-Packard company, and became a member of the Hewlett Foundation board, which he continued for many years. In addition, the Hewletts created a special foundation in honor of Mrs. Flora Hewlett, and Katchadourian served as the first president and established a high-caliber organization. So he earned respect in scholarship, education, and philanthropy—taking advantage of his cultural diversity in all of these. Moreover, he is as kind and loyal a friend as I have ever had and is beloved in a variety of countries as the *quintessential educator linking nations across boundaries.*

In this context, he developed much insight into the awful problem of genocide, with a deep grasp of the history of the Armenian genocide. When I was working on my book on the prevention of genocide and its associated documentary developed by Eric Hamburg and Rick English, Katchadourian was able to clarify the vital point that the genocide was not a last-minute surprise as so often was argued, but rather it developed gradually but clearly over several decades. This is a fundamental point in understanding genocide altogether: there is ample warning. The challenge is to know to respond at an early stage—prevention.

Another example of ways in which Stanford reached out to neglected parts of the world was illustrated by the distinguished surgeon, James Mark. During our primate research and education in Tanzania as part of the Human Biology program, I established a strong relationship with Professor Abdul Msanji, the scientific leader of the University of Dar es Salaam. He involved us in the educational program in biological sciences and asked for my help in strengthening the university's medical school. In response, I invited Jim Mark, an extraordinary, capable, and adaptable physician and surgeon, to spend a year in Dar es Salaam. He did so and established long-term relationships with some leading members of the medical faculty and did everything in his power to help the school.

Laboratory of Stress, Conflict, and Evolution of Human Aggression

The evolution of human aggressiveness has been a recurrent intellectual curiosity and subject of active research throughout much of my career. There are different facets but the central themes are consistent over many years.

The interests in genetics and evolution were closely related, as they are conceptually and indeed operationally in the field of biology. Having gotten that bug as an undergraduate, it really never left me. As the stress research evolved, I got more and more intrigued with the question of individual differences in response to stress situations. They were very manifest on the psychological level, but then it seemed to me that, given the enormous biological variability on almost any measurable dimension, there probably were big individual differences biologically in stress response. Let's say, for example, if you and I had an argument and we both got approximately equally upset, it might be that the level of adrenaline circulating in my blood would be three or four times yours, or it might last three or four times longer than yours. I really wanted to investigate that kind of possibility.

There are a lot of places in which the individual differences could be genetically determined. It might be in the rate of synthesis of the hormone in the adrenal gland, it might be something about the way it's transported through the blood to reach all the tissues of the body, it might be something about the way it's excreted in the kidney. There are a number of places where a genetic variation could influence an individual's biological response to stress. In any event, it was clear to me that, as Sonneborn had predicted, genetics had a great future.

So I recruited into our department at Stanford, when I went there in 1961, people with backgrounds in genetics and biochemistry and evolution, and brought the different disciplines together and began to develop the study of what I came to call a behavior-endocrine-genetic response to stress. The acronym was BEG—behavior endocrine genetic. We tried to get at that kind of question. It had to be done mostly in animals, where you could really look at the synthesis and transport and the metabolism of the hormones.

So, we helped to advance that field, which has gone far beyond where it was in the beginning. We were able to show that there were, in fact, major genetically determined variations in the way the body processed the stress-related hormones. It would have been fascinating to go on with it myself, but as in much of my career, for whatever reason, I would tend to stimulate superb people to get going on a line of inquiry, and they would carry it far beyond what I had done myself. Two of the most extraordinary young people in neurobiology, Jack Barchas and Roland Ciaranello, pursued this line of inquiry very effectively. They both went on to become leaders in neuroscience and psychiatry. Genetics has become very important in the stress field and in psychiatry generally at the present time. Barchas comes into this story later as one of the most remarkable people I have ever known. At NIMH, I "stole" William Bunney from his residency at Yale and we became collaborators and permanent friends. He has made major contributions in biology and psychiatry right into 2015.

When Barchas came to Stanford, we were short of "wet labs" (biological and chemical), since the planners of the new Stanford did not think of the field in this way. So I gave Barchas my own lab and he never ceased to be grateful. No "what have you done for me lately?" Over the years, our family and his did a great deal for each other.

I had long wondered whether it would be possible to learn anything about chimpanzees in the natural habitat because of their very close biological relationship to humans. The new work in genetics and biochemistry was showing that over 98 percent of the genes of chimpanzees and humans are identical. In fact, it's hard to figure how we could be so different from chimpanzees, since we share so many genes. But be that as it may, it seemed to me a great advantage if you could learn something about chimpanzees.

I began searching for opportunities in the 1950s. But how best to implement this difficult and dangerous enterprise? Within a year, Clark Howell, a distinguished physical anthropologist, brought the eminent Louis Leakey around to see me. This is before I moved to Stanford, when I was still at the NIH.

I thought a unique and valuable arrangement would be to have a field research unit in the natural habitat of chimps and a seminatural laboratory on or near campus—gaining insights from each.

Stanford had a lot of land, and they were wonderful to me and set aside twenty-seven acres to build a seminatural laboratory for chimpanzees. They could live in groups, not like solitary confinement. But we knew very little about how they lived in the wild. What's a day in the life of a chimp? Nobody knew at the time. At first I was going to try to find a young zoologist to go out and set up a field station to do that; also, a medical school classmate of mine, who was a medical missionary in the Congo, had identified an area that seemed very promising. Then the civil war in the Congo broke out, and that clearly wasn't a feasible proposition. I wasn't going to ask anybody to go and do something so dangerous.

Leakey told me that he had started a young woman named Jane Goodall on chimpanzee observational studies just a few months before in Tanzania, on the other side of Lake Tanganyika from Congo. So I started corresponding with her. Then she came for a visit to the United States, and we became friends. She and her husband, a great animal photographer, Hugo von Lawick, had a marvelous treasure trove of film, even at this early point, of chimpanzees in their natural habitat. We learned a lot from each other and this mutual benefit helped us and our students for some years, until an African political conflict led to a hostage episode that drastically ended the joint venture and put great strains on the relationships of those directly involved.

So, to fast-forward, I eventually got out to Africa. In the earlier years I didn't go because my kids were young, and I just felt to go away for a long time wouldn't make sense. But in 1968, my wife said to me, "Why don't you take Eric with you?"

He was fifteen at the time. Then Peggy, our daughter, when she was fifteen, went with us. I began this pattern of going to Africa once or twice a year throughout the 1960s. When I first went out there, it was almost time for Jane Goodall to leave. She had finished the work for which she would get her PhD at Cambridge University, and it didn't seem a practical proposition to stay. Hugo needed to do filming elsewhere on other subjects. But it was clear that they really wanted to stay; they just had no support for doing it. So I offered to try to get funding, some organizational support, make a relationship with the Tanzanian government that would give them an official blessing, and find young people with good scientific backgrounds to extend the range of their work.

We made a real field research station out of it, and it was a wonderful collaboration that lasted the better part of a decade. We were able to get graduate students and very good undergraduates and postdoctoral fellows, so at any given time we had perhaps twenty or so people working there from Stanford, from Cambridge University in England (influenced by Robert Hinde and Pat Bateson), and from Tanzania. I felt it was very important that it be international and interdisciplinary and that Tanzanians be included in it.

A lot was learned. We made much more systematic and, to the extent possible, quantitative observations of the behavior of chimps in their natural habitat, and moved from studying a single community to studying two adjacent communities so the interaction between the communities could be studied. That turned out to be extremely illuminating because of the violence between different communities.

Then we also built this seminatural laboratory at Stanford, where we wanted to be able, for example, to train the chimps to hold out their arms to have blood drawn, which it's possible to do without much difficulty. So we had the seminatural laboratory at Stanford and the natural habitat studies in Africa. We informally called them Gombe East and Gombe West. People went back and forth, students working first at one place, then the other. There are different things you could do in a laboratory than in a natural habitat. Each has its own limitations; each has its own strengths. It was, I think it's fair to say, unique in the world at that time, and may still be.

THE HOSTAGE EPISODE

This could be a book in itself, but I'll condense the essence of a dramatic story. The chimp research came to an end with a hostage episode in 1975. That's a great irony since I originally thought the Congo might be the best site for chimp studies. It was Mr. Kabila, who later became dictator of Congo, who masterminded the hostage episode. He was later assassinated by his own people, and his son has taken over. Millions have been killed since then, especially involving nearby African countries in search of precious resources.

The experience was, to say the least, intriguing. I was at the time spending a year at Caltech as a visiting professor, and my wife, Betty, was a visiting professor at UCLA (University of California, Los Angeles) that year. We were living in Pasadena. I gave a lecture at the University of California in San Diego on May 19, 1975, and we came back to my office at Caltech to check for messages toward the end of the day. The system they used at Caltech was that they would stick any messages for you on your office door. Normally I'd come back after a day or two away and I'd have a few messages. This time it was a blizzard. The door was covered with dozens of messages, so I thought it was a practical joke. But it wasn't that at all. These were emergency messages that four of my students had disappeared in Africa. There were calls from the State Department and the press and families and others. Betty, as usual, plunged in to help, answering half the messages, and then we put together a picture.

All we knew was that about forty heavily armed men had come in off Lake Tanganyika into our camp on the lake shore, taken four people, and disappeared on the lake. A few shots were heard, and nobody had any idea. Were they killed and dumped in the lake? Who took them? What was it about? We knew nothing. So I decided immediately I would go over there and see if there was anything I could do. I hadn't the foggiest idea if there was anything I could do that would be useful. We were all quite scared. It was just a surreal experience, the kind of thing that you may read about, but that doesn't happen to real people.

It was some days before we found out that these were rebels against the government of Mobutu, the longtime dictator in Congo. He renamed the country Zaire. (Now it's Congo again.) They had sent a harsh letter of demands to President Julius Nyerere of Tanzania. The story had been very secretive and complex. These rebels against Mobutu lived very high in almost impenetrable mountains that rose dramatically out of Lake Tanganyika on the other side of the shore. Lake Tanganyika is about the size and shape of Lake Michigan, about thirty miles across, three hundred miles long, a very deep mountain lake, rather dramatic, aesthetically appealing in some ways.

But anyhow, they'd come from across that lake. Our group did not know that they were there. They'd taken these students and were holding them hostage. The point was that they had had a secret supply line for a thousand miles from the Indian Ocean at Dar es Salaam, the capital of Tanzania, across Tanzania to Lake Tanganyika, and they had been getting supplies that way. They were derivatives of the Lumumba group that lost the civil war in the Congo, lost to Mobutu and the CIA, and they were getting some supplies from a few Communist countries, China, North Korea, and Cuba, as we came to understand later. That supply line had been shut down by Nyerere in a trade deal with Mobutu, so they were furious with Nyerere—whose economic tasks were exceedingly difficult. We were pawns in an African political-economic struggle. We were meant to bring pressure on Nyerere. They saw us as very powerful "Europeans," meaning white, and they attributed great power to me as an American professor—very amusing. American professors are not in the habit of thinking of ourselves as very powerful.

We were somehow supposed to get their people back who were operating the supply line, get the supply line reopened, or something to help anti-Mobutu efforts. So it was quite a surreal experience. All the way over on the long plane trip, I was very apprehensive about how I would react in the situation. I had no great confidence that I would have the foggiest idea what to do or that I would hold up well or any of that, but I was determined to do whatever I could.

It turned out that Nyerere was furious with the rebels because they were very insulting in their note to him, in their demands on him and so on. Our own government, unknown to me, was negotiating with Mobutu to be our strong man in Africa vis-à-vis the Angolan proxy war that was about to begin in Cold War fashion between us and the Soviets. I only learned that months later. So our own government had very little sympathy for our exercise. The last thing they wanted was for Americans to be talking to rebels against Mobutu when they were cultivating Mobutu as our great asset in Africa. I won't comment on the irony of that situation.

So we did not have a sympathetic response from the host country, Tanzania, or from our own government, or, of course, from the government of Zaire/Congo. So I was in business for myself. There were some wonderful people in our embassy in Dar es Salaam, especially Ambassador Beverly Carter and one of his senior staff, Lewis MacFarlane, who were very resourceful, courageous people, who helped me, as it turned out, at the risk of their careers. So we set out to do whatever we could, first of all to find out who had taken the students, and then to make contact with the hostage-takers. We didn't know how to do that. Eventually we made contact, and then had to see whether we had any conceivable negotiating leverage.

We devised a very complicated mid-lake fail-safe transfer, which failed because Mobutu had located our group and set up heavily armed gunboats in the lake. So it was Mobutu who blocked off the transfer this time, not the rebels against him. The only option that remained was to meet the hostage-takers on their beach at night. So under their guns, they released all but one of the hostages—a male student, Steve Smith. His life was now in great danger.

The only way to free this student was to involve President Nyerere. As luck would have it, his official Tanzanian representative (an anti-American bureaucrat) went out of town, so the American ambassador made an urgent plea for a meeting with Nyerere, which was readily granted. The Tanzanian representative had proved to be a real obstacle who misled us into believing that Nyerere would be of no help. The opposite was in fact true. Nyerere was determined to help free Steve and made necessary concessions to these rebels—privately held.

The students, at the reunion celebration that evening at the hotel, gave me an "Honorary Degree in Contingency Planning" written on the only available piece of paper they had. I have many honorary degrees, but this one is the best and will always recall the courage, affection, and ingenuity of these students. Anyway, after two and a half months, all four were free. It was a very important experience. It was the end of our work in Africa, and it certainly *influenced the rest of my life, as I explain in the next chapter.*

One further point on the life-changing influences: the *courage and integrity* of the student hostages (Emilie Bergman, Carrie Hunter, Steven Smith, and Barbara Smuts). Fortunately, they were allowed to stay together and their *mutual support* was of inestimable value. Moreover, and deeply touching, they were convinced that I would immediately come to Africa and find some way to get them freed. While that was a hope-sustaining fantasy since I had so little preparation and so little leverage, it taught me an unforgettable lesson in *human solidarity*. The themes of this experience in Africa echo through the remainder of this book.

There was no alternative but to provide some ransom, which we had to raise privately. My wife simply signed for it at a Palo Alto bank. It was wonderful of them to do that, because we didn't have the capital to back it up. Then some friends of ours were arranging some skullduggery, something called a "rat line," which turns out to be a covert way of sending cash around the world. There were other details that aren't important. But we did get some money over there, which we urged the rebels strongly to use for food and medicine, but we had no control over how they would use it. In all likelihood, they used most of it to buy arms. We couldn't control that, but we did the best we could to build that into the negotiation.

HUMOR IN CRISIS

If there is humor in a situation of this kind, it is almost inevitably in retrospect. There is very little that seems funny when you're in the midst of such a crisis. But we did have an episode involving some of the money in the deal with the rebels that would have been very funny had it not been so serious. In the middle of the transaction, when only Barbara Smuts had been freed due to a serious illness, the world's news media reported that we had taken a large sum of potential ransom money to the Kigoma area. (We had reason to believe that this leak came from someone in the Tanzanian government, though we could hardly take the time to track down the source.) Lewis MacFarlane and I were staying in a shack once built by the UN for research on the lake. In it we found a beat-up old trunk that served no useful purpose and it occurred to us that this might aid in a useful bit of skullduggery. We filled the trunk with obsolete papers and trash, then conspicuously carried it from our little house down to the Kigoma bank, such as it was, barely qualifying as a bank by any normal standard. We made our trek in a very conspicuous way and told the banker we had befriended earlier that he should take the utmost care to protect this trunk since it had objects of great value in it. We mentioned this "fact" to a couple of other Kigoma citizens. The implication was clear: the trunk must contain the money referred to in the media. We then quickly faded into the bush and remained out of sight. We could observe from a distance that the Mobutu people then staked out the bank and we got information that their plan was to observe it closely until we came to get the money whereupon they would take it and kill whoever came to get it. Of course, it was not money and no one came to get it. These days, we sometimes laugh at the possibility that the bank is still staked out approximately four decades later and they are still waiting for the money.

Anyway, the recognition in the world press was step one, and the ransom was step two, and the establishment of a diplomatic point of contact with the Tanzanian government was step three. But in bargaining with them, I could sense that this was not a trustworthy bargaining relationship, that they were going to try to trick me if they could, and I arranged a very complicated mid-lake transfer, which they resented and tried to avoid, and I was simply adamant, consulting with the parents all the time, that we would not give them the money except in the middle of the lake under certain conditions—we get the students first and then you get the money.

Finally they agreed to that, but unfortunately when we got out on the lake, in the meantime, Mobutu had located us, and he had some heavily armed gunboats, very powerful gunboats, that were lining that portion of the lake, and it was impossible to get across in daytime. So that hard-won plan fell through. There were so many steps that I can't even remember them now and my notes are long since gone. But we tried. For example, through some friends, I got the Swedish Embassy to intervene to help with the mid-lake scenario. We got a UN fisheries research boat to assist, and various neutral intermediaries in the international community to give legitimacy and so on, but it all fell through.

The kidnappers said they knew the lake very well, they were very skillful, and I didn't doubt that. If we were willing to do it at night, we could still do it. They could get through between the gunboats, but it would have to be on their beach; it would not be mid-lake. So, after discussion with the parents, it was clear that that was our only option. It was a lousy option, but it had to be done, and when it happened, under their guns, they gave us not all four hostages, but three of the four, keeping one, Steven Smith, a fine young man. So they had now given us the three women, but the one man they kept, and his life was in great danger.

I don't think they were actually bloodthirsty. They were certainly unreliable as negotiating partners, but I didn't have a sense that they were eager to kill anybody—though I believed that they were perfectly willing to do it if they thought it had political advantage. The political advantage would have been something like this: they would kill Steve Smith and drop his body in front of Nyerere's house in Dar es Salaam, and the message would be, "Look, Nyerere, we can get you or any of your people anywhere. We can go anywhere," as they had just done in coming there a few weeks before to the embassy.

So I finally felt that there was no way to do this last piece to save his life unless we could get Nyerere to do something, and by a great stroke of luck, I learned that this man who had been our obstacle, the official Tanzanian representative, was going out of town. He called me to say that he wanted to give his wife, Jane Goodall, a vacation, and was going off to a national park. We said good-bye, I called Ambassador Carter promptly, and we made an urgent plea for a meeting with Nyerere, which was readily granted, because it turned out that this Tanzanian representative had been the only obstacle—he had misled us grossly about Nyerere's role. Nyerere told us he had always said that he would help if it was clearly needed to save the hostages' lives. He looked shocked when we told him his representative had conveyed exactly the opposite.

Nyerere said that although he was very angry with Mobutu's people, he wasn't angry with us, and assumed we were trying to save lives, and if it were necessary for him to intervene, he would do so. I had formulated a set of sort of minimal proposals that I thought would be adequate to get Steve freed. As it turned out, Nyerere did more than I had asked. He was quite determined to get Steve freed. So he did that, only he asked us not to describe in detail what he'd done for ten years. He did not want it known that he had made a serious concession to these people. He could not give them back their leader because he'd been killed by the Tanzanians; I had found that out earlier and had leveled with rebels about it. It turned out to be useful. I had a terrible turmoil when I found it out, whether to tell them, to be the bearer of bad news, in the hope that perhaps they would find me a more trustworthy interlocutor, and the latter proved to be the case. I told them. They had thought it was probably true earlier. I confirmed their suspicion, and they seemed to have some sense that at least I was an honest man. Anyway, they couldn't get all that they wanted, but at least they got something out of it.

Fundamentally it revolved around the opportunity for them to have a continuing relationship with the government of Tanzania, at least an opportunity to see what advantage they might eventually get. Nyerere also returned a couple of people that were being held, not the high leader, but a couple of others, and so that combination was enough for them. He did not promise to reopen the supply line or anything like that, and I don't know what happened later.

Years later, I had occasion a couple of times in New York to thank President Nyerere publicly in a general way for his role in it, for his humanity and compassion. So as a matter of fact, it was really very nice. The International Peace Academy gave several simultaneous awards, on their twenty-fifth anniversary, to Nyerere, to me, and to Gro Brundtland, the prime minister of Norway. I felt very honored to be in such company, and it did give me a wonderful chance to tell our audience in short form the story of his humanitarian behavior.

Anyhow, it's gotten pretty hazy over the intervening years since 1975, but that was the gist of it—making contact with them, finding out what they stood for and what they believed in, where we might have negotiating leverage, what we could do to free the students, and to persist long enough to do it. Toward the end of that two-and-a-half-month period, about a week before the end, my wife came over. She had sensed, though I had not said it to her, that I was considering going to their camp across the lake. There was a journalist in that part of the world at the time who knew the area and who talked with me and said that if I'd be willing to go, that he'd be willing to go. He had some contact with the rebels in the past, and he thought he could find the location, and he thought it would be a very dramatic story, but he thought it would only make sense if I would go and that the two of us might be able to do something to get Steve Smith out. I was planning to do that, but only as a last resort. It was obvious that it gave them the opportunity to just hold us hostage as well and thus have two more hostages, which might, in some sense, be of greater value to them than the one that they were still holding. And that was of course a very real risk. But if I had no other options, I was going to do that, and Betty sensed it, and I don't recall how. She is a very sensitive person. She then set out from California to Tanzania.

Our son and daughter were deeply concerned to have us both in this situation. It was a vivid and poignant circumstance. But they trusted our judgment.

One final episode. When Nyerere did what he did, he just went ahead and did it. He didn't make it an exchange. He sent these two guys back and sent the message, and he was convinced that they would then release Steve Smith, but there was a day or two of great tension, and then we got the call. I was back in Dar es Salaam at the time when Steve appeared in Kigoma, and we sent a plane out to pick him up. It was a great reunion. When he got to the airport, the Tanzanian official, the same official who'd been a problem to us all along, arranged for the Tanzanian secret police to suddenly arrive. We had a lot of troubles in the airport itself. Our ambassador was misled about the time of arrival and kept out of the way. Dishonesty rode high.

But there I was, I went out to the tarmac to greet Steve. Suddenly a jeep full of troops came up, knocked me down, took Steve Smith off, roaring away. They turned out to be Tanzanian secret police. The plan was to interrogate him before we brainwashed him. So they interrogated him. By that time, the US ambassador arrived and we were making a tremendous international howl. The ambassador called Nyerere, and I don't know if he got through to him or not, but he got through to somebody, and so in a couple of hours they released Steve, but that episode was an unpleasant coda to the whole affair.

So when it was all over, that night we had a big party at the hotel, and the students gave me, just on a shabby piece of paper—the best they had—an "Honorary Degree in Contingency Planning." It was from "Kasakale University." Kasakale is a valley where the chimps had very rich fruit to feed on, so they invented Kasakale University, and somewhere in my papers I have that treasured honorary degree. I have a lot of other honorary degrees, but that's the best one. I can never forget the courage of the four hostages: Carrie Hunter, Emilie Bergman, Barbara Smuts, and Steve Smith.

Anyway, you see what that experience did. For those two and a half months, I was immersed in dreadful problems of hatred, violence, deception, abject poverty, cruelty, disease. It just left me with a sense that if I could contribute anything, even the slightest contribution at the margin to some of the great problems of that kind, that I would like to try to do so. I didn't fully realize it, actually, until I had a thoughtful letter in Dar es Salaam from the president of the National Academy of Sciences, inviting me to reconsider the presidency of the Institute of Medicine. He had the perception that an experience like that might change what I'd want to do with my life, and so he renewed the offer that I had turned down in May.

I did wrestle with what was the best way to do something that would be effective in linking the scientific community and the policy community to address such great problems. It was really a rare opportunity and I should take it, so the hostage episode did change my life drastically. There was this total immersion in the depths of degradation, and at the same time it brought out the best in some people, wonderful people like MacFarlane and Carter, and the students, for example Michelle Trudeau, who now broadcasts for National Public Radio, and Barbara Smuts, now a professor at the University of Michigan, who was so gravely ill with a parasitic disease she had acquired in the hostage zone—as well as the other hostages. Courageous, wonderful people. Stress tends to do that. It tends to bring out the best in some people and the worst in some people, and we saw both in these stressful months. It gave me an impetus to tackle crucial problems of human survival.

Ambassador Carter was a wonderful man. He was one of the two black ambassadors that we still had in our ambassadorial corps at that time. We were down to a very low ebb at the ambassadorial level. At the end of the episode, he asked me, had I ever thought about doing other things? He said that he'd known a lot of people who dealt with difficult situations, and he was impressed that I could really do that and I should think about larger problems.

1975: THE TURNING POINT

Toward the end of the hostage episode, a dangerous twist occurred, and Betty and I collaborated to cope within it. It's a great tribute to Betty's ingenuity and sensitivity. We've been terrific collaborators for about sixty years. She's an extremely resourceful person.

During the episode, when I first got to Dar es Salaam, our ambassador told me that the Tanzanian Secret Service was quite up in arms about the whole thing, and they were going to bug my hotel room—which they did, in a very clumsy way: they came in repeatedly to "fix the light in the bathroom." But anyway, what I could say on the telephone connections, tenuous at best, was extremely limited by that fact, because we were going to do things that clearly the Tanzanians didn't want us to do. I was going to do whatever was necessary to save the students.

Betty and I were able to improvise a code. From our relationship, partly out of US idiomatic language and partly some shared experiences that nobody could know about but us, we were able to get certain key symbols for the code to communicate what I needed her to do. Since it was an African political problem, the US side of it was very important in a number of ways, and she took charge of that. But over a period of time, she did figure out—and I didn't intend to tell her—that I was considering going to the kidnap location on the other side of Lake Tanganyika if necessary, as a last resort to try to bargain for the fourth student.

As I mentioned above, there was an American journalist who knew that area very well because he had had a number of scoops there in the past. He told me that he thought he knew where the camp was. He was willing to go himself, but he didn't think it would amount to much. He thought if we went together, we would have a chance, and that was plausible. But there was also the chance they would simply take us hostage.

In my negotiating with Kabila people, there was nothing that engendered confidence. I mean, they were not trustworthy negotiating partners. I wouldn't say they were bloodthirsty, but neither were they trustworthy. So it wasn't a congenial proposition. On the other hand, if that was all I had, the only card I had to play, then I would do it.

Somehow Betty sensed that and got on an airplane and came over to prevent me from going and doing what she thought would be quite foolish. She thought they would simply take us hostage and they would have more bargaining power with us than with the student. And I suspect she was probably right about that.

Anyway, it did work out. It's a tribute to her as an individual, and it's also an interesting commentary on close human relationships, that you can, under great duress, invent a code and sense each other's responses over thousands of miles of poor communication. It was also a tribute to Peggy and Eric that they had the courage to trust both their parents in a situation of great risk.

Those years were extremely stimulating, and an opportunity to get some insights into human evolution, and I wrote quite a number of papers alone, with Goodall, with Washburn, and with others, and, more importantly, stimulated students, some of whom are now professors at Harvard, the University of Michigan, Duke, the University of California, and elsewhere—making very good contributions to the field. So I view it as a very good time and a fantastic set of experiences of a kind that I never would have dreamt. I never dreamt of going to Africa in the first place. I never dreamt of doing primate research. I never dreamt of dealing with a hostage problem. But there it was.

POST-HOSTAGE: THE NEXT CRISIS

Ambassador Beverly Carter was one of only two remaining black ambassadors in our ambassadorial corps at the time. To my surprise, I had to save his career after the kidnapping. To us, he was a hero. It was shocking that his career should now be in jeopardy. It was a dramatic experience, as if we had not had enough drama already. We stopped off in London on the way back, my wife and I, to thank our British friends, especially John Bowlby, the pioneer in child development who had been very helpful, particularly with Barbara Smuts when she was so ill, and in other ways, getting information that we needed, getting to the BBC and so on; we wanted to thank them personally. After a day there, we went home. We dropped off the students at this hospital in Britain that's so good for tropical diseases, to have them thoroughly checked out. I had diarrhea and lost a lot of weight. I thought I'd go back home and get medical care at Stanford, but I thought they should be checked for exotic tropical diseases just in case. This London place was tops for tropical diseases. After a morning farewell, we took off for California.

To my utter astonishment, it was a great homecoming. There were hundreds of students at the airport with banners and photos and cheers. We all went to our house, and out in the yard they had set up a microphone, and I explained to them what happened. Got to bed about midnight or so, and a couple of hours later, I got a call in the middle of the night from Ambassador Carter, who was back in Washington. He'd been called back to Washington, and I thought naively that they were going to honor him for his contribution, but no, he'd been fired. His career had been ended on the grounds that he'd violated US terrorism policy. This so-called policy was extremely vague. After all, this was the first episode of its kind. Carter had done his best to keep within the limits prescribed.

Friends in the State Department and the media gave me some background and context: Kissinger did this sort of thing periodically. A couple of times a year, he would show his authority in some really flagrant way, and he also was upset about this Angola problem. That, no doubt, inflamed him further, but in his view, this man had been insubordinate or something like that. It was done in a very public way. Kissinger's style was to denigrate ambassadors generally to flaunt his authority from time to time. I can't read the man's mind, but he had done it, and it was, of course, in our view, all of us who knew Carter, just an outrage.

The "welcome home" middle-of-the-night call was poignant. Carter, a six-foot-eight, powerful, composed person, got through a few sentences, and broke down. His wife had come on the phone to explain to me what had happened. All he wanted was for me to come to Washington in a couple of days and stand with him at his resignation press conference and say that he was a decent human being. I said, "Well, those kids were held hostage for some time, and, in my view, you are now hostage, and I'd appreciate it if you'd give me a chance to get you freed. Let me work on it now."

He said he didn't feel he could do anything himself. He felt it was professionally inappropriate. He was a very disciplined person. But if I wanted to do that, he would hold off any public announcement and just wait. So I then devoted the next six weeks to trying to find ways to get him reinstated. This was another part of the experience of getting into new territory far beyond any of my prior experience. We first tried all the proper routes, talked to the person that Kissinger had designated at the State Department, and although the man was personally sympathetic and I've gotten to know him in later years, he said there was nothing to be done; it was finished.

So having tried the proper routes, I decided the only real possibility would be through media pressure, particularly on the president, if we could manage that. I had a friend, luckily—it was a very good piece of luck—named Fred M. Hechinger, who for some years was the education editor of the *New York Times* and a member of the editorial board of the *New York Times*, who, oddly enough, in later years was on the Carnegie board and then he was on our staff after he retired from the *Times*.

I told Fred Hechinger the story, he said he would think about it and get back to me. He got back to me that afternoon, and he read me a draft of an editorial—and then the *Times* ran it the next day as the lead editorial. They titled it "Humane Diplomat," and they said it was an outrage to fire a man in his mid-fifties who'd done what he'd done throughout his career, and so on. That was very, very useful.

Then Carl T. Rowan, the columnist who knew Carter and who himself had been a black ambassador, one of the few, got interested. I talked with him, and he wrote a column about it and made various calls. The State Department was very leaky, and Rowan was able to find out a lot. Some other people were also helpful, including Daniel Schorr, the distinguished journalist, then with CBS. So we got some media coverage.

Then we got one of the networks to do a little bit on the evening news about one of the families, the family of the student who'd been held the longest. So with that, with several indications that I wasn't just some long-haired professor, but that we had the capability to mobilize media, I asked for an appointment with President Gerald Ford. I didn't get that, although I later got to know and respect President Ford. He helped us on the Carnegie Commission on Science, Technology, and Government. I had a very interesting conversation with him later about all of this.

But anyway, I did get to talk to his then chief of staff, Donald Rumsfeld, and essentially my message was, "Look, here is the *New York Times* editorial, here's the Rowan piece, here's a summary of the ABC piece. I have had invitations to go on the air with these students, very sympathetic, appealing students. We've turned them all down so far, but the *Today Show*, the *Tomorrow Show*, and other popular television shows were persistent." These were morning shows and evening shows with large audiences, the talk shows of the day in 1975. "We've turned all these down, but unless Ambassador Carter is reinstated, we simply will have no alternative but to go on the air and tell the essential story, and it is a nasty story in which American lives were put in jeopardy by the American government, not just the ambassador's career, but this is what we would say." And I outlined what I and the students would say.

His response was at first very cool, but when I laid out the media options, he got rather agitated. In fact, he misunderstood me. He thought we were going on the air that day because I had mentioned the *Today Show*. I said it would be soon if necessary but I would prefer to avoid the show and instead get a constructive response from President Ford, especially since I know he had been immersed in the vital Helsinki conference. His chief of staff said, "Put it off. Please put it off a day. Give me a chance to look into it. It's probably all a misunderstanding."

So I said, "Fine. Of course," but I said that in order for us to feel confident, Carter would need a choice—he'd already been replaced in Tanzania; they had quickly appointed another ambassador. We felt it right for him to have a choice of several positions so that he could have an appropriate one. We weren't going to have him reinstated in the lowest possible position. It would have to be appropriate and acceptable to him. Anyway, the White House got back to me in a few hours and said it was all a misunderstanding and the president certainly never knew about these events. And our request was legitimate. The president was in Helsinki during much of our turmoil (leading to a great human rights initiative vis-à-vis the Soviets). I doubt whether the president knew about it. He had a lot of other things to worry about. In any event, that's what Rumsfeld said, "The president didn't know about it, and once it was called to his attention, he said he certainly wants to be fair about this, and Ambassador Carter will be offered a choice of positions." That was all done, and he was reinstated.

To jump ahead on that story, about a year later, when Cyrus R. Vance became secretary of state, I didn't know him then, but I wrote him a letter explaining what had happened and saying that I thought it would be a public service if he were to find a good position in the new administration for Ambassador Carter, and he did. He actually created a special position for Beverly Carter. Little did I know that Vance and I later would become fast friends and collaborators for years.

But that additional experience with Carter after the hostage episode made me feel that I should try to do things that would deal with deeply serious problems. I didn't have great confidence that I could, but at least I had some encouragement toward it. Then, for example, when I got to the presidency of the Institute of Medicine, it was early in the history of the Institute, and I was able to lay out a program for dealing with major issues, including diseases of poverty at home and abroad. We created an international health program, which dealt primarily with the diseases of developing countries. There was some direct carryover, both in spirit and in the substance of what I did in the ensuing five years. It was a transforming experience that opened the way to totally unexpected developments—the *twists and turns of opportunity*.

WHAT COMES NEXT?

It so happens I had an invitation early in May to become president of the Institute of Medicine, which is the medical part of the National Academy of Sciences (NAS). Or to put it another way, the search committee, looking for a president, wanted me to be the lead candidate. It would have had to be approved by the academy system, but they had taken informal soundings that determined that, in fact, there was support in the academy system, and in all probability, if I said I would be interested, that I would be president of the Institute of Medicine. The NAS is a very special place in the American and, indeed, world scientific community.

I was enormously pleased, but I said no on the spot in May. It was at a luncheon in Pasadena. My wife was there with me, and we were on leave that year. I felt I couldn't leave Stanford, including the linked work in Africa and on campus. I had developed a configuration of responsibilities that was unique to me, and I thought if I pulled out of it now, it probably wouldn't be sustained. In any case, I loved what I was doing. Our kids had grown up on the Stanford campus with wonderful attributes. I never envisioned leaving at all.

That was early in May. The students were taken on May 19. Two and a half months later, it was over. When I got back to Dar es Salaam at the end of it, there was a letter from the president of the National Academy of Sciences that essentially said something to the effect that, an experience like this can be a deep experience. It can affect your whole life. It can make you rethink what you want to do. We're asking you to rethink. Would you like to consider the Institute of Medicine? Please come and visit and let's talk about it.

It rang a bell. I wasn't sure that that was the right thing to do, but that, combined with what Ambassador Carter had said, made me rethink. I had been immersed in the worst problems of the world during those few months—of disease and abject poverty and ignorance and deception and violence. My nose was rubbed for months in all these dreadful problems. I had thought that maybe in some way, if I could turn my energies to settings and institutions that could do something about those problems, the smallest bit could affect policies that would have some kind of ameliorative or preventive effect on terrible problems of that kind. That would surely be a good thing to do. But how best to do it? I thought maybe to construct something at Stanford different from what I'd been doing before the kidnapping.

I did go to visit with the president of the Academy and others, and decided that in point of fact, that was a very strong institution, had worldwide standing, was policy oriented, and had ways of bringing the strength of the scientific community to bear on great policy issues, policies within the scientific community and beyond the scientific community. So I was, in a way, a changed person, and from then on, both in that position and later at Carnegie, I was fundamentally trying to find some way to do what I could on these great issues.

We had several strands to work at the Institute of Medicine, and then later for a few years at Harvard when President Derek Bok urged me to develop a university-wide health policy program modeled on the Institute of Medicine. So there was a total of about eight years at the Institute of Medicine and at Harvard where I was basically putting together sets of people who could bring great strengths from different angles on health policy issues—and learning about the broad, fundamental value of international, interdisciplinary research as related to domestic analysis and education. We had the opportunity of linking the scientific community and the policy community—a project with enormous potential for making the world better, in health and beyond.

INSTITUTE OF MEDICINE (IOM): BUILDING AN INSTITUTION, CONTRIBUTING TO WORLD HEALTH AND PEACE; THE NATIONAL ACADEMY OF SCIENCES (NAS)

After well-meaning perplexity in the early seventies, groping for a way to put health into the National Academy of Sciences (NAS), with my arrival we set out to build an enduring institution that would explore all factors influencing the health of the American people and beyond. The strength of the NAS setting was a strong asset. The NAS was created during the Civil War by Abraham Lincoln and did much to advance the basic sciences. In the 1960s, a National Institute of Engineering was created, and at the outset of the 1970s, an Institute of Medicine. This rapid broadening of the NAS to include engineering and medicine involved transitional stress, but in the long run has proved valuable for the institution, the nation, and indeed the world. By 1977, the IOM knew that the president of the United States and the secretary of health, education, and welfare to bothok a keen interest in its activities. Evidence was accumulating that the IOM could have an enduring effect on the nation's health policy. Historians who did a study of the IOM credited me with five years of inspirational leadership (1975–1980).

In June of 1975, the IOM Council had designated me as its first choice for the presidency. The NAS Council moved quickly to confirm the selection, and President Philip Handler agreed. He wrote to me that month and offered this leadership position. My acceptance of the offer depended on a set of circumstances as bizarre as the IOM would ever encounter. Because I was in Dar es Salaam, dealing with the hostage episode, Handler's letter reached me very slowly. On July 19, 1975, I reported to Handler that three of the four students had been freed without harm (but not without danger), but the negotiating process for the fourth was very difficult and dangerous. Handler was exceedingly helpful in reaching out to the world scientific community to save these students in the spirit of free scientific inquiry. Most of the world's active science academies signed Handler's open letter. After wrenching consideration and valuable consultations, I accepted Handler's offer with deep appreciation and high hopes.

In November of 1975, I delivered my inaugural remarks to IOM members who attended the annual meeting. I was not a stranger in IOM circles, having been selected as an initial member in 1971, served on the Council from 1971 to 1974, and chaired the Program Committee between 1972 and 1973. In inaugural presidential remarks, I described the key features of the IOM. The organization must make a serious, thoughtful attempt to face difficult issues and to do so in a way that cut across traditional specialties and perspectives. Unlike other organizations, the IOM held no overriding doctrine, no party line, no cow too sacred to be examined, and its views reflected deeper analysis and reflections than those of most others in the health field at that time. After listing the organization's assets, I considered its liabilities. I wondered how the IOM could coax sufficient time from its busy members to examine the key issues, how a Washington-based staff could relate to a geographically dispersed membership, how the IOM could preserve its independence and be of use to both the government and to private institutions, and how the IOM could achieve cross-specialty collaboration to tackle the policy problems of health care, prevention, education, and the science base underlying it all. These problems deserved thoughtful attention and I intended to get it—by quiet, respectful inquiry if possible; by relentless harassment if necessary.

The historical study of the IOM described me as speaking with an inspirational eloquence in exhorting the members to contribute to the work of the organization. When I learned of staff-member tensions in the infant organization, it raised questions. Although I wanted more member participation, I realized how important it was to treat our high-quality staff, for example Sarah Brown, Elena Nightingale, Fred Solomon, Delores Parron, Karl Yordy, and Roger Bulger, with respect and maintain good relations with the governmental staffs who were interested in having the IOM create and maintain a solid factual basis for considering health policy. I wanted to make the IOM relevant to this new policymaking structure, yet do so in a way that would not turn the IOM into a consulting firm.

We grappled with the IOM's identity during my first year in office. I initiated a major review of the IOM's progress with a long-term view of institution building. This analysis lasted from the fall of 1975 through the fall of 1976 in the search for a well-founded, enduring vision of its future missions and basic themes. The review, extending to all levels of the IOM's operation—from the staff, to the IOM Council, to the IOM membership—moved toward a consensus as to its future directions, and reshaped the organization to reflect this consensus. There were crosscutting pressures. Some wanted a sole preoccupation with medical practice; some with basic research; some with national health insurance; and still other options as well. In the end, we adhered to the original mandate of the preorganizational planning group that urged the IOM to cover all the factors that affect the health of the American public. Among the distinguished members and public health figures who were helpful were Julius Richmond, Daniel Tosteson, Don Kennedy, Walsh McDermott, Walter Rosenblith, Josh Lederberg, and others too many to mention.

In management, I realized that we would have to clarify the expectations that project staffs (Washington-based) and steering committees (national) had of one another. We arrived at four tentative conclusions. First, the IOM should work on some big issues, but not at the expense of monopolizing IOM money or staff talent. Second, the IOM should develop the ability to perform policy analysis on a quick-response basis if necessary. Third, the IOM leadership should reflect diverse talents and institutional centers—for example, clinics, health associations, and research institutions. Fourth, the IOM should use the broad-based interests of its members to clarify important national and international problems, not narrow political preoccupations or partisan preference. Operationally, we had to clarify the relationship between the staff and the steering committees and integrate the variety of skills in a respectful atmosphere.

I turned early and often for advice to the IOM Council and to IOM members as well as the brilliant context of the Academy as a whole. They considered how much emphasis to give to major policy themes and how much of the Institute's efforts should be devoted to large studies, policy statements, background papers, conferences, and seminars. Organizations of high quality and integrity should provide us help for organization and function.

Several institutional settings and several superb mentors gave me an extraordinary education in the newly emerging biobehavioral medicine. In taking on this role, I was determined to serve as the first *full-term* president of the IOM, holding a clear structure to pursue the original mandate of the institution. On November 6, 1975, Senator Edward Kennedy, then the leading member of Congress in health matters, gave the inaugural address. The enthusiasm of the members and staff was most encouraging.

Early IOM studies concerned the costs of medical education. Congress then asked it to consider the related problem of how the Medicare and Medicaid programs should pay physicians in teaching hospitals for their treatment of elderly (Medicare) or indigent (Medicaid) patients. Congress also wanted to know how much federal money went into the support of foreign medical school graduates and how Medicare reimbursement could be used to avoid gluts of physicians in some areas and shortages in others. How could the IOM consider ways in which Medicare reimbursements might be structured so as to encourage a greater number of physicians to enter primary care fields? A perennial dilemma in modern medicine. While these were important questions that have enduring significance, there were other issues of at least equal significance.

Before reaching conclusions about basic themes, I wanted a mandate from the IOM Council arising from thorough consideration. Toward this end, I scheduled a series of retreats for the Council that took place in July 1976. Julius Richmond (a highly respected elder statesman with long vision) presided over the first one in which five IOM Council members held a long and unstructured discussion of IOM priorities, deciding that the IOM should devote its time and skills to crucial public policy questions. I affirmed this point at a meeting of the Program Committee a week later. I said that the Institute would not be doing so many "responsive" studies in the style of the Medicare-Medicaid reimbursement project, useful as they were, but would instead diversify its portfolio and turn more toward private foundations to support smaller studies with sharper focus.

Richmond said that the IOM should begin to attack major problems such as national health insurance and biomedical research policy. I floated an idea that appealed as a rational way to assess our prospects. I would ask the staff and key members to "map out the terrain" in five major policy areas, giving staff a definite role in the "new IOM" and staking out the major issues that should be addressed. I thought that the five areas should be (1) health services, with special attention to national health insurance; (2) health sciences policy; (3) prevention of disease; (4) education for the health professions; and (5) mental health. This proved to be the major idea that emerged from the meeting and was well agreed upon with broad participation.

In a communication to IOM members in September 1976, I synthesized the staff, committee, and Council discussions of the IOM's mission. Here again, I announced my intention to map the terrain of health by means of the multiple perspectives so distinctively available in the IOM. In the past, IOM studies had been initiated by Congress and the executive branch, but the terrain maps would make it easier for the IOM to initiate its own studies while still being responsive where appropriate to government requests. Although I did not believe that the IOM's five principal foundation benefactors would indefinitely provide the sort of flexible money that would make such initiatives possible, the IOM should be able to obtain foundation grants in particular program areas, allowing for flexibility within each area as necessary and feasible. Concomitantly, we should establish constructive work relations with policymakers in both parties and both houses of Congress as well as the executive branch.

Thus, the IOM moved toward reorganization. In March 1977, we created six operating divisions, each with its own staff director and its own advisory board of IOM members and other experts. The divisions meshed with the work of the Program Committee and terrain maps. Before the reorganization, staff had worked on projects of the moment without a long-term perspective. The new plan made it possible for staff members to develop specialties and for the entire IOM program to have more coherence from year to year.

Two people who worked with me over several decades wrote to express their joint appreciation and their appraisal of why they stuck with me for so long and in different institutions. One is Elena Nightingale. She is a remarkable person who worked with me at the Institute of Medicine, other components of the National Academy of Science, Harvard, and the Carnegie Corporation. She was an authentic pioneer in molecular and cellular biology, earning her PhD at Rockefeller University. Having lived through part of the Holocaust in Italy, she was acutely aware of clinical needs, and so augmented her basic science by earning an MD at New York University. There she met her remarkable husband Stuart Nightingale, a leader in preventive medicine and global health, and they have been great collaborators ever since.

It is difficult to imagine how she juggled the various balls she had to cope with between Rockefeller, NYU, Harvard, and the Academies. While doing all these things at a high level of achievement, she raised two wonderful daughters and helped to strengthen each institution where she worked, not only at the project level but also at the structural level.

A singular achievement was the large role she played in the years-long series of studies on vaccines, initiated at the Institute of Medicine and carried on to subsequent institutions, as they have become increasingly valuable both in this country and in developing countries. Together, we built the framework of the program for Dr. Fred Robbins, who had earlier earned a Nobel Prize for his work on the polio virus, and carried on by joint design after I left the institute. With my strong support, he became my successor as president, with Elena Nightingale at his side for the vaccine program.

Another colleague who wrote to me in appreciation was Susan Smith, who came to me at a very young age and served as my administrative assistant at the Institute of Medicine. Later, she joined the staff at the Carnegie Corporation, again as my administrative assistant. She was extremely skillful in both institutions as an effective interface between the internal staff and board on the one hand and external contacts on the other. Her extraordinary judgment, kindness, practical wisdom, and adaptability made her invaluable, and I will always be grateful. She has moved on to important positions at Columbia University. With my encouragement, she undertook formal education and was very effective getting a bachelor's degree from New York University, a master's degree at Columbia in international affairs, and a second master's degree in public health.

The joint statement Elena and Susan recently wrote me on their perception of my leadership is as follows: "*Interpersonal Skills.* Our initial encounters with David Hamburg were different than those either of us had experienced with other employers. These encounters were marked by his unfailing enthusiasm, support, and recognition of our potential.

"*Institution Building and Organizing Work for Action.* He would organize work—from the largest-scale initiatives to day-to-day tasks—into interconnected pieces, each of which had a specific mission and set of milestones. At IOM, Harvard, and Carnegie he created an organizational structure that endured for many years.

"*Willingness to Take Risks.* He led the IOM to take on controversial issues that hadn't been touched before, such as the Adolescent Health Conference and issues relating to recombinant DNA research, a controversial topic in the 1970s. At Carnegie, David added health as a new topic for support and launched the Avoiding Nuclear War program in 1983, a time when the Cold War was in full swing. Other foundation leaders were reluctant, if not downright fearful, of entering into this area."

We had exceedingly productive working relations and I am very grateful for their extraordinary contributions.

Sarah Brown worked closely with me in the early IOM years and later in outstanding advancement in adolescent development and women's health. So, too, with Lee Schorr, Betty Hamburg, Belle Sawhill, and Anne Petersen. One outgrowth of their efforts was the creation of an organization to avoid teenage and unwanted pregnancies, spearheaded for years by Sarah Brown and Tom Kean.

Lee Schorr is a member of the Institute of Medicine of the National Academies, and served on its Governing Council from 1975 to 1977. From 1965 to 1967 she headed the health division of the Office of Economic Opportunity when the original Neighborhood Health Centers were developed and funded. In 1979 she was Senior Scholar-in-Residence at the Institute of Medicine. From 1981 to 1986, she was a member of the Working Group on Early Life of the Division of Health Policy Research and Education at Harvard University.

Building a Structure for Long-Term Value; Leadership Roles

Sketching these people should give an idea of the diversity, dedication, and intellectual stature of the IOM atmosphere. Many deserve credit. The creation of program divisions and the initiation of terrain maps transformed the way in which the Program Committee functioned. What before had been an unstructured discussion of disparate projects became a much more disciplined conference on the six program areas. I chaired the group in charge of writing the terrain maps in health science policy and in prevention. It was an invigorating experience. At the end of 1978, I announced that we would create a new Division of Mental Health and Behavioral Medicine, an appropriate choice given the gravity of the problems, new scientific opportunities, and my own commitments to the field.

The new organizational structure achieved several aims. It increased the participation of members in IOM activities. Not only would members be able to serve on the Program Committee, they also would be able to shape an advisory board in their specialty area. The new structure also expanded the role of the staff, because they would have to collaborate with the advisory boards and help in the creation of terrain maps. Moreover, it enabled interested parties to observe what areas of inquiry the IOM regarded as most important and hence what projects most deserved to be funded. In short, we were seeking to build an enduring structure for the institution that would make full use of its talents and members. This has been confirmed in public statements by subsequent presidents.

One focus, still salient today, is that when medical schools admitted students, they should favor those who wanted to go into primary care fields, and all medical schools should provide undergraduates with clinical experience in a primary care setting as well as training in epidemiology and aspects of the behavioral and social sciences that were relevant to patient care. The report included a checklist of the steps that medical schools could take to implement the changes advocated by the committee. Thus, we built on the emerging molecular and cellular biology with such great promise for the future of medicine—and also broadened the horizon of health-related education and research.

Disseminating Reliable Information

Aware of the need to distribute the results of its studies, the IOM made efforts to place a summary of some studies in a well-respected journal. Two examples are the report on medical school education and the polio study. Articles appeared in the *New England Journal of Medicine,* and are now read by doctors in many different specialties. The reports carried names of multiple authors, from the project staff and the membership. Thus, the IOM disseminated the results of its work and gave professional recognition to staff as well as members. In all of this work, we recognized that long-term efforts would be essential, measured in decades and even generations, to meet the scope and complexity of the problems.

The Polio Study and the Promise of Immunization Worldwide

The polio vaccine study illustrated how the IOM could use its expertise to resolve public policy disputes. Polio vaccinations constitute one of America's greatest public health advances. After the introduction of the Salk vaccine in 1954, new cases of the disease virtually disappeared. By the 1970s, the number of new cases each year could be counted in single digits. Public health officials worried as much about people not getting vaccinated as they did about the safety of the vaccine itself. For greater ease of administration, authorities substituted the use of an oral vaccine for the injected vaccine in 1962. All a person had to do to prevent polio was swallow a sugar cube. Unlike the Salk vaccine, this Sabin oral vaccine was prepared with what scientists called "attenuated live virus." Although this oral vaccine was generally safe, it did lead to rare cases of polio—forty-four cases between 1969 and 1976, among people who took it or came into contact with someone who had taken it.

The problem acquired more visibility in 1976, in the wake of the effort to prevent an epidemic of swine flu. A number of people who were vaccinated against this flu suffered adverse reactions, creating a public scandal and raising questions about whether the government or the vaccine manufacturer was liable for damages. In September 1976, a Health, Education, and Welfare (HEW) official testified before a Senate subcommittee that the government was having trouble entering into contracts with private companies for the manufacture of vaccines of all types, including those against measles, rubella, and polio. Thus, a shortage of vaccine caused widespread concern.

Against this background, Dr. Theodore Cooper, the Ford administration's assistant secretary of health (and later, head of the IOM Program Committee), approached me about responding to a request from senators Edward Kennedy and Jacob Javits (R-NY): Would the IOM look into the relative merits of live (Sabin) versus killed (Salk) polio vaccines? They wanted the report in the spring of 1977. The sooner they received an answer, the better. I took a keen interest in this problem and we responded with alacrity. In less than two months, well-informed and effectively organized Elena Nightingale of the IOM staff made arrangements for two committee meetings and a two-day workshop. We persuaded Bernard Greenberg, respected dean of the School of Medicine at the University of North Carolina at Chapel Hill, to chair the study, and we recruited a steering committee that contained Fred Robbins—a Nobel laureate for his research on polio, a person notable for his good judgment, and a future IOM president—as well as Byron Waksman, a professor of pathology at Yale. We were dealing with a terribly severe disease, made famous by President Franklin Roosevelt's extraordinary struggle to overcome it.

The committee met its deadlines, first convening a working plan and then an international workshop a month later—for example, consulting with experts from the Netherlands, which had not switched from the dead to the live vaccine. The committee assembled working groups on practical questions: for example, how to obtain informed consent from those who received polio shots, and the safety and efficacy of polio vaccines in the United States. There followed promptly an executive session that reached decisions on the major public policy questions. In early April, the committee presented its findings at a scientific conference devoted to immunization; nine days later, exactly on schedule, it delivered its report to the Department of Health, Education, and Welfare.

The committee recommended that the United States continue the use of the Sabin oral vaccine as its chief means of preventing polio, but with caveats. Those with heightened susceptibility to infection or adults who were being vaccinated for the first time should continue to take Salk polio injections. The committee also advised that there be a new round of immunizations, to be given orally to all children as they entered seventh grade. The interest of this practice was to protect the children in their later years when they became parents and thus eliminate cases in which parents contracted polio from their immunized children. The committee emphasized that the country could achieve a higher rate of immunization against polio. In 1974, only 45 percent of all nonwhite children had been vaccinated against polio. The committee sought a 90 percent immunization rate within a few years. Toward this end, the committee advised that all liability from the immunizations, except in cases of gross negligence, be assumed by the government.

This study attracted a great deal of serious attention. As I've mentioned, the *New England Journal of Medicine* ran an article that summarized the study, as did the widely circulated *Scientific American*. Elena Nightingale reported that she had been besieged by requests for copies of the study from groups around the world, including the Belgian government and the World Health Organization. Nightingale emphasized that the study helped to calm the national agitation that had followed the swine flu vaccine debacle. She noted strong interest in poliomyelitis vaccination. She and the IOM earned much respect for the excellence of this study. It showed her capacities, which in future years would serve the IOM, the United States, and other countries as well.

In the Nixon and Ford eras, IOM staff eventually developed and maintained many close ties to administration officials, such as HEW secretary Elliot Richardson and assistant secretary Merlin DuVal. During the Ford administration, in particular, I worked closely with Theodore Cooper, the assistant secretary of health, and Guy Stever, the president's science adviser, and formed a lasting friendship with Elliot Richardson that began when he was secretary of HEW, a man of wisdom and courage. After Cooper was fired by Califano in the Carter administration, he received an invitation from me to come to the IOM as a visiting scholar. As these examples show, these were not partisan enterprises. They were health professional enterprises based on biomedical science and public health research.

As I had said in my final president's report to the IOM, "We must take a sympathetic interest in government efforts and try to be helpful where we can. But the Institute can be most helpful in the long run if our actions have the degree of insight and objectivity." So the IOM would continue to speak truth to power and make an impact in accordance with the evidence.

In March 1977, for example, I told the Council that an ad hoc group had been convened to offer strong suggestions to the Presidential Commission on Mental Health, since there was well-known serious interest on the subject within the IOM. I was very appreciative of the respect bestowed on us by both scientific and policy communities. I also reported on a bipartisan congressional request that the IOM study urgent needs and promising leads in the field of *international health*, something I had wanted since my days in Africa. Senator Edward Kennedy and his congressional colleagues from both parties expressed an interest in how America's medical research capacity and its experiences in organization and delivery of primary and preventive care might benefit other nations, an interest in the international dimensions of health that the Carter administration adopted and President Carter has pursued vigorously ever since. In May, members of the IOM Council had dinner with Secretary Califano and met with Donald Kennedy, commissioner of the Food and Drug Administration (FDA), and my former colleague at Stanford. In the same month the Council learned that Julius Richmond, who had played such a valuable role in the origin of the IOM, was chosen by President Carter to be his chief health officer.

IOM, NAS, and World Health

Each of these administration ties led to work for the IOM. Already interested in the field of international health after my experiences in Africa—indeed you might say I brought Tanzania with me to the IOM—I urged the IOM Council to accept the congressional invitation to do research on this subject. At its own expense, the IOM convened an International Health Committee that prepared a report on research opportunities in the field of international health. The field became integral to the IOM's basic activities, with a program division devoted to it. In 1978, I made international health a major focus of the IOM's annual meeting. Although I was not sure how much interest members had in the topic, I believed that the gravity of disease conditions in other parts of the world merited serious attention from the Institute.

In July 1977, the IOM Council learned how important international health activities were to President Carter. It heard from Peter Bourne, a Carter White House staffer and former student of mine, that health was an increasingly pivotal concern in the administration's strategy for improving relations with other countries. Bourne said that the president's human rights initiative included policy, problems in food supply, health care, and shelter were likely to receive as much emphasis in dealings with other countries as civil rights. In the remainder of his long career, President Carter increasingly emphasized health in developing nations. Congress mirrored the president's interest. Aware that the IOM was doing work in the field, members of the Senate Committee on Human Resources attached an amendment to a public health bill that provided for an IOM study to determine opportunities for broadened federal program activities in international health. This study became the first formal product of the IOM Division of International Health.

It appeared in April 1978 with the steering committee chaired by John Bryant, director of Columbia's School of Public Health. The report reflected the work of four subcommittees that, taken together, provided a powerful overview of the field. These were the hard cases: (1) the major diseases of low-income countries; (2) the ecological, socioeconomic, and cultural factors involved in health; (3) environmental control programs and health education possibilities; and (4) the feasibility of US involvement in international programs to help with the problems identified. The committee concluded that the current base of knowledge and experience provided the possibility of ameliorating many problems with realistic amounts of resources from both developing countries and economically advanced countries. The report thus marked a credible IOM entry into a new field of endeavor. This case was one in which the interests of the Carter administration were influenced by the IOM and in turn helped to shape the IOM's pathways as well as my own.

Health and Behavior

Something similar happened in the area of mental health. Once again, the interests of the Carter administration coincided with my own to produce a series of IOM studies. These concentrated on the links between health and behavior, which had long been a focus of my research. Before leaving Stanford to take the IOM job, I told my colleagues that one of my top priorities was to try to get the IOM to look at the whole range of health reform, including health and behavior. The work of the IOM for the President's Commission on Mental Illness presented an opening to pursue this interest. Betty Hamburg's role as Director of Studies, in conjunction with Mrs. Carter, the first lady, gave IOM an expanded role in the field of behavioral medicine. There emerged a dynamic interplay of shared interests among the scientific, medical, public health, and policy communities. This led to a major IOM project, "Health and Behavior: A Research Agenda." Delores Parron, fresh from her graduate work at Howard University, took major responsibilities, substantive and organizational, and for years did much to advance the agenda, from White House to IOM to NIH.

The project began with a series of IOM conferences, each of which generated its own report, on specific questions in the field of health and behavior. Then, a comprehensive volume synthesized the conference results, suggested promising research leads, and integrated available information into a perspective of the frontiers of the biobehavioral studies. To make this complex effort as effective as possible, I decided to chair the steering committee, which met for the first time in November 1979. Other committee members were leading figures in a wide range of biological and behavioral sciences. Because so many different federal agencies were involved in the task, the contract for the project was complicated and the final report—a sort of grand synthesis—did not appear until the summer of 1982. It became a landmark in the field, stimulating research, education, and practice across the nation.

The first conference volume in this multiyear program, on the links between smoking and behavior, followed an interest shared by Surgeon General Julius Richmond and HEW secretary Joseph Califano. This had been a major feature of the IOM annual meetings, with much support from great basic scientists like Joshua Lederberg. It featured an introduction by Richmond in which he noted that the IOM volume supplemented the work he had undertaken for a 1979 report on smoking and health. Both the conference volume and Richmond's report emphasized the disparity between the large amount of biological research that showed the deleterious effects of smoking and the small amount of behavioral research on what caused people to smoke and what might encourage them to stop.

Five more conferences, each on a topic of interest to one or more federal agencies, followed the conference on smoking. Robert J. Haggerty, president of the William T. Grant Foundation, chaired the Conference on Combining Psychosocial and Drug Therapy. They concluded that behavioral science has a powerful role to play in conjunction with biologic research for both the individual patient and the entire society. In a subsequent conference, participants brought social disadvantage into the mix. They noted, for example, that rates of severe mental illness were higher among members of the lower social classes, and pointed out that inadequate resources, low-status jobs, social stigma, and inadequate education interact with differential immunity, nutrition, environmental risks, and coping styles to create a convergence of disadvantage. Indeed, the boundary between the personal and the social realms was significant for participants in all of the conferences. In aging, for example, researchers had to distinguish among events that were biologically determined, culturally determined, and personally determined. In a similar vein, Leon

Eisenberg, summarizing the results of the Conference on Infants at Risk for Developmental Dysfunction, said that efforts "to understand … the various risk factors experienced by both mothers and children during pregnancy … and early infancy make sharply evident the need for research that integrates sociobehavioral with biomedical paradigms."

Overall, this report on health and behavior acquired great stature. Within the Academy complex, the IOM had a distinctive advantage in such an initiative because of its ability to engage in interdisciplinary work that combines biology with behavior. The IOM study found that as much as half of the mortality from the ten leading causes of death in the United States could be traced to a person's lifestyle. In the typical hospital population, there are a disproportionate number of people who have engaged in alcohol abuse, cigarette smoking, or overeating to obesity. Pregnant mothers carry the problems to the next generation. Cigarette smoking doubled the risk of having a low-birthweight infant; mothers who drank heavily faced a far greater chance that their babies would suffer from fetal alcohol syndrome. Altogether, relationships among the stress of life events, social supports, and various styles of coping offered a crucial area for research. Through this research, health care practitioners can come to understand just how social and psychological influences affect disease course and outlook. The project amply demonstrated that the leading causes of illness and death have substantial behavioral components, so approaches to preventing or managing them must include a strong biobehavioral perspective. This is a fundamental concept of education for a healthy public and has moved ahead remarkably in the past two decades. We had indeed turned a corner for American society. In 2014, it is clear that this work stimulated many initiatives throughout the country.

The process of working with the Carter administration extended well beyond the area of health and human behavior. In fiscal year 1979 alone, the Institute reviewed HEW's planning process, reported on food safety policy and on the proper use and health hazards of sleeping pills for the FDA, investigated the research agenda of the National Institute on Alcohol Abuse and Alcoholism, and studied health in Egypt for the US Agency for International Development. It also tried to clarify issues of national health insurance that would have to be addressed over the years to come, as we have indeed seen since then.

One major project stemmed from Surgeon General and Assistant Secretary of Health Julius Richmond's desire to issue a report with a focus he and I had long considered. It was on *prevention* as a major theme of health policy altogether. In February 1978, the IOM held a conference on health promotion and disease prevention, a subject that had received a great deal of attention from the Carter administration and carried over into subsequent administrations and public education in schools and media. Richmond asked the IOM to prepare a report, based in part on the conference, that summarized the field. A contract was worked out and Secretary Califano announced that Richmond would issue a major report in the autumn to tackle obesity, alcoholism, and many other costly health problems of everyday occurrence. (On completing government service, Califano devoted most of his career to addiction and made important contributions.) The IOM staff, assisted by a special advisory committee, rushed to get key information to Richmond by October. The IOM also commissioned a series of papers on particular aspects of the subject, such as reducing tooth decay in children and lowering the number of motor vehicle accidents. The IOM tried to be as helpful as possible to the surgeon general in writing a Surgeon General's Report on Prevention.

Healthy People: The Surgeon General's Report on Health Promotion and Disease Prevention appeared in August 1979, and Joseph Califano signed it as one of his last official acts as secretary of HEW. The book drew heavily on the material that IOM had prepared and on which HEW had put its stamp. A second volume of the surgeon general's report consisted entirely of the background papers that the IOM had commissioned, with a special contribution made by Elena Nightingale.

Secretary Patricia Harris, for her part, held many fruitful discussions with me and proved to be very supportive of the IOM's international health efforts. Still, her time in office was brief and the possibilities of collaboration were fewer during her tenure than during Califano's.

Even as I periodically reassured foundations that the IOM was worth supporting for the long term, I also courted new ones. A notable success came with the Charles H. Revson Foundation. Asking IOM Council member Lisbeth Bamberger Schorr to serve as an intermediary, I set up a meeting with Revson Foundation director Eli Evans. "I think our interests overlap in many ways," I wrote to Evans after the meeting. Three months later, I learned that the Revson board had appropriated $200,000 for the IOM to conduct four Revson seminars on biomedical research.

Teresa Heinz, John Heinz, John Kerry: Accomplishment, Tragedy, and Philanthropy

During my years of establishing the Institute of Medicine, one of the serious efforts was to get to know leadership people in major foundations that had existing or emerging health interests. Some of the foundations were troubled by the first couple of years prior to my arrival, when the IOM seemed to be floundering, and they alerted me that I might have serious difficulty in getting foundation support. I nevertheless believed that there was a strong rationale for establishing such connections in order to give the IOM flexibility. So I tried, visiting headquarters and spending time with the leaders of a considerable number of major foundations. The results were rewarding. One of the strangest turns of events was that the Robert Wood Johnson Foundation helped us substantially; another was that I had a chance to open the door to a major role for us in another large foundation, the Heinz Philanthropies. It is a very good illustration of the value of being alert to unforeseen developments, even tragic ones, to see whether unexpected opportunities might emerge.

One of the programs established by the Robert Wood Foundation at the Institute of Medicine was to select a set of mid-career health professionals each year for a twelve-month stay dividing time at the Academy, paying special attention to new developments in biomedical research that might well have profound significance for clinical medicine and public health in due course. The other part was an assignment to the office of a member of Congress (and later of the executive branch) in which the mid-career fellows could see both substantive and organizational examples of important opportunities. As we distributed the fellows over a considerable number of offices throughout the government, it became clear that one of the most respected of all the members was John Heinz, a relatively young senator from Pennsylvania. In understanding and facilitating these relationships, I got to know a good many government officials, including Senator Heinz. He was chairman of the Aging Committee of the Senate, which had no authority to pass legislation but had with his leadership a splendid "bully pulpit" to educate Congress and indeed the American people about the emerging pathways of our aging society. Demography is destiny, and more so all the time. But Congress was slow to see the significance of these trends and only a few leaders like Heinz took the initiative to move into this difficult area of medicine and public health. Moreover, both he and his wife Teresa had strong interest in education, clearly seeing the lifelong value of learning in a sound and stimulating way. Through John, I met Teresa and thought very well of her. She in turn met my son Eric. He was recently out of law school and eager to learn about the policymaking processes of Congress. To my surprise, she promptly informed her husband that she had found an exceptionally gifted and nice person who could certainly help him as an intern on a pro bono basis. Moreover, it would give Eric an opportunity to learn about "The Hill" and open future possibilities for him. Since we had not known them before, our family was surprised and delighted and will always be grateful to her for her foresight and kindness. Eric had a very good summer with Senator Heinz and then moved on to a regular Senate job for Senator Kerry where he had four rewarding years.

Senator and Mrs. Heinz were both concerned about the problems of television and violence. They foresaw a growing range of media possibilities for reinforcing overly aggressive tendencies of children and particularly adolescents. I discussed these interests with Newton Minow, who was then chairman of our board and deeply informed in these issues. We hit upon the notion of establishing a high-caliber commission, in the best Carnegie tradition, on the problem of television violence and child development. In order to sustain the long nonpartisan tradition of Carnegie, we suggested that there be co-chairs: Heinz, who was a highly respected Republican, and Minow, who as a young man was President Kennedy's chairman of the Federal Communications Committee and since then had been associated with almost every facet of the communications industry, always bearing in mind a strong sense of the public interest. We were very near the point of announcing the appointment of this commission when one of my staff burst into the room to tell me that Senator Heinz had been killed in an airplane crash. He was campaigning for reelection, and his small plane collided with a helicopter that was checking to see if his plane was functioning properly. Although for years I had studied stress and coping situations with special attention to denial as a mechanism of defense in an unexpected tragedy, this event hit me very hard. I simply couldn't believe it for a while. It must be a mistake. Here was a person of great quality, vitality, and a brilliant future who was now lost to all of us. Of course, I contacted Teresa Heinz and expressed my deepest sympathy. She asked me to give some time to their sons, who were close to their father and hit very hard by this disaster. I did so in the ensuing months and formed a high opinion of them, doing everything I could in my capacity to give them a full sense of the enormous respect their father had earned and the splendid future they could have by following in his footsteps one way or another.

In the meantime, Eric was working for Senator Kerry, whom I got to know quite well. Indeed he often asked me to meet with him to discuss the pros and cons of a complex policy issue. Although I did not introduce them, I was one of the people who knew the Heinzs and Kerrys well and saw important shared interests and values. Over time, John Kerry and Teresa Heinz were drawn to each other and eventually married, as they are to this day. Along the way, Teresa was asked by the family to take over the multiple Heinz philanthropies, which in aggregate amounted to a very large foundation. She told me she was concerned with her lack of knowledge in this field and asked if I could help. Of course I wanted to, so I consulted with Newton Minow and the other board members, and we invited Teresa to join our board so that she could benefit from whatever our experience might be worth. She was convinced in advance that it would be worth a good deal.

In addition to that, we thought through a way of turning John Heinz's tragic loss to the benefit of humanity by giving awards each year to people who were making outstanding achievements in fields of his wide interests—for example, environment, arms control, science education, public service, the arts, and more. We ended up giving ten awards a year, paying special attention to outstanding people who were not necessarily well known but showed great promise and dedication to a field of John Heinz's interests. So, for about a decade, I helped Teresa build that institution, and it has been very successful. It was a rewarding experience and certainly not one that I would ever have anticipated. Today, the Heinz Philanthropies are among the most dynamic and progressive in the world, and Teresa has given Carnegie public credit for helping her in this process.

An Overview of Five Remarkable Years

Although relations between the NAS and the IOM tended to be calm in my years, differences of opinion did arise over such issues as the report review function. Both Philip Handler and Saunders Mac Lane, who was a University of Chicago mathematician and NAS vice president as well as chairman of the Academy's Report Review Committee, offered critiques of some reports. These typically led to constructive revisions even when differences persisted. The IOM has always had to clarify differences between basic and applied science—what would today be positively called translational medicine. Nobelist Fred Robbins, who succeeded me as IOM president, stated bluntly that the Institute could not limit its study to the hardest evidence and still carry out its mission. I invited him to spend a year as visiting scholar during my term in the hope that he would succeed me, and this indeed did come to pass.

It was clear that the IOM walked a fine line between the scientific commitments of the National Academy of Sciences and the social questions of policymakers. It also tried to identify the most appropriate projects of those that its members suggested and those that the government brought to it. The fact that it could filter these proposals through separate divisions, each with its own advisory committee, helped lend coherence to the effort. The IOM, although it had clarified neglected themes in primary care, health education, quality assurance, and prevention, still had basic themes to clarify for the long term.

At the beginning of 1979, I appeared before the IOM Council and summarized the institution-building foundation of the past few years. These were rewarding years. Council members had suggested that I serve another five-year term. I told the Council members reluctantly that I had decided not to do so. I would complete this term and then open the doors for new possibilities—for the IOM and for myself. I announced my intention to solidify valuable, long-term directions for the Institute during the remainder of my term. In the meantime, the IOM would have plenty of time to search for a successor. I was deeply touched when the members greeted my decision with genuine disappointment; they really wanted me to stay. They emphasized my inspirational leadership, the establishment of

IOM's clear mission, and its relations with the NAS and policy leaders, important for the nation yet sometimes difficult. We learned a lot in those years of establishing the IOM on a strong basis.

I hoped the lessons being learned from the unique experience of the IOM could be applied in other great institutions, especially universities with major health investments. Indeed, three Harvard leaders who were familiar with evolving patterns of progress in the IOM—President Derek Bok, dean of Medicine; Daniel Tosteson; and Graham Allison, dean of Government, saw great potential in going that route with my leadership by creating a university-wide Division of Health Policy Research and Education, which took advantage of Harvard's extraordinary intellectual and organizational assets in health to unite multiple scholars and hospitals with latent health policy interests.

At the end of my tenure, Philip Handler wrote me a graceful letter that eloquently captured what I tried to do for the IOM:

Under your leadership, the Institute of Medicine has been brought to maturity. It has earned a place in the Washington scene and become the instrument to which we aspired when it was created. Our country has yet a long way to go in the development of an accepted philosophy which will enable us to frame a consistent national health policy. Thanks to you, I am confident that the Institute of Medicine will make cardinal contributions to that process. We have enjoyed your boundless good humor, basked in the warmth of your compassion, and been stimulated by the keenness of your intellect. All of us are richer for your stay among us.

Knowing his high standards, and the inevitable vicissitudes of the early years, that tribute meant a great deal to me. He also kidded me about needling him to create what became CISAC (Committee on International Security and Arms Control). He said my "punishment" would be to serve on CISAC. As it turned out, described in the section of this book on Carnegie war and peace, my membership on CISAC was good for me, for the NAS, and indeed it was not an exaggeration to say that CISAC made a contribution to world peace. This conclusion was put forward not only by distinguished scientists but by world leaders such as Gorbachev.

HARVARD AND HEALTH POLICY:
THE EVOLUTION OF A UNIVERSITY-WIDE PROGRAM
IN HEALTH POLICY RESEARCH AND EDUCATION

Whatever else may be true, this was a novel venture in the extent of its conjunction of knowledge and skills across traditional boundaries. The biomedical, clinical, and public health competencies need enduring linkage with economic, political, ethical, and legal competencies. In a community of Harvard's scope and quality, such enduring linkages are feasible though difficult.

This concept has potential for other policy-oriented domains. The great problems surely do not come in packages that fit the traditional disciplines or even schools, however excellent they may be. Universities can make a much greater contribution than they have in the past if they can organize effectively to share information, ideas, and technical abilities widely across traditional barriers and systems.

The establishment of this university-wide Division of Health Policy Research and Education became a reality at the outset of 1980. The university setting, including its clinical assets, made possible many initiatives. The Division provided an institutional link among administration and faculty at three Harvard schools, in order to use their complementary strengths in the field of health policy. It was also able to draw on the full range of talent at other schools, the Harvard-affiliated hospitals, and a large health maintenance organization. It had many opportunities—suggesting new research initiatives, stimulating educational activities, fostering university-wide resources for work in health policy, coordinating research and educational efforts, promoting multidisciplinary analysis of complex health policy issues, and disseminating health policy findings through publications, conferences, and informal meetings with policymakers. These initiatives were greatly enhanced by President Derek Bok, Dean Daniel Tosteson (Medicine), Dean Graham Allison (Government), professors John Dunlop (former secretary of labor), Julius Richmond (father of Head Start), Jack Rowe (a pioneer in geriatrics), Martha Minow (now dean of Harvard Law School), Leon Eisenberg (a distinguished child psychiatrist), and Arnold Relman (editor of the *New England Journal of Medicine*).

The Division was helpful in ongoing activities in health policy, stimulating latent interest in health policy, and providing a focus for broad cooperation in analyzing crucial problems as well as for training students and policymakers. By keeping informed about pertinent efforts in health policy throughout Harvard, such a Division can draw upon areas of strength, minimize redundancies, and promote interactions among disciplines that seldom interact. It can encourage deliberation on problems that may have appeared too difficult to tackle or may not have been explicitly recognized before.

Six major programs were established in 1980 as the focus of the Division's effort to address health policy problems. These were (1) health science policy, (2) disease prevention and health promotion, (3) mental health policy, (4) early life and adolescent health policy, (5) health policy and aging, and (6) innovations in the organization and financing of health care.

The research, teaching, and Harvard-wide coordinating activities in each program area were guided by a group of fifteen to twenty people, mostly but not exclusively drawn from Harvard faculty throughout the university. The faculty was joined by selected fellows, research staff, and students in the meetings and the conduct of the groups' work—for example, Charles Czeisler (since elected to IOM) and David Blumenthal (recently appointed president of the Commonwealth Fund).

Such working groups have the combined competencies to examine critically the complex factors influencing health, and the policies and programs designed to promote health. The multiplicity of disciplines represented in each group ensures that a broad range of evidence and ideas is taken into account. Although enjoying independence from government, the working groups consult widely with people in government as well as with voluntary health agencies, foundations, industry, and other relevant groups.

The goals of such working groups are (1) to develop intelligible, credible syntheses of research relevant to health policy issues; (2) to make objective, science-based analyses of policy options, taking into account the political and economic realities faced in implementing proposals; (3) to provide a broadly based, long-term view in analyzing policy questions; and (4) to disseminate information on health policy to students, scientific and professional groups, policymakers, and the general public.

The fundamental function of the working groups is to stimulate and guide. They begin with mutual education, and this underlies all the rest. As projects evolve, students and other faculty are brought into the process. From time to time, a working group undertakes a consensus statement on behalf of all its members. But this is not the main function of the groups, and in this respect they differ from commissions and the like. One of their best functions is to stimulate and encourage outstanding individuals to pursue novel questions in depth—for example, Professor Thomas Schelling's superb work on smoking cessation and prevention, well deserving of his Nobel Prize. The publications are broadly based and multifaceted, analytical rather than polemical, and explicit about their limitations. Over the years, this work has drawn in faculty, students, and policymakers.

Policy studies are followed up with a concerted effort to inform policymakers about what has been concluded and why. Activities may include executive sessions with policymakers, formal briefings for congressional staff and other relevant bodies, and informal meetings with leaders in various sectors. Dissemination, stimulation, and consensus-building activities include leaders in science, the health profession, industry, foundations, and educational institutions as well as government.

The Working Group on Health Science Policy had three major areas of interest: the allocation of resources for the health sciences, the credibility of scientists and the integrity of their research, and the relationships between universities and industry in the health sciences.

The Working Group on Health Promotion and Disease Prevention was particularly interested in helping people to orient their behavior toward health-positive goals. The chair, Professor Alexander Leaf, viewed this as the major issue in preventive medicine. The 1982 book, *Health and Behavior: Frontiers of Research in the Biobehavioral Sciences*, was a collaborative effort between the Institute of Medicine and Harvard's Division of Health Policy Research and Education. This volume was the result of the deliberations of more than 400 professionals on various aspects of health and behavior and has provided a useful stimulus for consideration of this subject in the prevention working group and also in the working group on early life and adolescent health policies. Starting from the background information and its uses delineated in the book, the disease prevention and health promotion working group selected smoking cessation as a major focus for study.

Strong evidence implicates cigarette smoking as a risk factor for many diseases, including respiratory diseases, lung and other cancers, coronary artery disease, and stroke—in sum, an immense burden of illness for the nation. Much needs to be learned about the initiation, maintenance, and cessation of the smoking habit. A conference entitled "Smoking Cessation: A Research Agenda for Health Policy" was organized and held by the working group on November 12, 1982. The forty invited participants represented active scientists and scholars in different aspects of the smoking problem as well as people from contributing disciplines. The keynote speaker, Professor Thomas C. Schelling, later a Nobel Prize winner in economics, posed penetrating questions that formed the basis for the discussion of promising lines of research that range from the effects of taxation policies to social network effects on cessation.

The Mental Health Policy Working Group, after a systematic survey of individual members followed by in-depth discussion, set priorities as follows: (1) care of the chronically mentally ill, (2) organization and financing of mental health care services, (3) manpower policy in the mental health field, and (4) mental health care in general health services. Panels were established to pursue inquiry in each of these areas.

The Working Group on Early Life and Adolescent Health Policies had as its goal the generation of studies leading to policy options for the prevention of morbidity, mortality, and other impediments to development in early life. An agenda of policy issues was developed, structured around problems critical to child and adolescent health as well as normal development: strategies for reducing infant mortality; health policy implications of advances in prenatal diagnostic technologies; monitoring child health outcomes; organizing and financing health services for children; interventions designed to prevent "rotten outcomes" in adolescence; ethical issues in health policies for children; and factors influencing outcomes in school-age pregnancy. Thus, children had the benefit of the deep commitment of people who had dedicated years to these issues, for example, Julius Richmond, Mary Jo Bane, Lee Schorr, Martha Minow, and Betty Hamburg.

Interwoven in all of these efforts are the *international* considerations, especially in regard to developing countries. It is interesting that it was difficult to get funding for this, yet in 2014 there was large support. There has been a transformation.

Infant mortality is intrinsically important and also serves as an indicator of general health status, especially of child health. A broader study, "Interventions Designed to Prevent 'Rotten Outcomes' in Adolescents," represents quite a different approach. The study group, chaired by Lee Schorr, examined some of the worst outcomes for adolescents and potential preventive strategies. The "rotten outcomes" considered were those that entail significant suffering for the individual and family and place a heavy burden on society—such as violent crimes, suicide, substance abuse, pregnancy before age fifteen, and leaving school without the ability to read. The heterogeneity of these outcomes would stimulate the consideration of multidisciplinary approaches to their prevention. The social significance of these outcomes poses a special challenge for health policy and vividly demonstrates the scope of the enterprise.

A subgroup on school-age pregnancy stimulated an interdisciplinary set of studies to gather in-depth, systematic longitudinal data on factors that influence outcomes in adolescent pregnancy. It went beyond the exclusive reliance on age, race, and economic status that characterizes so much of the work on this problem. The inquiry covered the following domains in addition to demographic variables: biologic maturity, psychosocial maturity, problem-proneness, depressive symptoms, sexuality beliefs and values, parenting beliefs and values, health history, relationship of adolescent mother and her own mother, and social support systems, formal and informal. All facets of the study include an emphasis on the early adolescent mother. This emphasis reflects our concern with the serious limitations of knowledge about these mothers and the special risks they bear.

Over many subsequent years, I was seriously involved in a long-term effort of this project, led by my colleague from IOM days, Sarah Brown, as well as President and Mrs. Clinton, Governor Thomas Kean, and Belle Sawhill, a distinguished economist. They played a major role and the success has been remarkable. An organization to avoid unwanted teen pregnancy grew partly out of this initiative, in conjunction with the White

House and Carnegie. It is still dynamic in 2015 and shows evidence of desirable outcomes. Its stimulating, nationwide effects were nonpartisan—for example Republican Governor Thomas Kean as long-term chairman (at my suggestion) and Democrat Hillary Clinton, who made substantive as well as public education efforts.

The Working Group on Health Policy and Aging was formed because the aging of our population has rather suddenly presented a profound challenge to our system of health and social concerns. Currently 11 percent of the population is over the age of sixty-five years. In the next fifty years, 20 percent (more than 52 million persons) will be in this age group. The fastest-growing group is the old-old, or those over the age of eighty-five—individuals most likely to require health care and long-term care services. Closely tied to the increased elder population are increases in health care utilization and federal expenditures for health care. Those over the age of sixty-five bear a great burden of disease and currently about 30 percent of the health care dollar.

Geriatrics is perhaps the most interdisciplinary of all clinical areas. The substantive advantage of interdisciplinary approaches to both clinical and basic issues in geriatrics is powerful. An interdisciplinary project was developed that examined the interaction of the formal health care system with other patients, focusing on areas of difficulty. The system of health care for the elderly is marked by fragmentation, gaps in service, and widely differing intake procedures and eligibility requirements. There is an institutional bias in federally funded programs and significant unmet need for services in the community outside institutions. Despite spiraling health care expenditures, lack of coordination and inappropriate service provision abound. The working group considered innovations that addressed these problems. Dr. John Rowe was a pioneer in this field and played an increasing role in the entire program. Elsewhere, I describe the extraordinary turn of events in his career.

At the request of the Veterans Administration, the group planned a conference to examine the organization of care for older veterans, the interaction of the Veterans Administration with other services and entitlement programs, and the potential coordination of services for the older veteran and spouse. The study of chronic care of the mentally ill (Mental Health Policy Working Group) and of the organization and delivery of services for the elderly have basic themes in common, and the two efforts are mutually beneficial. The two working groups joined in sponsoring a national conference on Science Policy and the Dementias. The frustrations of research in this area were vivid. Yet there were hopes that the emerging new neurobiology would in due course become valuable.

The Working Group on Innovations in the Organization and Financing of Health Services created a novel mix of skills bearing on health care. Projects have been selected that, while diverse, relate fundamentally to the pursuit of innovative solutions to existing health care system problems. A wide range of issues was reviewed: the effects of ownership on the delivery of health services, medical technology assessment, the competitive approach to the control of health care costs, primary care networks, health care and the poor, prospective payment in the hospital sector, allocation of health care costs to different activities and institutions, organization and motivation of the medical profession, new kinds of health insurance, and, finally, visions of the future: What will the health care system look like in the twenty-first century, under alternative assumptions about finance, organization, level of spending, and ownership?

Another project of special interest is the effect of ownership on the treatment of end-stage renal disease, led by Dr. Arnold Relman, longtime editor of the *New England Journal of Medicine* and one of the nation's most distinguished medical scholars of health policy. His role in this entire health policy enterprise was highly significant. He was chair of this study group, studying end-stage renal disease as a way of analyzing the effect of ownership on health care. End-stage renal disease units care for a well-defined population and deliver a relatively uniform type of care. The care process can be concisely described and its outcomes readily measured. In subsequent years, Relman became a truly major figure, a wise man in health policy, who tragically passed away in 2014.

Crosscutting Themes

Although the work of the Division encompassed a wide range of topics, certain themes emerged as bright threads that weave in and out of the tapestry of health policy. Among these threads are the following:

- The *organization and financing of services*, addressed specifically by the Working Group on Aging, Mental Health, Early Life and Adolescent Health Policies, and Innovations in Health Care. Also, monitoring the impacts of new health programs and of changes in existing programs. Whatever the program of concern is to a particular working group, monitoring the impact of change is important from *health status, economic, and ethical perspectives*. We sought to identify major characteristics of children that can be assessed objectively and used to monitor changes in programs affecting *children and their families*.
- The Health Science Policy Working Group, the Prevention Working Group, the Early Life Working Group, and the Aging Working Group were all directly concerned with the *impact of new technologies on health*, particularly as utilized in medical care. The Innovation Group has expressed serious concern about the assessment of technology in medical practice. The Health Science Policy Working Group, in its survey of university-industry relationships, has noted that recent advances in molecular biology, cellular genetics, and biochemistry have created unusual opportunities for the development of new technologies and commercial applications of basic research, but also raised new problems. Their particular interest is in comparing different patterns of relationship between universities and industry, clarifying the conditions under which substantial mutual benefit is likely to occur. They also seek to clarify the risks of such cooperative arrangements.
- *The impact of new technologies*. The Working Group on Early Life and Adolescent Health Policy was particularly concerned about the health policy implications of advances in prenatal diagnostic technologies. This is a subject that was of interest also to the Working Group on Disease Prevention and Health Promotion because of the preventive implications of prenatal diagnosis. A study group, headed by Dr. Elena Nightingale and sponsored by both working groups, was organized to develop a comprehensive framework for decision making in the field of prenatal diagnosis. Some of the rapid developments in the technologies enabling diagnosis and treatment emerge from cell biology and genetics—of concern also to the Health Science

Policy Working Group because they are associated with compelling policy issues. How can we best resolve the asynchrony between the rate of development of the capacities to diagnose disorders prenatally and systematic planning for assessment and application of these technologies? How can the less tangible but no less important factors—economic, ethical, legal, societal, and personal—be integrated in the development of policies that are both equitable across populations and responsive to individual values? The Prenatal Diagnosis Study Group was formed to address issues concerned with decisions ranging from prenatal diagnosis of disorders in an individual fetus to determining how to provide optimal means of prenatal diagnosis for the national population.

- *Health and behavior.* Several groups share common issues. The Working Group on Early Life and Adolescent Policy, Disease Prevention and Health Promotion, Health Policy and Aging, and Mental Health all have projects that deal in a major way with the positive and negative impacts of behavior on health. The "Rotten Outcomes" Study, the Smoking Cessation Study, and the Study on Health and Illness Behaviors of the Aged (among others) highlight the profound importance of dealing with this neglected subject from an interdisciplinary perspective. The book *Health and Behavior: Frontiers of Research in the Biobehavioral Sciences* has provided an important focal point for advances in this field. I constructed and edited it, with splendid collaborators from Harvard and the IOM.

- *Ethical concerns.* The Prenatal Diagnosis group included ethical questions in its assessments. The Early Life Group convened a study group that, after consideration of the wide range of ethical issues pertinent to health policies for early life and adolescence, selected several for inquiry: informed consent by children and adolescents; access to health care in general, and particularly prenatal diagnosis and genetic screening; and decisions to forego therapy. The Mental Health Working Group had a strong interest in the ethical problems in deinstitutionalization of mentally ill individuals. The Working Group on Innovations in Organization and Financing of Health Services was concerned with ethical issues in the effect of ownership of health care facilities by physicians on the delivery of health care services. The Health Science Policy Working Group was concerned with credibility and fraud in research. This brief summary indicates the pervasiveness of ethical concerns in formulating health policies and the necessity to keep ethical considerations a priority in the Division's work.

- *Health policies for the disadvantaged.* A recurrent and deep concern of each working group was the impact of the issues under study on socially disadvantaged people. The Early Life Working Group, in its infant mortality project and its concern with the ethical issues in access to health care for children; the Aging Group in questions of access to quality care and long-term care; the Mental Health Working Group with delivery of quality care to the poor and to the chronically ill; the Innovations Working Group with care of the poor in Massachusetts vis-à-vis changes in financing and organization of services—all these studies reflect interest in the special needs of disadvantaged people. This last crosscutting issue is one that is of concern not only nationally, but worldwide; in the developing nations the disadvantaged constitute a large majority of people and the degree of poverty is extreme.

The Division stimulated conferences in many fields. These conferences shared common features:

- They are stimulated by major clinical and public health problems that require interdisciplinary consideration.
- They deal with social, legal, and ethical problems as well as biomedical science.
- They delineate scientific opportunities and how they can be enhanced.

These conferences have a national function of *calling attention to neglected problems* and *to the need for interuniversity cooperation* toward their resolution, as well as to possible linkages of university activities to the government. Within the university, they increase the likelihood of interrelated research and scholarly activities providing stimulation of biomedical, behavioral, and policy studies on neglected problems of national importance.

Where Working Groups Can Lead

The working groups are fundamentally stimulating and guiding bodies, each concerned with a large domain of health policy. Their process has been briefly described already. Clearly, they can delineate key issues, generate study groups, develop proposals for support, hold conferences of wide significance, and foster faculty and student interest throughout the university. A highly positive feature of the working groups is that they contain such a wide variety of talent, mostly available on a part-time voluntary basis. We also need scholars who devote all or a large portion of their time to a particular project or a particular working group. It is important to have senior scholars with major commitment to health policy research and education; otherwise, the many competing commitments elsewhere in the university will interfere with the productivity of the working groups. These scholars can also serve as role models for students and fellows working in the Division who may consider health policy as a major career commitment. The interdisciplinary approach to health policy has been viewed positively by virtually all participants.

Dr. John Rowe, who chaired the Health Policy and Aging Working Group, foresaw additional benefit from enhanced interaction among the groups, particularly the chairmen. This work led to his extraordinary career, which now deserves some attention as it illustrates the ways in which these activities can open doors of great potential. This book concentrates on *unexpected opportunities*, opening doors that could be closed in much of the world. Jack Rowe's extraordinary career is a valuable illustration of this.

At Harvard, Jack was largely focused on physiologic studies of normal aging. Until he and I met in the first phase of the health policy program, he had not taken much interest in policy, and my involving him in our policy program at Harvard had a very important influence on the rest of his career. It opened his eyes to the feasibility and value of translating scientific evidence into policies that will help individuals and our society adapt to aging.

Later, I was chairing a search committee for a new president of Mount Sinai, a great hospital in New York with high ambitions for its next phase. The search committee was a very distinguished one (e.g., Bob Rubin, later secretary of the treasury), but they were not thinking in terms so special as a pioneer in geriatrics who had not run a large organization. Still, my experience with Jack Rowe at Harvard encouraged me to engage him in our enterprise, and he provided great leadership over a decade when he moved from Harvard to Mount Sinai.

Mount Sinai had too small an engine to get the big clinical chassis up the hill. The academic weaknesses spanned basic science and public health, health services research, and health policy. Hence we set about to build more labs, recruit more and better scientists, and establish new policy and health services research departments.

Rowe also led the institution's very effective response to the beginning changes in the organization and funding of health care. We began to build the Mount Sinai Health System through a careful set of acquisitions and partnerships. We became the largest and in many ways the most respected clinical health system in the region, and this has continued to the present with the leadership of Dr. Kenneth Davis. The success of the Health System makes available substantial funding for the School of Medicine in addition to its clinical value. The health world noticed Rowe's success and remarkable personal qualities. The Aetna health insurance company, a failing giant at the time, made a surprising comeback similar to the one we made at Mount Sinai. They recruited Rowe to be CEO. In six dynamic years, he transformed Aetna for the better, and so we see another transition of great practical significance.

One More Twist: Toward the Broadest Sense of Health Policy

During these years in developing the health policy program, I was drawn increasingly to the Kennedy School of Government (KSG), which was doing well with a galaxy of scholars in various fields, and David Blumenthal as my deputy. At the same time, there was no doubt of the prime attention by KSG faculty to the dangerous Cold War situation. A number of scholars, spearheaded by Graham Allison's classic study of the Cuban Missile Crisis, were able to contribute a lot to the war and peace issues—for example, Richard Neustadt on the presidency; Ernest May, history; Joseph Nye, political science and government; Al Carnesale, nuclear engineer and arms control; Sissela Bok, study of violence; Abram Chayes, international law; and Toni Chayes, conflict resolution. As Carnegie pursued us to see what its foundation could do to decrease the immense danger of nuclear war, I began assembling faculty with relevant knowledge and experience to see if we could elicit cooperation to develop a program on avoiding nuclear war. A cooperative fascination evolved that led us to seriously consider a move to the foundation in order to help build such a Cold War program.

The Harvard health policy leadership was in good hands of the highest caliber, like Julius Richmond, the father of Head Start, the recent surgeon general, and a broad, highly respected leader. This opportunity seemed unique, especially since the Carnegie foundation could have the scope, flexibility, and resources to influence the course of action. We were trying to diminish the immense danger of the Cold War. Betty was supportive of the crucial effort, even though her situation at Harvard was excellent. Not only was she assembling excellent scientists, clinicians, and public health experts in child health, she was elected to the leading body of faculty members guiding the Harvard academic program. Yet there was a unique opportunity now. A group evolved across schools inclined to try to work toward avoiding nuclear war and in time to help wind down the Cold War altogether. Our previous shared interests in developing crisis prevention pushed us in this direction. So I began to solidify the Health Policy Program and move toward the high-risk, high-gain, interdisciplinary, international work on the Cold War dangers and what opportunities we might delineate through Carnegie.

The eminent Harvard scholars who worked on these dreadful war problems also cooperated with counterparts at other great universities such as Stanford (e.g., Alex George, Bill Perry, and Sid Drell) and Columbia (e.g., Robert Legvold and Marshall Shulman). We were in a position to take advantage of the permeable membranes between government and universities. The pull of these factors was compelling. I continued a close relationship with Harvard as I had before with Stanford and with the National Academy of Sciences. This was a rare and special chance to *link the scientific and policy communities* for tackling the most urgent needs. So we went to the Carnegie Corporation of New York, the first general-purpose foundation, established in 1911 by Andrew Carnegie, whose philanthropic interests were formed on education and peace. When I moved from Harvard to Carnegie, there was considerable continuity in values (especially the *prevention* approach) and collaborators (e.g., Graham Allison, the highly successful dean of the Kennedy School and an emerging expert on prevention of nuclear crisis, who came with me to Carnegie for over a year to collaborate in developing the Avoiding Nuclear War program at both Carnegie and Harvard). The flow of interest was from prevention of illness in medical practice to prevention of mass violence on a scale beyond any other danger.

Because of this natural flow from Harvard to Carnegie, it is salient to mention a few people who were especially helpful to me and in turn I made special efforts to foster their professional work.

First is Graham Allison. He and I worked closely together with Alex George. Alex was especially important, as I have explained in an earlier work, as a great scholar devoted to preventing war and an extraordinary inspiration not only to me but also to young scholars in the entire field. He and Graham Allison were natural partners and effective ones—especially in formulating the crisis prevention approach and carrying it to both American scholars and policymakers on the one hand and Soviet scientists (and policymakers after Gorbachev came to office) on the other. Graham was instrumental in recruiting me to Harvard, together with Derek Bok and Dan Tosteson. All of us shared a deep concern about avoiding nuclear war, and, as I have noted in the section on Harvard as an institution, we drew in a wealth of talent across fields who had latent or overt interest in coping with Cold War problems. When Allison completed a long and successful term as dean of the Kennedy School at Harvard, he joined me at Carnegie as a visiting scholar, originally for one year, but then he stayed on longer. Together we took many initiatives, widened the horizons of the prevention approach, and worked together for years on a variety of initiatives for peace.

The second person I'd like to mention is Astrid Tuminez. Having grown up in the Philippines, she came to Harvard for graduate work and in the depth of the Cold War became our person in Moscow. She had an extraordinary facility for understanding conflict resolution, for reaching key people in the Soviet hierarchy, for getting around the obstacles of their formidable bureaucracy, and for opening avenues of sensitive communication. When she finished her doctorate I invited her to join the staff at Carnegie, which she gladly did, and served brilliantly for several years until I left the presidency. She served importantly as a liaison function with a number of Soviet leaders, including

Gorbachev, and helped them create a center in Moscow that to some degree was modeled on the Carter Center created by President Carter in Atlanta. Later, she worked on efforts to resolve the serious conflict in the Philippines and spent successful years in Hong Kong and Singapore.

Another person I'd like to mention is Frederic Solomon. Having done outstanding biomedical research at the University of Chicago at a young age, he landed with me at the Institute of Medicine, serving as head of the unit on mental health and behavioral medicine. He organized and saw through to completion a landmark book published in the depth of the Cold War, *Medical Implications of Nuclear War*. This volume brought to light new findings of great practical importance. It drew heavily on experts from Harvard and Stanford.

Martha Minow worked with Betty in the White House on the President's Commission for Mental Health. This was an encouraging interlude for her in the midst of the inevitable rough edges of law school. Later, I played a very active role in recruiting her to Harvard, though I am not a lawyer. I saw from her extraordinary analytical ability, intellectual curiosity, and profound values that she would be a very valuable member of the university-wide program I was developing on health policy, particularly with respect to children. After I left, she co-chaired with Julius Richmond—the great leader in child health and health policy—the Working Group on Child Health, and she has been an outstanding contributor for many years.

It was in another line of inquiry, directed toward relief of human suffering, that I fostered communication between Martha Minow and Sadako Ogata, the great United Nations High Commissioner for Refugees with whom I had the privilege of working for a decade. They focused on preventing recurrence of mass violence after war. UNHCR worked with Harvard Law School on a program called Imagine Coexistence. Their initiative spread through several parts of the world. Minow has greatly clarified education for coexistence, including reconciliation after hateful outbursts. She described several methods of education for coexistence, each one providing a useful example. Later, Betty Hamburg brought her on to the board of the Revson Foundation with such distinguished scholars as Joshua Lederberg. In due course, she became chairman of the board and the foundation was one of the best during her term of office. In recent years, she has earned great respect as a superb dean of the Harvard Law School.

Arthur Kleinman, professor of psychiatry and anthropology at Harvard, is a logical person with whom to close this section. For years, he has spoken publicly and privately about being inspired when he was an undergrad at Stanford about a lecture I gave as a young professor in the mode of "Welcome to Stanford." It gave him a sense of a newly emerging psychiatry that could help many people in a world badly in need of such help. The relation of stress and hormones interested him very much, as did my evolutionary perspective. As his career has developed, we have kept in close touch and I have been fascinated to see his deep grasp of Asia. As with Martha Minow, I put him in touch with my dear friend Sadako Ogata, and one of their highlights was a symposium at Harvard in preventing mass violence in Asia. It is a major regret that illness prevented me from participating, but I know that it was a wonderful occasion. For some years, Kleinman chaired a department of social medicine and health policy that I helped to create when I was at Harvard, and every year he would invite me to come to a lecture for his African students. Over the years, he conducted research in education in both Asia and Africa and followed up with his students in their home countries. He has been revered in the field of international psychiatry and anthropology. Tragically, he lost his wife to a neurological disease much too early, but he turned it into an experience that would help others by writing about it in an extremely meaningful way.

Delores Parron, who provided a link between the IOM and Harvard in the large project of Health and Behavior, came to work with Betty in the White House fresh out of graduate school in social work, making a significant contribution to the President's Commission on Mental Health, which was of great interest to both President Carter and Mrs. Carter. The latter continued this interest after they left the White House and has been a leader in mental health to the present day. Betty then recommended Delores to me and she joined our staff at the Institute of Medicine during my presidency and stayed on for some years afterward as a bulwark of the mental health program, including prevention of violence. She was instrumental in our major enterprise covering broadly biobehavioral sciences and mental health. Later, she rose to a high position in the NIH and contributed in various ways to increasing diversity in the health professions. We have been very lucky that she has been in Washington during our stay here in recent years. Her kindness and loyalty are unbounded.

There are so many others from whom I have learned a great deal and whose professional careers I have tried to foster at every opportunity that it is on the one hand deeply gratifying almost beyond imagination, and on the other too long a list to be practical. There are many more besides those listed here and I apologize for those I have left out. Perhaps there will be another opportunity.

CHAPTER 4

The Carnegie Years

A. WAR AND PEACE: PREVENTION OF MASS VIOLENCE

Coming to the Carnegie foundation was a big transition for me and for the staff. Remember I mentioned earlier that major transitions are inherently stressful. For myself, every time I made a move, I always had doubts as to whether I really would be able to respond well in the new situation or take advantage of the opportunities. And for the staff, I think they were a little apprehensive about me, though it helped that I'd been on the board and they knew me. I wasn't so threatening as an individual. I think there was some question whether I was going to medicalize the foundation. The staff did not have a substantial background in the health field.

There was some apprehension about it, but we all threw ourselves into the new tasks enthusiastically, knowing the importance of the problems we faced in finding ways to be useful. I had certain issues that I wanted us to address, which had a lot of continuity with the Andrew Carnegie tradition going back to his philanthropic priorities of peace and education. We organized mixed staff and board groups, working groups to look at these issues and to do as I'd done at the Institute of Medicine, that is, to make what I call terrain maps, papers that would in some depth examine a problem area and see where we could maybe find a hot spot on the map, where we had an opportunity to make a contribution. Everybody, I think, got engaged.

We had valuable outside consultants—authentic experts with a range and depth of knowledge. I opened up the foundation quite a lot to outsiders to come in and tell us what they thought about these issues. There was a zest to it that people got caught up in. The staff could see they were going to have substantial inputs, as was the board.

I had no feeling that I needed to make big changes in the staff. I felt that there were a lot of devoted people who were knowledgeable and good in philanthropy. It might be necessary to move some of them around. They might have to change what they worked on and show adaptability, but I certainly didn't feel that I had to clean house to get my own staff. I had some advice from the board to do the corporate thing and get my own staff, replace Alan Pifer's staff. I just didn't feel any necessity for that. I thought I would look at it one by one, case by case, first year, second year; and there were some changes I made, quietly, not blood on the floor. But most of the people were very smart and experienced and adaptable, and they threw themselves into it. This was reassuring.

Operationally we did make a change. I organized program groups. I felt that the topics we were tackling were sufficiently complicated that we would need to have several people working together. That was my style anyway, from way back. Rather than have each staff member be a mini-foundation, we would need to have groups that would work out together the priorities for grant making and the evaluation of specific grant proposals. The working group system was fruitful.

There was some transitional stress, but I don't think it was a very big deal. There was a lot of continuity and there were some changes, but the changes were worked out together. Now, the biggest change, of course, was in the Avoiding Nuclear War program. That was strange to almost everybody, except for David Robinson. I must say, I'm very glad, from the standpoint of the tradition of the foundation, that we made this major initiative, not only in terms of contributions we were able to make, but also in terms of what had been important to Andrew Carnegie. He didn't require that the foundation follow in his footsteps. He gave the broadest possible mandate. It's extraordinary what he did. He invented the concept of the general-purpose foundation, and he said, in effect, "Nobody can be wise enough to know what will be important in thirty years or fifty years or a hundred years, and the greatest tribute the board can pay me is to decide what's important at a given time."

Nevertheless, it's very clear that he had deep commitments to *peace* and *education*, and those problems have hardly gone away. It made a lot of sense to pursue these great themes. But how we were going to do it in avoiding nuclear war was not obvious at all. I didn't know if we could make a contribution. All I knew was that the Cold War had a relapse, the Soviets had recently gone into Afghanistan, and they were vastly expanding their nuclear and biological weaponry. If they could make such stupid and dangerous decisions, who could tell what might happen? There was a certain amount of talk in both Washington and Moscow in those days that perhaps a nuclear war was inevitable and maybe somehow you could "prevail." Nobody talked about actually winning, but you could prevail, maybe just 100 million dead or something like that. Truly beyond imagination. One of the big arguments at the time was whether, in the case of a nuclear war, the human species might actually become extinct or not. Well, that's some argument to have. So it was a dreadful situation. But how could a private foundation make any difference? Wasn't this a function for governments? So we had to figure out what we could do. And that was, I think, the most innovative thing. It is hard to reconstruct now the readiness of leading people, military and nonmilitary, to risk nuclear war and yet to educate their high-level colleagues on the danger. Presidents Eisenhower and Kennedy in the 1950s and 1960s had to fend off influential members of their own administrations to use the incredibly powerful hydrogen bomb. Traditional aggressive attitudes jeopardized rational thinking.

For me it was a complex transition in regard to levels of education, and I made the decision that we were going to focus on *pre-collegiate education* to strengthen its quality and widen its availability. We were going to use the universities to help clarify those problems, but we were not going to concentrate primarily on the well-being of universities. We were going to concentrate on the well-being of elementary, secondary, and even pre-elementary. I used to say education doesn't begin with kindergarten, it begins with prenatal care. We were going to go from prenatal care through high school, because I felt the most serious problems were there. The foundation had a track record in that field, had some expertise, and very little was being done in other foundations on pre-collegiate education at that time. In fact, it scared me, because I asked the staff to do a round-up of who's doing what in this field. The answer was, next to nothing at that time. I felt, well, maybe they knew something I didn't know. Maybe this was a poisonous field to enter.

Nevertheless, we did. We developed fundamentally a sort of zero-to-fifteen strategy on education, child development, and adolescent development, and a program in avoiding nuclear war, which later got broadened into preventing deadly conflict. It's all of a piece with special attention to find ways of *preventing* disaster. And then a developing countries program, in which Carnegie had some up-and-down, in-and-out history, but a serious interest in Africa. And that suited me from personal experience. So we could pursue a developing countries program focused primarily on South Africa, in light of the grave apartheid oppression. Those were the main strands of what we did.

Those three priorities were clear in my annual report introductory essay, "New Contexts for Grants," in 1983. They were separate and distinct programs, but with a lot of informal interplay. On every level, *accurate objective education of the public* was fundamentally important. What evolved was, in effect, a fourth program, a *democracy* program, strengthening democratic institutions both in the United States and abroad. There were very different problems in different places. South Africa, one problem. Russia, another problem. United States, another problem. But still, that fundamental commitment: building and strengthening democratic institutions. And as the underpinning for that, an informed public.

So, for instance, vis-à-vis the universities, in all of our program areas we got major involvement of outstanding scientists and scholars in universities, and one of the things we tasked them with was what I called *education beyond the campus*. Why must education stop at the boundaries of the campus? If there is elucidation of an important problem, whether it be in arms control or crisis prevention or disadvantaged minority education or the role of women in development, whatever the topic may be—if there's something solid to understand, why not explain it insofar as we can, in an objective, clear, and cogent way, at least to the American public and to such other publics as we might have opportunity to reach?

One of the big struggles was to try to get access to the Soviet public in the bad old days, and we actually did get some, not nearly as much as we would have liked, but a process began. Anyway, that commitment to *broad education of the public* was a *crosscutting theme* of fundamental importance throughout most of my career.

Science and Public Policy: The Carnegie Opportunity

During his presidency, my predecessor Alan Pifer was deeply committed to the issues of poverty and racism, the social agenda that had really come to the fore in the 1960s, and he was determined that Carnegie would do whatever it could to improve opportunities in education and the like. Those were values that I admired. The issues were quite interesting. They had a good deal more experience in elementary and secondary education than I'd been exposed to before, and the need for improvement in that arena was clear. But how? This was a challenge of first-rate importance.

There were, however, some problems in the board. There were members of the board who felt that it had too little to say about the agenda, and so Alan appointed a few of us to a committee to consider what to do about that, and we came up with the notion of an Agenda Committee, which continued throughout my term—a combination of board members and senior staff who would keep rolling forward the agenda of future meetings, what did we need, what would be helpful, and so on. I thought that was a constructive response on his part to a certain discontent in the board, and I was glad to be helpful.

There were some board members at that time who were, I think, rather controlling, who wanted to dip into management or, at any rate, didn't understand very well the distinction between policy and operations. It seems to me that the board sets policy, and the operations are handled by the chief executive and the staff. I was very sympathetic to the position of the president and the staff, and felt we board members oughtn't to be too intrusive. We had ample opportunity to say what we wanted to say at board meetings. But the Agenda Committee was a good innovation.

Alan had had a nasty injury in falling from a ladder, so he wasn't as deeply engaged in his last few years as he had been earlier. I wasn't aware of that at the time. But from my standpoint, it was a well-functioning educational foundation that dealt with important issues, and I was happy to be a part of it. It was a unique pioneer, the first general-purpose foundation. It celebrated its centennial in 2012.

My unexpected opportunities and rich experiences in several great institutions opened the door for *relating science to public policy* broadly. Some of it had to do with innovations in health care, basically the application of the burgeoning life sciences to health care problems. Part of it had to do with disease prevention, health promotion. Part of it had to do with health in early life, in childhood and adolescence, which was the main part that carried forward to Carnegie later. Part of it had to do with the emergence of an aging society, health care and disease prevention in older people. And part of it had to do with health in developing countries, the immense disease burdens carried by those countries, which I'd been exposed to, and there I had the great opportunity to create a Division of International Health in the National Academy of Sciences, and ever since have been working with the academy on broadening its international functions, in health and other matters. This also applied to the American Association for the Advancement of Science (AAAS), the other umbrella organization of American science. Among other positive outcomes, President Carter became deeply interested and gave these issues priority for the remainder of his career. After constructing the Carter Center in Atlanta on leaving the presidency, he focused on the diseases of poor, tropical countries as well as conflict resolution. Carnegie gave support for such serious, even desperate problems.

So that was very satisfying. In fact, we had the opportunity to bring the strengths of a variety of sciences to bear on clarifying policy issues and formulating policy alternatives in important fields, and some of that carried over to Carnegie, mainly the part on children and youth and the part on developing countries, and especially the prevention of mass violence, above all reducing the nuclear danger.

I was very surprised when they asked me to become president, and I at first said, almost reflexively, no, both from their standpoint and mine. That is, from the standpoint of the foundation, I felt that it would be odd to have a person of a medical background as president of the foundation. It really had never been a health foundation, though it had health components. It didn't intend to be a health foundation. The perception might be wrong, my background might be wrong.

Furthermore, I was getting increasingly concerned about the dangerous situation of the Cold War, and I felt that if I were to be associated with the foundation, that I would really want to do something about the Cold War if possible. The nuclear danger was then nowhere near the agenda of the foundation (the same was true of the other major foundations), and it seemed to me that would be a wrenching transition to make.

From my own standpoint, I had only been at Harvard a few years, Betty was very well established as an academic leader at Harvard, and I was building a novel program. I had become friends with scholars at Harvard who were studying the Cold War, for example Graham Allison, Joseph Nye, Al Carnesale, Tom Schelling, Paul Doty, and others. I had good people with me and it was clear that somebody could take over the health program (e.g., Julius Richmond, the "father" of Head Start and recent surgeon general); that wasn't so much the issue. But I didn't feel right about leaving after only a few years. So I felt, on both counts, from the standpoint of the foundation and my standpoint, it wasn't very appropriate. Yet the special opportunities of building a coherent program on the desperately urgent problem of avoiding nuclear war were very attractive, not least in working toward ways of winding down the Cold War with a worldwide network of scientists, scholars, and practitioners of every kind—and linking broad education with the dreadful dangers of such a war.

The then vice chair of the Carnegie board, Helene Kaplan, later the chair of the board, was chair of the search committee. Luckily for me, she was quite persistent, and at some point she talked to Betty about it. She understood my reasoning was that I didn't want to uproot Betty again. Betty had been an awfully good sport about moving with me wherever I went. She was always supportive, helpful, and collaborative, and I felt, "Enough already. She has a very good position and is making a valuable contribution." Furthermore, by that time our daughter Peggy was a medical student at Harvard, and I loved being with her. The whole thing didn't seem sensible.

But Betty was the one who said, "Well, you really ought to think about it. You ought to open up your mind to the possibility." She wasn't recommending that I do it, necessarily, but I really should think about it, particularly when the response of the search committee, especially Helene and board chairman Bud Taylor, was, "Why not try to help in avoiding nuclear war? Why shouldn't we?" Andrew Carnegie had a passion for peace. I knew that, too, but for a long time the foundation had largely gone away from war and peace issues. Indeed, to a very considerable extent, the foundation left that when he died. Although it came back from time to time, as far as I could make out, it was really not central to the agenda of the foundation after Andrew Carnegie's death in 1919. Still, John Gardner, a distinguished prior president and a good friend, urged me to do it.

So I didn't really know whether it was appropriate or not, but the then trustees seemed to feel that yes, the Cold War was the greatest conflict in history, the most dangerous situation in history, and indeed was a threat to humanity, and why not see if there was something useful to be done? So that was very significant to me, because it opened up a possibility to move into an area in which I otherwise had no way to do anything useful. That was very exciting. I guess Betty's reaction and the opportunity to tackle Cold War issues were the pivotal factors for me.

Avoiding Nuclear War: The Ultimate Health Crisis

I had been very interested in intergroup relations from an early time, no doubt as a personal and family matter in the first place with World War II and the Holocaust in the background. Professionally it was very striking to me. One phase was human evolution: How did we get to be the way we are? In the primate work, I wanted to try to clarify relations between primate groups. Our research effort discovered that those can be very menacing and even lethal relations, especially relations between *different communities* of chimpanzees. You would see many indications of positive feeling, affiliation, proximity, and conflict resolution and all that in the higher primates, but you also saw that there was a condition of great risk and even lethality in the crowding of strangers or lopsided power relations in the presence of valued resources. That was a particular conjunction of deadly circumstances for chimpanzees. Richard Wrangham, now a professor of human biological anthropology at Harvard, has pursued this line of inquiry most effectively. In the early work, David Bygott made an important contribution.

This question led me to do a lot of inquiry, starting with the year at the Center for Advanced Study in the fifties (the first time I was there; I came back for a second year a decade later), and going on after that to do research in a variety of behavioral sciences, particularly in social psychology, but to some extent in other fields, about in-group/out-group relations and this remarkable human propensity to form distinctions between one's own group and other groups very quickly.

In fact, experimentalists in that field (with humans) have found that even when they are neutral or want to avoid any negative implications, it's hard to avoid. Once you get a group forming, even a short-term, transient group, the members begin to make invidious distinction between their group and other groups. And where you have more enduring groups, it seems to be rather a pervasive human attribute that it is very easy to learn invidious distinctions between my group and others, between me and others. Egocentrism and ethnocentrism go hand in hand. Mind you, there's a very positive side, an affiliative, loving, tender side to human nature, which has also been important to me, but I think there's no gainsaying the fact that we have a worldwide propensity for depreciating other groups and thus predisposing to violence.

A fundamental question in human adaptation for me is, can we get the sustaining quality of identification with our own group, without severely depreciating other groups? I think that ought to be possible. But the fact is that education everywhere is to some degree ethnocentric. I think humans have a tendency to amplify small differences and to find a basis for depreciation of others. Of course, that was carried to the nth degree by Hitler's maniacal attitude toward the Jews particularly. It showed that there's almost no limit to which this human propensity can be carried. I don't think it dooms humanity, but it is something we have to take account of in a really serious, sustained way. That's part of the human reality, and we have to learn how to cope with that tendency, which becomes more and more dangerous as our capacity to destroy is enhanced.

I felt that was a background feature of the Cold War, but there were many other aspects to it. And always in these situations it's a zealot leader, an ethnic entrepreneur, a pyromaniac, who will put gasoline on the embers of intergroup hostility and cause a great conflagration, whether it's Hitler or Stalin or whoever, a political leader to activate people on the basis of these differences and to use the intergroup hostility for his own diabolical purposes.

In any event, I felt we had to take that as a background for what, if anything, we could do about the Cold War issues. To make a long story short, what I set out to do was to get the maximum possible expertise on Cold War issues and to bring people together from different backgrounds to work on it. So I felt a great sense of urgency, and together with the staff, especially David Robinson, Fritz Mosher, Jane Wales, Pat Nicholas, David Speedie, and Deana Arsenian, we went to major universities and research institutes and tried to identify people, some from my prior knowledge and some not, who knew about nuclear weapons, who knew about arms control, who knew about nuclear crises and confrontations and how we got out of them, who knew about decision making in the Soviet Union and security decision making in the United States, who knew about Third World flashpoints, who knew about Eastern Europe, where the Cold War began.

So when we faced up to it, there were *different bodies of knowledge and skill* and expertise that were needed to address Cold War issues. In effect, we mainly went to some major universities and scientific institutions and said, "If you can get people who have a number of these competencies together, to *work together in a sustained way*, then we'll make a grant, a sizable grant by foundation standards, to get that kind of conjunction of talent brought to bear on Cold War problems." Nongovernmental organizations oriented to conflict resolution, human rights, and democratic development were also helpful.

We had these interdisciplinary groups working at a number of universities and research institutes, and then pretty quickly we moved to get some joint study groups between the United States and the Soviet Union, mainly through their Academy of Sciences, the only chance we had to have some stature and independence beyond the political control of the dictatorship, not to have KGB hacks who would be controlling the process, but distinguished scientists and scholars. That was our only chance, and it worked pretty well.

So, through the US Academy, the Soviet Academy, and US universities, we got working groups starting on *arms control* and *crisis prevention*. Those were the main ones during the dark days. Later on, *after Gorbachev came to power*, it was possible to broaden out into joint study groups on a wider range of issues, and ultimately toward concentrating on building democratic institutions in the Soviet Union in its last phase, and then in Russia and Ukraine after that. It was a good start but it will necessarily be a long haul. There has been a lot of slippage since Gorbachev left office. What a tragedy. Gorbachev did more for his people in a few years than had been done for several centuries. In 2015, the repression is serious. But it may not be too late.

Our joint study groups were useful. First were the interdisciplinary groups in the United States, then the international joint study groups. These groups were primarily scientists and scholars. Some other kinds of expertise were represented. Then we moved toward linkage with policymakers, getting independent experts together with policymakers in our own country, in both houses and both parties in Congress and with the administrations and then, after Gorbachev came to power, with policymakers in the Soviet Union. Through some members of our joint study groups, scientists, I was able to meet Gorbachev early and form a relationship with him. I could see that he genuinely wanted to have access to Western ideas and information and analysis, and to some degree I became a broker, to bring or send experts to meet with him and some of his closest colleagues, to discuss arms control and crisis prevention and then the winding down of the Cold War altogether, what they might do to ease the yoke on Eastern Europe.

It was a fantastic opportunity that I never expected to have, but the upshot of it was, we not only had a policy linkage with our own government, which we thought would be possible in our democracy, but also with the government of the Soviet Union, which had seemed, I must say, like a very long shot before Gorbachev.

So those were the three main strands of that program: the interdisciplinary study groups generating a wider range of policy options in this country, the joint study groups between us and the Soviets, and then the policy linkage with our own government and the Soviet government.

There were some obstacles, which turned out to be less severe than some had anticipated. There were one or two people in the Reagan administration early on, in his first term, who were not friendly to any kind of nongovernmental involvement, be it foundations or universities or the National Academy of Sciences. They thought this was a sole governmental authority and we ought not to be involved in it. We were basically outsiders in that perspective.

But it turned out that President Reagan himself didn't feel that way, and Secretary of State Shultz didn't feel that way, nor did Jack Matlock, Reagan's special adviser on the Soviet Union. So we had some pretty significant allies. By the spring of 1984, I must say to my surprise, President Reagan himself was engaged in one of our activities that involved restarting the scientific and scholarly exchanges with the Soviet Union, so that was reassuring. This was a year before Gorbachev came to power.

In terms of Congress, there had been people who anticipated there might be resistance, but it turned out to be minimal. On the contrary, members of Congress welcomed having a chance to be with independent experts, and we began a much deeper engagement, particularly in a retreat format, of independent experts with members of Congress, than I had ever anticipated. Members of Congress then were deeply concerned about the Cold War—both parties, in both houses. They were really impressed with the danger and wanted to play a role. This was a unifying influence. They didn't feel that it should be just the executive branch that had something to say about that. So we had pillars in both parties, like Senator Simpson on the Republican side, and Senator Nunn on the Democratic side, who were deeply engaged with this all the way through the program of policy linkage.

Earlier, the Cuban Missile Crisis was a turning point for me. In 1978, when I was still president of the Institute of Medicine, I was keenly aware of the dangers of the Cold War, partly because the academy in which we were embedded was trying very hard to save Andrei Sakharov's life (a great physicist and visionary), and our academy was very much aware of the pressures under which the Soviet scientific community was operating, and the dangers of their buildup of weapons of mass destruction. Incidentally, Sakharov had a remarkable broad view of our *common humanity*, even though he was involved in creating the Soviet hydrogen bomb—a weapon of unprecedented and almost inconceivable destructive power. Through the *new foundation, suggested by Gorbachev* and *implemented by us*, we made it possible for Sakharov to come to the United States, his first-ever travel outside the Soviet Union. Gorbachev sought an independent, international vehicle for grasping our common humanity.

What was particularly concerning is that there seemed to be an inclination over there, at least of some people, to take the nuclear issue right up to the brink, right to confrontation, like the Cuban Missile Crisis or the earlier Berlin situation. They were very resentful of the United States going on nuclear alert during the 1973 Israeli-Egyptian War. That was an unexpected development, and very dangerous. To this day, nobody knows for sure about the interacting effects of nuclear alerts on the two sides, and the possibility that it could get out of control in such a way that each side would have to fire, even though neither head of state wanted to do it.

So I felt in the 1970s that we ought to get some people together who were experts on nuclear confrontation, on crisis management, to meet in a pleasant, neutral setting and talk about it, first of all, as a kind of technology transfer. We had learned something from the studies of great scholars like Graham Allison at Harvard and Alex George at Stanford, on crisis management, above all the Cuban Missile Crisis, but other crises of the Cold War, and, to some extent, earlier crises like the interaction of mobilizations in World War I that led inexorably to the war, even though the leaders were in a great muddle about whether they really wanted to start the war.

So we had a body of knowledge, and I thought we ought to explain to the Soviets what we'd learned. There were principles of crisis management that Alex and Graham had formulated. So, under Pugwash auspices, we got together a few Americans, a few Western Europeans, and a few Soviets in Geneva, and we spent the better part of a week there. The aura of Albert Einstein, the cofounder of Pugwash, inspired me. I was the chair. We started out with a docudrama on the Cuban Missile Crisis that Graham Allison had adapted from an earlier docudrama made in this country, which was historically accurate to the extent possible, but also condensed and dramatic, and conveyed a sense of how close we were to having the whole thing go wrong. We were apprehensive about how the Soviets would take it. Indeed, they were very perplexed. Were we trying to put them down? Because, in the end, they had backed down fundamentally. We weren't trying to put them down. We were trying to get across a sense of how dangerous and difficult these crises are to manage. So we spent two or three days on that.

In the 1950s, a number of prominent Americans, military and nonmilitary, put heavy pressure on President Eisenhower to go to the brink and even to initiate a nuclear war using hydrogen bombs. With great difficulty, he managed to fend them off. So this was a persistent and immense danger. Yet analytical work both in and out of government was limited, and the issue of a prevention agenda scarcely arose.

The Crisis Prevention Approach

And then we began to make the transition from crisis management to crisis *prevention*. I said at the turning-point day in the middle of the 1978 Pugwash week, "Let us begin anew. Let us recognize how hard it is, when you get to the brink of a nuclear catastrophe, to prevent some accident, some inadvertent development, from leading us into a nuclear war. We certainly don't want one. So let's think. Could we *prevent the crisis*? We don't need to assume that the nuclear weapons stockpiles will be coming down soon. We don't need to assume that the level of animosity between the two countries will come down soon. All we need to say is, we've got to be smart enough to keep back a few steps from the brink.

We don't want to fall off the brink. The slope gets very slippery at the edge of the brink of nuclear confrontation.

"What could we do to avoid that? Could we strengthen the hotlines so that communication in urgent circumstances would be easier? Could we develop other mechanisms like the Incidents at Sea Agreement—rules of the road at sea so that our vessels don't crash into each other—so that we don't inadvertently shoot nuclear weapons? Could we have some rules of the road in the air, on the land? Could we move toward notification about troop movements or vessel movements or missile tests so that it would minimize nasty surprises? Because, confronted with a nasty surprise, the decision maker may panic and hit the button. Let's begin thinking about *preventing* the crisis, even if we remain locked deeply into the Cold War."

Well, I should say in that week I thought we failed, although it was a very good, substantive meeting. Toward the end of that week, we had an expert on Iran—the shah was still in office—an expert who had been a consultant to Iran for many years, a Swiss scholar. We took Iran as a case in point. If the shah falls, must we and the Soviets go to nuclear confrontation? There's a lot of oil there that we both care about, a strategic position. We tried to look at ways of managing a crisis over the shah's fall that would not lead us into a nuclear confrontation. But it was also very illuminating to me that this expert from Switzerland on Iran put it to us, "There's really no need to discuss if the shah falls, it's when the shah falls. He will within the year. I'm very sympathetic with the shah. I've counseled him for fifteen or twenty years. He's finished."

That was news to me, to all of us. We were astonished. I came back and tried to get word to President Carter. It got to him, all right, but not in a way that it was persuasive to him. That was a great pity.

But the more fundamental part, from my standpoint, was that we needed to continue this discourse, and it didn't look very promising. I thought we'd failed because the head of the Soviet delegation was quite a nasty character. He wanted to talk to me in the evenings, as was the style during the Cold War. The chairmen of the delegations would meet privately in the evening. And he wanted to know why we were so hostile to the Soviet Union. His picture was of Jimmy Carter and Cyrus Vance as almost maniacal fiends who were looking for a nuclear first strike. That was crazy. If you knew Carter and Vance, you couldn't think of more peace-loving, reasonable people. I realized this was really dangerous, that these relatively sophisticated people had grotesque distortions in their understanding of our leaders and our country. So the crisis prevention need was greater than ever, but it looked to me like we'd struck out.

But about ten days after that, I got a cable from Georgy A. Arbatov, who headed their Institute of USA and Canada, which was their main scholarly institute that specialized in the US-Soviet interface, asking if I would come and spend a week or two there and talk more about crisis prevention. Well, that made me know that they were interested, but I didn't feel that I was the big expert on the subject, and furthermore, I had a very demanding job at the Institute of Medicine. But I did persuade Graham Allison and Alex George to go separately—we had no money—on their own money, their own good nature. They went and spent time and began to arrange meetings in different places. There was a professional meeting of the Political Science Association, where they would meet with some Soviet counterparts.

At least a discourse got going, erratically, on crisis prevention, and that was one of the things that went through my mind. If I had some money at my disposal and some legitimate organizing capacity, I could make this crisis prevention approach move vigorously. We'd already had a very good thing under way at the academy, on arms control, which I personally helped to start and participated in, from 1980 onward—for which continuing appreciation was expressed in 2014. And so the Carnegie option was very appealing.

As soon as I decided to take the Carnegie job, which was in the middle of '82, I sat Graham Allison down and said, "Graham, you're a very successful dean of the Kennedy School of Government at Harvard. You've built it up wonderfully. You cannot do that anymore, not just the deanship. You've got to get help administratively, for example, rely more on your excellent deputy, Hale Champion, so that you can come back to the crisis subject. You know more about it than anybody in the world. You've got to spearhead a joint crisis prevention group." I hadn't even moved to New York yet from Harvard, but I felt it was such an emergency, that if I could get him committed to it, as soon as I got to New York I could persuade the board to make a grant. And that happened.

So that Pugwash '78 meeting in Geneva, which was improvised and which had no obvious follow-up, grew into this joint study mechanism and major follow-up in crisis prevention in other fields. And it gave me great encouragement that maybe I could do something when I got to Carnegie that wouldn't be foolish.

So the crisis prevention group got going, and then it was steady. It was formally meeting twice a year, once here and once there, and established a flow back and forth of younger scholars in between to prepare for the meetings and exchange materials. In due course, it got to be a broader discourse—not only crisis prevention, but ways to wind down the Cold War. That's what evolved from it. I think it was a significant part of the mechanism, with feedback to Gorbachev years down the road. We started before Gorbachev and continued with him when he came to power in 1985.

Arms Control and Crisis Prevention

So, the arms control was one piece. Crisis prevention was another. It got to the point where many of the proposals made in and around the crisis prevention group were adopted. Early on in my term, we supported Senator Nunn and Senator John W. Warner, with Barry Blechman, to form a group looking at *nuclear risk–reduction centers*, places where we and the Soviets would both have expert professional people, day in and day out, year in and year out, examining all the risks of inadvertent launch and accidental war and ways of reducing those risks, just in the same way we had challenged the scholarly groups early on to ask how a nuclear war could actually happen. And then the centers would examine *preventive interventions on each pathway* to make the slippery slope a little bit less slippery. That was the concept behind the nuclear risk reduction centers. They did eventually get established on a modest scale. Senator Nunn later produced a proposal to strengthen those for other purposes, related to terrorism and weapons of mass destruction. The concept would be the same.

So we pursued a number of proposals, like strengthening the hotline and creating nuclear risk reduction centers, and having new rules of the road to avoid nasty surprises, and starting *regional consultations*. That was one of the ideas, primarily from Alex George, and at first the governments were quite awkward, but then they became rather skillful. That is, we and the Soviets would meet about different regional conflicts. At the least, we could delineate what is our vital interest, and each side could go very carefully if they recognized that the other side had a truly vital interest at stake. "Don't push me too hard there, because I can't let you." In other places we could bargain; we could give and take in mutual accommodation. So the regional consultations were another part of that whole scheme of *avoiding nasty surprises*, getting gradually *more transparent*, with troop notifications and major weapons movement notifications, so that you won't think we're going to war when we move troops around.

Thus, the whole field of crisis prevention grew and developed and provided an impetus for what came to be called *confidence-building measures*. That's still important on the international-security stage today. In addition to the excellent scholars I've already mentioned, we got valuable input from people like Bruce Jentleson, Joshua Goldstein, Roald Sagdeev, Robert Legvold, Bill Perry, and others.

I think it's significant to recognize that the studies we supported got out into the general discourse, certainly in the democratic countries at home and abroad, and to a certain extent in the Soviet Union through its scientific community. For example, the studies that we supported on arms control and crisis prevention, the studies we supported on Star Wars (Strategic Defense Initiative), and the studies we supported on Soviet decision making were in newspaper columns and op-ed pieces and magazine articles. In congressional hearings, I think it's fair to say that after about 1985, in the ensuing decade, there was hardly ever a congressional hearing that didn't have reference to one of the Carnegie-supported studies or have testimony from one of the Carnegie-supported experts or members of one of the Carnegie-supported panels. It was just part of the discourse. There were a lot of other sources; I'm not suggesting Carnegie was the only one. It is true we were, for a few years, the only foundation deeply engaged in this kind of work, and then we gave great encouragement to the MacArthur Foundation to come into it. It's a long story, but we played a very active and cooperative role with MacArthur (discussed later in this chapter).

Patience, Analysis, and Persistence

We wanted to play a role in the analytical underpinnings for major reductions in nuclear weapons and the missiles that would carry nuclear weapons. We wanted particularly to focus on the first-strike capability. We wanted both sides to cut back on the capacity for the first strike, because that's so enormously threatening. The more you build up first-strike surprise capability, the more I have to build up to match it. So we simply wanted to get the ablest people we could anywhere in the world to do the analytical work that might be useful, if and when the political leaders wanted it.

Now, it's interesting that in our early arms-control ventures it was not uncommon for me to say something like this to the groups we were supporting: "I don't know when, if ever, the work you put in will be put to use. It all depends on the political leaders and public opinion. What I want is for us to have on the shelf, so to say, good analytical work that shows how we could both reduce the weapons and reduce the danger, both the structural arms control in reducing numbers and the functional arms control in reducing the risk of an inadvertent firing, to do that work so that sooner or later someday, somehow it may be useful." And great physicists and engineers and behavioral scientists spent a huge amount of time, energy, and aggravation in that work, knowing the importance of it potentially, but not knowing if it would ever be put to use.

Now as it turned out, it was exceedingly valuable once Gorbachev and Reagan got around to making the political decisions. That kind of analytical work, which had diffused into the arms-control community, into the government, and into public opinion, was helpful. You have to be patient and take some risks, and people have to invest valuable time in a mission they believe to be terribly important. If you make the least little contribution, it's worth doing, and you have to be patient and persistent in trying to bring it to fruition.

The Emergence of Gorbachev

My first meeting with Gorbachev—in 1985, shortly after he came to office—was dramatic, and it was one of many points in my career when I really had to pinch myself. I have to say I wish my grandfather could be around to see it. To some degree there was always within me the kid who grew up in a small town in Indiana, close to people who had fled from persecution, and feeling somewhat insecure, and lacking in chutzpah. But I felt if you had a chance, you should try. President Kennedy once said something to the effect of, "what's influence for, except to use it?" If you have it, you should use it.

So we had these arms-control meetings between the US Academy group and the Soviet Academy group from 1980 onward—and I was a member of the group, though not a financial sponsor. But in my participation, I became friendly with a couple of leading scientists in their group, the chairman at that time, a physicist named Velikhov, who was well respected by our physicists. So I would meet on the side with one or two of their leading people and have other discussions. I figured maybe there was something else I could do with the academy or with the foundations or universities, apart from the arms-control issue. What's happening? Are there openings to improve the relationship, to reduce one danger or another?

So it happened, by chance, that a meeting of the arms-control group—which we called CISAC, the Committee on International Security and Arms Control—was in Moscow a few months after Gorbachev came to power. So I had my meeting, I remember, under some steps in their academy, with Velikhov, my ritual advance meeting. I said to him, "You've got a new leader. I don't know anything about him. I apologize for my ignorance. I'd never heard of him before he was appointed. I'm certainly nowhere near a Soviet expert. I don't know if he's good for us, for the cause of peace, for the United States, for friendship, any of that. I don't know. Maybe good, maybe bad. But I do know this. New leaders, when they come to power, like to have a distinctive ecological niche, to say to themselves, 'There's some way in which I can make a contribution different from my predecessors or exceeding my predecessors.' I wonder how Gorbachev feels about that? I wonder if we could help him see that a great contribution he could make might be to begin to wind down the Cold War. Is that possible?"

So Velikhov got excited, said, "Let me think about it. I have to think about it. I'll get back to you in a while." What I didn't know was, he was going to talk to Gorbachev that night. I had no way of knowing his relationship with Gorbachev.

The next morning, he was waiting for me when I came in. I was five minutes late. People said, "Velikhov's been looking for you all over." Very uncharacteristic behavior. The Soviets were never very punctual. He was excited. He had brought some ideas from Gorbachev. There was a whole series of rapid-fire interplays that first year.

My first meeting with Gorbachev was really dramatic because he gave me a severe critique of the Soviet Union. He told me of the damage that had been done over the past seventy years, and then he sort of beat me about the head and shoulders, as if I were criticizing, and said, "We are great people. We have great mathematicians and novelists and musicians and artists. We are a great country. We've just been hamstrung for so many years by dictatorial regimes—Czarist and Soviet. Dictatorial regimes cannot bring to full flower the creativity of people, and our people are great people. Don't put us down. My task is to bring out the creativity and to free the Russian people."

Velikhov had introduced me as a leader of the scientific community. I was at that time president of the American Association for the Advancement of Science (AAAS). I guess he told him about that. So, for instance, he said to me, "Your scientific community should be helping us." He said, "In the social sciences, you should be advocating objective social science. Our social science has been distorted by ideology. I'm supposed to be a policy-maker. How can I decide when I have no honest facts before me? I don't know what to believe in economics or social trends. What is the truth? We have to have a disciplined collection of social information that's reliable, and you have to help us with that, because we have no background, no tradition in it. We have great mathematicians, you know. We can do it." It was extraordinary.

So, toward the end I said to him, "It seems to me you're very interested in ideas outside Russia. If I could be of any help I certainly would." I felt he might kick me out of the room for being so presumptuous to say I could help bring in people and ideas, but, no, he put his arm around me and said, "That would be a great thing. Would you be willing to do that? Would you be willing to bring people to see me, send people to see me and my colleagues? We must open up. We have good ideas. We have very good people, but we don't have all the good ideas and need more."

I really couldn't tell—it could have been a terrific act. On return, I went to see Senator Nunn, who was one of the few Americans at that time who'd had any substantial exposure to Gorbachev, and we had to compare notes. He had the same reaction I did. We weren't sure what to make of it. Perhaps he was a terrific actor. One thing that made me think that he wasn't an actor was, when we got talking about nuclear weapons (back to my research on stress), he began to tremble and sweat. Now, I don't know, maybe some very good actors can do that, some method acting that permits you to evoke these autonomic responses, all my old adrenaline observations, but he had it. Let me tell you, when we talked about nuclear weapons, he said, somewhat like Reagan had said to me in 1984, that he'd learned a tremendous amount about nuclear weapons after he came to power, and he couldn't believe that anybody could think of using one. What responsible person would order a weapon to be fired that could cause millions of people to be killed in a minute? Just crazy.

So I didn't think it was an act, but still it took a while to sort out. But I saw no harm. I did clear it with key people in the White House and the State Department to confirm that they didn't think it was subversive if I were to begin to organize delegations to go and visit and increase contact in various ways.

I have up on my wall some photographs that were taken by Deana Arsenian, who was on our staff and still is, who grew up in Russia and left in adolescence from Moscow. Her first trip back to Russia was on a particular delegation that I took, that had five distinguished scientists and five members of the Senate. Some wonderful pictures of Nunn, Simpson, Cranston, and Bill Cohen—who later became secretary of defense—were of that delegation, and some very distinguished scientists who are arms-control experts. That was perhaps the peak visit—ten of us for a whole week-long meeting with Gorbachev's top military people and his top economic people and so on, and then a half-day meeting with Gorbachev at the end.

There's a kind of amusing story. This was in early 1988, as I remember. At the end of a half-day meeting with him, he was talking to us in ones and twos, and I said to him, "Mr. President," or whatever was the terminology we used, "if you stay on the track you are on now, I think the Cold War might just be over by the year 2000, by the turn of the century." And when I walked out with Nunn, I said, "Gee, Sam, did I get carried away by that?"

And he said, "No, no, no. The spirit was right. It was right for the occasion. You were probably just too optimistic about the timing." Well, you know, a year later, depending on what criteria you use, one or two years later, it was all over. The year 2000 was way too pessimistic, not too optimistic a projection. Who anticipated it?

Cooperative Threat Reduction: Nunn-Lugar Program (and Carnegie's Role)

The Nunn-Lugar program, the cooperative nuclear threat–reduction program, has been going on for several decades. Senator Nunn and Senator Lugar would tell you—they've often said publicly—that this grew directly out of some Carnegie-sponsored activities. What happened was the following. There was the coup against Gorbachev. We arranged two quick emergency meetings, one in Budapest and then one in New York. The one in Budapest had a number of Russians involved, some of whom had been involved in the coup—not coup plotters, but coup defenders, pro-Gorbachev, pro-Yeltsin (short-term), pro-democracy forces. We tried to make an assessment, members of Congress and independent experts in Budapest, of what had happened, how dangerous it was, what to make of it. We concluded it was very dangerous, that Gorbachev might not hold power much longer, that the Soviet Union might fall apart, with indeterminate consequences, with all those nuclear weapons and launching vehicles—"loose nukes" and the like.

So when we came back, I got together all of our grantees who were experts on the Soviet Union, plus a few consultants with great experience, like Bob McNamara, who'd been secretary of defense during the Cuban Missile Crisis; Mac Bundy, who later was a resident scholar with Carnegie; and some retired military people, in addition to our grantees, and we spent a day or so trying to figure out what we could usefully do.

One of the things that became clear was that we needed to know, to the extent possible, where the Soviet nuclear weapons were. There was a lot of information available, and we had a study, led primarily by Ashton Carter of Harvard (later deputy secretary of defense and in 2015 becoming secretary of defense) with a number of colleagues, and we therefore soon had a reliable map of where the weapons were and some knowledge of how well they were supervised, how they could be made secure and scarce, because our concern was, what would be the fate of the nuclear weapons in the disintegrating Soviet Union?

A couple of years before, I had set up the steering committee on the Prevention of Proliferation (POP). The steering committee consisted of me; William Perry, who was then a professor at Stanford, later to be secretary of defense; John Steinbruner from the Brookings Institution, who headed their international program, a very respected scholar; Senator Nunn; and Senator Lugar, the five of us. We met regularly to talk about what the United States could do in the world to minimize the proliferation of weapons of mass destruction. It was thoughtfully supported by Carnegie's chairman of the board, Warren Christopher, who was later secretary of state.

So I called an urgent meeting of that group to hear Ashton Carter's report about the Soviet nuclear weapons, and Nunn and Lugar were very excited and very creative in thinking about how they could translate this knowledge into legislation, especially funding. They asked us to come back in a few days to meet with a larger group of senators. They convened twenty-some senators several days later for an emergency meeting on what they could do about this problem. The conclusion was twofold. First of all, could we put up money through the Defense Department to work with counterparts in the then Soviet Union, to make sure that their nuclear weapons were safeguarded to the maximum extent possible, that they were in secure places, that they didn't fall into the hands of terrorists, that they weren't sold on the black market, any of that?

Secondly, we needed to provide scientific work for their nuclear-capable scientists and engineers so they wouldn't be inclined to go to Iran or Iraq or Libya or someplace like that—and moreover to help them turn their work gradually to civilian uses.

So, with advice from us, Nunn and Lugar drew up legislation to do that, to help safeguard the weapons, move them to safe storage, with responsible stewardship, and set up scientific centers in Russia and Ukraine to employ nuclear-capable scientists and engineers. That went through.

Then before long Perry was secretary of defense (first deputy, then secretary), and Carter was with him as assistant secretary in charge of nuclear weapons policy, and there they were implementing the very thing that they had earlier analyzed. In implementation they had a lot of cooperation from senators Nunn and Lugar. Some billions of dollars have now gone into that since its inception. A huge amount of actual destruction of nuclear warheads and other nuclear-related technology has occurred under that program, as well as a lot of stabilization of their scientific and technical community. It's moved more slowly than we would have wished, both here and there, but the movement has been substantial. It is recognized globally as a model for international cooperation to reduce the nuclear danger.

In early '92, Nunn, Lugar, a couple of other senators, Perry, Carter, and I went to Russia and Ukraine to see if we could speed up implementation there and back home. This was Nunn and Lugar's initiative. On return, they met with President Bush Sr. and Howard H. Baker to expedite it even before Perry was in the government. Perry and Ashton Carter gave great attention to that in government. They wrote a follow-up book with Carnegie support on that whole program and the concept of *preventive defense*. That concept was continued by them for years after they left government in a Stanford-Harvard collaboration. In 2014, Carter had left government and, at Stanford, continued the collaboration. Now he has returned as secretary of defense. They did a great deal over the years to establish the prevention approach in a military context.

Every foundation talks about leverage. Carnegie spent a very modest amount of money, but it leveraged billions of dollars, federal dollars, on a huge international program that materially reduced the nuclear danger. If there was ever a success story in the foundation community, this is one. Not only my testimony—Nunn, Lugar, Perry, Carter, and others have very often spoken about that. Nunn joined the Carnegie board when he left the Senate. He views Carnegie's achievements in this field as something very special.

I don't claim it personally. What I claim personally is that I had the sense to have an affinity for exceedingly able people like Nunn and Lugar and Perry and Carter, and to feel a comfortable sense in the American democracy of moving back and forth across that permeable membrane of government and nongovernment. My attitude is, the president of the United States has at his disposal, if he wants it, all the expertise in our country. It's all available. And it ought to be not just those in government, it oughtn't to be turf issues, it oughtn't to be this foundation or that university or that department of government. The whole country is his to use, and we tried to put that kind of concept into operation as best we could. We had very good cooperation from presidents Reagan, H. W. Bush, and Clinton. All of them have asked me about things the foundation world could do: "Could you do this faster than we could, or better than we could? Or could you stimulate something to happen across national boundaries that might be sensitive for the government to do?" And we've tried. Some of that goes under the name of Track II diplomacy.

As I mentioned, when I met President Reagan in the spring of '84, he told me he'd learned a great deal about nuclear weapons since he got into office, and he realized that they were incredibly dangerous. He did not consider them useful military weapons. He sincerely believed, as Gorbachev made clear to me a year later, if there's a way to get rid of the damn things, you ought to get rid of them. Reagan hoped that Star Wars would do that, but if it wouldn't, then there ought to be other ways to do it. You ought to use public education. He came to be a true believer in the enormous dangers of these weapons. In recent years, both men have been referred to as nuclear abolitionists.

Reagan was a complicated person. He wasn't what he seemed to be at first glance. We had thought that he might be very angry about our messing around in this field, but he wasn't. His attitude was, "I need all the help I can get." But that wasn't true of everybody in his administration. He told me one time that it troubled him very much that his administration was often divided on these issues, like reopening the scientific and scholarly exchanges with the Soviets in '84, about a year before Gorbachev came to power. A number of his people didn't want to do that, but he did. He wanted us to be strong—we could defend ourselves militarily if we had to, we didn't have to be afraid of anybody, but from that position we could negotiate in profound and pervasive ways.

But those delegations, I think, were useful. Later, in speeches at Stanford and at the Council on Foreign Relations in New York, when he was still in office and since, Gorbachev has said the new ideas, the Soviet new thinking, which is a term they use, didn't just arise in the Kremlin; it came elsewhere. Some of the Soviet's best ideas came out of American universities like Stanford, came out of American foundations like Carnegie. He's been very generous in giving us credit. At least we played a role, a very stimulating role for a great leader. And the US leadership met him more or less halfway.

The spirit of preventing the deadliest conflicts pervaded our work, and still does (see Chapter 6). I think we've really come back to one of the great spiritual heirlooms we have of Andrew Carnegie in that work. As the Cold War ended, I felt that we were very likely to have an upsurge of ethnic and religious conflicts. I had written about that in my second annual report essay, in 1984, and had talked with some of the Soviet experts during the Cold War about what might happen in the Soviet Union with the many different ethnic and religious conflicts within and around their borders.

As the Cold War faded in the early 1990s, we adapted the program to focus more on ethnic, religious, and regional conflicts, and less on the risk of international war—though without abandoning international war either—and trying to make grants that would help us to understand and, above all, to prevent the emergence of an enormous rash of ethnic and religious conflicts around the world. We were always aware that such conflicts were likely for decades to come, that slippage from democratic progress of the sort fostered by Gorbachev could readily occur in countries historically weak in democratic traditions and institutions. But we felt that these dangers needed to be studied, understood, and pursued to the extent possible, especially by the world's most fortunate countries and the finest scholars available. So we continued grants and meetings to deal with these issues into the twenty-first century. There is much more to be done.

The Carnegie Commission on Preventing Deadly Conflict (and Its Ramifications)

The most visible part of the Carnegie peace program was the Carnegie Commission on Preventing Deadly Conflict. Now, the way that came about was that I had involved Cyrus Vance as an adviser, along with a number of other people, in our international program from the beginning of my term of office, and he was a very valuable adviser. Then I had tried to be helpful to him in some of the missions he did with the UN secretary general, providing him with background material and whatever intellectual support we could, to make it possible for him to do missions on short notice. Again, the flexibility of foundations to respond was key. So he had done troubleshooting for the secretary general in South Africa and Nagorno-Karabakh, and then in Yugoslavia, first vis-à-vis the Serb-Croatia conflict, and then in Bosnia, ultimately with the famous Vance-Owen Plan, which was the only three-party agreement ever achieved in the post-Yugoslavia conflict—but it was essentially ignored for domestic political reasons by the United States and Germany. It was two bloody years later when the Dayton Agreement was reached. For Vance and me, this was a stimulus for prevention—in the general category of "never again."

I visited him in Geneva toward the end of the time when he was working on Bosnia, and I said I thought he really ought to do a book when he got back, that we'd be happy to support a book that considered how that conflict came about and especially how it might have been *prevented*. Part of my motivation was that one of our expert groups in 1987, in a meeting in Europe with members of Congress, had focused on Eastern Europe, with special attention to Yugoslavia, where Tito had died in 1980. In 1987, this expert group concluded emphatically that Yugoslavia was very likely to have a violent disintegration within five years, by 1992.

Members of Congress asked me to report this back to the secretary of state. They took it very seriously. I did report it, and he took it seriously as well. The Europeans then basically said to the secretary of state, "It's a European problem. Don't be excitable. Leave it to us. We'll take care of it." And so for several years, as a matter of fact, the United States was happy to let the Europeans take care of it. In the end, no one took care of it. But the point that was so striking was that there *was* early warning. The experts knew that this violent conflagration was likely to come. Later down the line, Vance had written a letter, and the secretary general of the United Nations, at Vance's urging, had written a letter to the foreign secretary of Germany, saying, "Don't recognize Croatia, because if you recognize Croatia, then there will be a war in Bosnia." It's exactly what happened. Germany went ahead, and it happened.

All I'm saying is, there very often is *early warning*, but there's not effective action to respond to the early warning and prevent these terrible things. When the Rubicon is crossed, it becomes infinitely harder, with strong revenge motives. After the slaughter, after the mass raping and all that, it's so much harder to put Humpty Dumpty back together again, and it would be much better if we could prevent it in the first place, work toward some kind of just outcome, some mutual accommodation among the adversaries.

Vance came back to me after a few weeks and said, "It's too hard. I can't write a book, even with a collaborator. It's too complicated. What we should do is have an international commission to look at the whole problem." So that's what we did. We had an independent international commission. He was adamant that I should co-chair the commission with him, because we did work well together. We set up an international commission for three years, and then a two-year follow-up explaining all over the world what we've said and why. What we did was set out the nature of the problem, why it's so dangerous, why it's likely to get more dangerous in the next century, when everybody will have weapons and technological capacities for incitement; everybody will be able to destroy everybody else in the path we're now on. No part of the world will be too remote to cause terrible damage somewhere else. (See the Appendix for a list of members of the Commission and Advisory Council.)

So we laid out, in a comprehensive way, the tools and strategies available for prevention, partly on a *public health model*, and then we asked who could do what, who could use those tools to implement strategies effectively in the future. That's what it is, it's an overview, in the so-called final report at the White House and the UN; then we put out forty additional reports and books. So we have a sort of two-foot shelf of what there is to know on prevention. Many of the related publications came from our regular grant-making program.

Since this field moves slowly, I suspect that it's going to be gradually useful for decades to come. We must be patient and persistent with a steadily improving agenda for prevention. Each publication goes into depth on some aspect of the final report: what is known or could be known about one part of the prevention problem. So this is a big, visible, worldwide enterprise that in its first year after the final report concentrated on high-level government policymakers at the UN and regional organizations like the Organization of American States, the Organization of African Unity, and others. It's been adopted wholeheartedly by the UN secretary general and by many leaders in a variety of countries, I'd say especially the United States, Sweden, Norway, Japan, Canada, and one or two others, with more to come. There was a lot of interest in Russia (before the loss of Gorbachev), in Germany, and in the francophone countries being spearheaded by Boutros-Ghali, who was part of this venture when he was at the UN. When Kofi Annan succeeded Boutros-Ghali, he picked up the ball and ran with it for a decade. Other world leaders such as Hillary Clinton, Gro

Brundtland, Desmond Tutu, and Noel Lateef took it up as well. Gorbachev kept pushing this agenda. Now, too, Ban Ki-moon, current secretary general of the UN, is promoting it.

Along with that, there have been many grants to learn more about these issues and to put into practice on a small scale ways of defusing emerging conflicts. That illustrates a principle of Carnegie's operation during my time that I believe we carried to a certain level that's unusual. I don't recommend it for every foundation every time, but for us I believe it worked well—that is, the interplay between a commission-like body (a commission, a council, a task force) and the grant-making program. On one hand, ideas that come out of the grant making challenge and stimulate and inform the council or the commission, and, on the other hand, observations of the commission challenge the grant makers to go out and find somebody who can dig more deeply into the subject and understand it better, or to try out on a small scale some conflict-prevention idea that the commission thinks is promising—a useful interplay back and forth between the grant making on the one side and these commission-like bodies on the other, each helping the other.

This sort of work also brings to the fore young scholars who have much to contribute, for example, in the Carnegie foundation, Bruce Jentleson, Melanie Greenberg, Larry Diamond, Joshua Goldstein, and of course our invaluable staff director Jane Holl (now Lute), who made a magnificent contribution from start to finish. In effect, such ventures help to create a dynamic community of scholars and policymakers who are committed to peace and creative in developing preventive approaches.

Lessons from the Rocky Road to Democracy in South Africa

When I came to Carnegie in late 1982, the corporation's earlier activities in Africa had been largely closed down by my predecessor, Alan Pifer. He explained to me that he was very disappointed that the African countries, by and large, had not made the transition to democracy in the short time that he had expected after independence, and that he found it very frustrating. This struck me as inconsistent with knowledge of democratic transitions in various countries, as established by a variety of excellent scholars. These transitions are complex, difficult, and time consuming as well as susceptible to violence. But Pifer remained positive on South Africa, and, in his final statement when I took on the presidency, he requested to the board that in some way we continue in South Africa. I thought that was a very reasonable and constructive suggestion, because South Africa had not only the intrinsic substantive importance of an enormous amount of human suffering as well as human potential, but it had the symbolic significance, as I said later in a number of speeches and writings, that if a democratic transformation could occur peacefully in South Africa, then it could occur anywhere; this could give great hope throughout the world to those who were watching South Africa. And I thought we ought to be helpful in any way we could.

We had two main points of entry. One was the development of *public-interest law*, which had been fostered by a staff member, David R. Hood, under Alan Pifer's tutelage. David stayed a while during my term and then went on to other activities. It was a very interesting effort to create public-interest law. There was in particular one legal center in a university, under John Dugard of University of Witwatersrand, and also a practice-oriented center, and these were run by distinguished white lawyers. Then later there was a rural one run by a distinguished black lawyer. It was, in effect, an effort to test how far the judicial system would go in protecting the rights of nonwhite South Africans. Given Carnegie's constructive activities in South Africa dating back to the Depression, could we push at that frontier? And it turned out that to some degree you could, that some of the more farsighted and courageous judges interpreted the law in ways that would broaden its protections to a wider range of South African people.

We continued the stimulus to the development of public-interest law for some years during my presidency. For example, one of the Carnegie grantees, Arthur Chaskalson, became the equivalent of the chief justice of the US Supreme Court. That, by the way, is a general story, that many of the people who were involved in Carnegie activities became leaders in the new democratic South Africa.

South Africa: The Emergence of Democracy and Intervention for Africa

Our second point of entry into South Africa was the Carnegie Inquiry into Poverty and Development in Southern Africa, which was a really big effort. When I became president, I definitely resolved the question of whether you should place the Inquiry to the extent possible in the black community from the outset, or whether you should do it in the white community with as much outreach as permitted. These are not really dichotomous choices, but there was an important difference of emphasis. There were some who felt that it just wasn't practical to have a deep engagement of black South Africans; it would make us too vulnerable to the government shutting it down. And others felt that we had to take that risk because for the long term it would have a much greater impact if black South Africans were a part of it from the start and made substantial contributions.

We worked a lot with our grantees and friends in South Africa. Francis Wilson, the initial director of it, did a superlative job and was extremely significant for me, as was Mamphela Ramphele, who later became the vice chancellor of the University of Cape Town. Other South Africans were also important in the effort. Desmond Tutu was, and still is to this day, an extremely important guide to that territory and to other territories for me. We've become close friends over the years. I'd say those were the three South Africans that I consulted the most. Mandela was in prison. I will say a special word about Tutu later in this chapter. He is a truly great person.

We had US experts on South Africa. We convened some early meetings of consultants. We had one very interesting meeting in which we got a group of in-depth experts on South Africa together with a group of in-depth experts on the principles of conflict resolution and violence prevention, in about a fifty-fifty mix, and we tried to see how could you take the concepts and themes of conflict resolution and map them onto the dangerous South African situation.

Francis Wilson, a broad-based economist, was the guiding spirit. I trusted his judgment very much. I went to South Africa in 1984 for a preliminary airing of the Inquiry. It was an international meeting, but primarily oriented toward explaining to South Africans what the Inquiry was trying to do, and I took a group of seven of us, board and senior staff, and Alan Pifer, who was emeritus. It was a very intense experience, as we went not only to the conference, bringing out the first phase of the Inquiry, but also to a forced resettlement camp, one of their concentration camps, where they dumped vast numbers of people in utterly marginal conditions. There were not gas chambers and the like, but these were conditions in which the hold on life was so tenuous that the death rate was palpably high, and the gross malnutrition and disease were visible to the naked eye.

There was some effort by the South African embassy in Washington to intimidate us out of going to that awful place. They called me in advance and basically warned me that they couldn't guarantee our safety. I said to them that I took it as a threat from the government and would immediately notify the secretary of state. Having dealt with an African terrorist situation before, I felt a little more secure than I might have otherwise about that. And I did notify the State Department, and the South Africans then backed off, but it was a scary experience.

One of the things we did was to visit a village to which Mamphela Ramphele had been banished, and that's where I first met her, and was tremendously taken with her ingenuity and dedication. With hardly any resources, she'd made child care and health care facilities in that community, and I could see she was highly intelligent and courageous, so we strongly backed Francis Wilson's efforts to get her to the university, at first in a very modest role, to reassure the government, and then she steadily rose to co-chairmanship of the Inquiry with him.

I gave a speech at that conference in 1984, which I wrote while we were there. I found it was a very emotional speech to give, but we were trying to clarify the significance of this enormously important activity. There was an earlier Carnegie Inquiry in the 1920s and 1930s on poverty in South Africa. It greatly benefited the Afrikaners, and then they became the dominant group. We said they must consider the rest of the people in South Africa. And the Inquiry showed concrete ways in which that could be done.

A very good move that Francis Wilson made was to organize task forces that involved leading blacks. There was a task force on religion and poverty, chaired by Desmond Tutu, and there were task forces on education and poverty, health and poverty, commerce and poverty, you name it. But every one of those task forces had black, white, brown—all skin colors—and the South Africans made such a to-do about that, with all their elaborate racial classifications. But it did give distinguished, gifted black South Africans like Desmond Tutu an additional forum, and it gave younger black South Africans an opportunity for research training, particularly in the behavioral and social sciences.

So there were many publications that came out of it. Avery Russell, Carnegie's dynamic director of publications, did a great deal to help with those publications, and then the final volume was published, *Uprooting Poverty* (by Wilson and Ramphele). And with that, we undertook a very active dissemination program in the United States, Europe, and South Africa.

Along the way, as the Inquiry work became available, I tried to link Francis Wilson and Desmond Tutu and others from the Inquiry with American leadership, particularly in the US government. One of our trustees, John C. Whitehead, became the deputy secretary of state in the Reagan administration, and he had been interested in South Africa, to a certain extent, from his Carnegie experience. In any case, he and I were good friends, so I kept him well informed and he took the initiative to organize a government commission on South Africa. It came to be known as the Shultz Commission, because George Shultz was the secretary of state. He persuaded George Shultz to set up such a commission. I think it was an attempt to get the Reagan administration to reconsider its policies, which had not been sympathetic with the democratic movement in South Africa, and I think it was effective in shifting the attitude of the Reagan administration toward a more serious interest. This is one example of the dynamic interplay of governmental and nongovernmental expertise in democratic processes.

I helped John Whitehead put that commission together. He asked me to serve on it, but I thought it would be better if the foundation president on it would be Frank Thomas, president of the Ford Foundation, who was much more expert than I in South Africa, and I felt that Helene Kaplan, our board chair, should be on it, and she became a very active, constructive member. So, indirectly, I think Carnegie's experience was helpful to our government in the establishment and conduct of the Schulz Commission, and that in turn had a positive effect on American policymakers—as well as the general public to some extent. Several of us tried for years to arrange a personal meeting between Reagan and Tutu because both relate well in personal contact. Whitehead was helpful in arranging this meeting. But at least in the short run, Reagan's reaction was indifferent.

I tried to foster contact between these leading South Africans and leaders in Congress—in both houses and both parties—to convey the information coming from the Inquiry, and there were members on both sides of the aisle who took a growing interest. I remember that on the Democratic side, Senator Edward M. Kennedy took a great interest, as did John Kerry. On the Republican side, Senator Richard G. Lugar was very effective, as was Senator Nancy Kassebaum. We tried to see to it that people who really knew that situation in South Africa would meet with them or their staffs in an accurately informative way.

Gregory Craig, a distinguished lawyer who has served in several important posts (e.g., chief of the Office of Policy Planning in the State Department), came to see me on behalf of Senator Edward Kennedy. He was Senator Kennedy's man for Africa at that time and sought to understand what was going on and how Congress could be helpful. So we tried to help them get the facts straight not only about what was wrong, but also about what the opportunities were for constructive change in South Africa. This was typical of Ted Kennedy and many members of Congress at that time—reaching out for sources of accurate information on critical issues.

So, on the dissemination side, besides the publication, we had various conferences on uprooting poverty. We put out Carnegie Quarterlies. Then we had photo exhibits, in which Avery Russell was instrumental, with photographs that had first been shown at the 1984 conference in Cape Town. I must say, by the way, that the University of Cape Town was a wonderful base for the Carnegie Inquiry. Stuart Saunders, who was then the vice chancellor, protected the Inquiry and connected with his own government about it. The key people at the University of Cape Town were able to work with considerable ingenuity, given the circumstances, and they were courageous.

I had the honor of being denounced by P. W. Botha in the Parliament. He was the prime leader of the government at that time. When I made my speech at the conference, he made some remarks in the Parliament the next day that were in the papers, to the effect that, "Dr. Hamburg probably means well, but he doesn't understand the situation in South Africa," and basically saying that outside agitators don't help the situation. We have our own problems to face and we'll do it in our own way. Visitors not needed.

But I think there's no doubt that in the end, the ideas and constructive suggestions of the Inquiry gave a sense of hope within South Africa, a sense of concrete paths that could be followed. Also that the Inquiry, combined with the grant making by Carnegie and Ford and the US government, helped in building a civil society in South Africa and made a big difference in the transition.

On one occasion, Cyrus Vance and I organized a conference at the Waldorf Hotel in New York that included high-level representatives of the world's main democracies. Our aim was to move toward cooperation in policies toward South Africa.

When I went to South Africa in '84, I met Reverend Allan A. Boesak, who was a brilliant young leader, kind of a firebrand, and a person who had some of the attributes of Tutu and even some of the attributes of Martin Luther King Jr. In later years, he had some personal difficulties, but he was an inspiring speaker and courageous man. After that, I saw him when he came to the United States, and we kept in touch. He got arrested, and that was at a time when very bad things happened to people like that in South African jails. They slipped on a banana peel and fractured their skull. People died or disappeared. This was the mode of action that disposed of Steve Biko.

So I got quite alarmed. I called down there, spoke to his wife and some others, and found there was no organized effort to get him free. So I asked my colleagues, primarily Barbara Finberg, to take over the running of the foundation for a little while, while I devoted full time to organizing an international network to get him free. What I did was to get a set of distinguished university presidents and foundation presidents to agree on a joint statement. I needed some kind of platform, more than what I could say alone. I drafted a statement, which we worked over. My recollection is, it was the presidents of Yale, Stanford, Harvard, Columbia, Princeton, and maybe a couple of others, as well as the presidents of the Ford Foundation and the Rockefeller Foundation. I think those were the only two foundations besides us who were active in South Africa at that time. And I made various calls. As luck would have it, we were able to get excellent editorials in the *New York Times* and *Washington Post*, based on the statement we'd put out, and considerable press coverage in the international press about Boesak's case. The government aggression was in process of backfiring.

It suddenly became an international concern. It lit up the sky for the South African government, that the world was watching, and if anything bad happened to him, they would be held responsible. It was the same principle as when they tried to threaten me about our visiting this forced resettlement camp, the realization for them that they would be held responsible for anything bad that happened. He was shortly thereafter freed, and he thought that our intervention had something to do with it. I'd like to believe that it did. At least it didn't do any harm and may have done some good.

I was impressed when that happened. Here we had a group of outstanding university and foundation presidents interested in South Africa. It seemed a pity to just let that drop. So I organized, for a year or two, a foundation-university consortium on South Africa, and we had a series of meetings in which we brought counterparts from South Africa, like Stuart Saunders from the University of Cape Town as well as the chancellor of the historically black University of the Western Cape who later was Mandela's chief of staff.

So we had leading educators from South Africa meeting with American university and foundation presidents. We enlarged the group, and the result was that some additional foundations, like Kellogg and the Henry J. Kaiser Family Foundation, moved into South Africa, and some additional universities became engaged in educational activities for

South Africans, beyond anything that had been done before. That was a very gratifying experience. It was done in a very low-key way. It also stimulated student-led organizations to work with university presidents and trustees to help overcome apartheid. The universities had some influence (especially via trustees) to put financial pressure on the South African government, and there is general agreement that the banks became helpful—and the South African government foresaw grave economic troubles.

I was touched when Norman Brown, the outgoing president of Kellogg, a few years later came to visit me—this was years after our original convening of a foundation university group on South Africa's needs and opportunities. He thanked me for facilitating their entry into South Africa. They did it very thoughtfully with years of good work in South Africa. Once they made the decision, they really moved into education.

At a later stage, I also facilitated the entry of the C. S. Mott Foundation, which is a large foundation based in Flint, Michigan, into South Africa and also into the former Soviet Union. They even had a board meeting here in New York, in which I spoke to them, and Frank Thomas, then president of the Ford Foundation, also spoke to the Mott Board about international activities, particularly in South Africa. So that was one of the things that we tried to do to help other foundations move into crucial international arenas.

Carnegie had a historic role of trying to facilitate the interest of other foundations in critical issues. So the Boesak case became an opportunity to do that, and a number of programs were established that lasted for some years. Some of them have continued. William G. Bowen, who was the president of Princeton at that time, later became the president of the Andrew W. Mellon Foundation, and he brought that interest with him to Andrew Mellon and did very good things at the foundation.

There were doubts when I came to the presidency of Carnegie about continuing the corporation's activity in South Africa. They were similar to our doubts about what we could do with the Soviet Union. How can you get a foothold in an essentially closed, highly authoritarian society? Is there anything useful you can do? There was a question in my mind whether it was feasible to improve the situation. But I thought we ought to explore it actively enough in both cases for a couple of years, to see if we could get a handle anywhere. Particularly when we made the trip in 1984 and were engaged with that conference and read a number of the early papers, and talked a lot with and met many more people in South Africa than I ever met before, I began to feel that, yes, we probably could make a difference.

I would say both South Africa and the Soviet Union were largely terra incognita for American foundations. How do you work in highly closed authoritarian and often violent societies? What can you do there as an outsider? The question even arose, do you put your collaborators in those countries at great risk? I'd have to say, in all candor, the latter worried me very much. The strategy in both cases was to work with democratic reformers, but they were in some danger in their own societies. Those were serious concerns, but I finally felt that, if these brilliant and certainly courageous people wanted to push on with it, we should help them. My feeling was that the proper metric for the emergence of democracy in Africa, South Africa, or anywhere else, was not years, but decades or generations, and to measure from the time of independence.

The great scholar of democracy, Robert Dahl of Yale, said that the consolidation of democracy from the time of tangible beginnings is about twenty years, that you just cannot expect to see consolidation sooner than twenty years, and of course, in many cases, it's taken much longer than that. So that influenced my thinking, and undoubtedly my own experiences in Tanzania and Kenya influenced my thinking. I believed that where we saw evidence of thoughtful, dedicated people trying, however slowly, to build democratic institutions, we ought to try to help them.

Now, I have to say, there was some internal tension when we extended to South Africa, because there was a curious, very well-meaning sensitivity, widely distributed in the international community, particularly in the development community, that people with white skin didn't want to be in the position of pushing around people with black skin. There had been all too much of that, and therefore maybe it was improper for us to urge sub-Saharan African countries to go democratic.

I never accepted that, and I used to say, "If it's good enough for us to urge white South Africans to go democratic, why shouldn't we urge black South Africans to go democratic?" It seemed to me it was in the interest of the people of the sub-Saharan African countries to have some say in their own lives. Why should it be good for black Africans to suffer from the tyranny of black leaders? It didn't make any sense for black Africans to suffer the tyranny of white leaders in South Africa.

In any case, we worked out fundamentally distinct strands of our involvement, because you do have to focus. One was to help build democratic institutions in any way we could, although that moved rather more slowly than I would have wished. The African tyrants would hide behind the sovereignty issue: "We don't want outsider interference from any-body, including other African countries, and we certainly don't want outside interference from sanctimonious whites." Well, sure, but in that way, people like Mobutu of Zaire/Congo, who did enormous damage to their own people, were able to justify their position, and to some degree to scare off the development community. The idea was, if you were going to help with development, just give the money to the government and walk away. Well, that meant people like Mobutu would rip off most of it. So it was a well-meaning but misguided history of the development community, in my opinion, of not being very explicit about building democratic institutions.

Our approach was very similar in South Africa and in the Soviet Union and in various African countries: we'd like to help them work toward the building of democratic governance for the well-being of all their people, in their own way—not on a precisely American model. And so we would relate to democratic reformers. What we'd do would differ from place to place, depending on the opportunities—who are the leaders of the democratic community and what did they see as some way to get a handle on the problem in a particular country?

Another strand of our involvement in South Africa, which actually emerged very early, concerned the status and opportunities of women in Africa. And when I say Africa, there were a few countries where we could work more or less effectively. A particular point of entry was maternal mortality. Early in my term, I'd been interested in that problem from my experience with the World Health Organization. We were one of the early parties, and UNICEF got interested, under Jim Grant, who'd been involved with me at an earlier time when I was at the Institute of Medicine; he was on my first International Health Committee. And WHO also became interested, of course, under Dr. Halfdan Mahler, who was a great leader and somebody I worked with for many years. And then they got the World Bank interested to help finance it. So those were the main players: UNICEF, WHO, the World Bank, and some foundations, and we were certainly early and active players in that effort.

We formulated a plan for reducing maternal mortality in Africa, where the situation was much worse than Asia or Latin America. So that was the point of entry, although I was always in some ways uncomfortable with it; that is, to take it as an end in itself. Of course, we don't want women to die in childbirth, when most of it is preventable, but it seemed to me it was one branch on the tree of the low status and minimal opportunities provided to women in Africa. We worked on this problem in West Africa through grants to Columbia University in collaboration with West African universities. Alan Rosenfield, dean of the School of Public Health at Columbia, provided inspirational leadership.

That was also, at one time, sort of a delicate thing to talk about. Maternal mortality, yes; that was the women who were dying. But the larger issues of the subjugation of women in Africa, that was considered impolite to discuss. But it was very severe. It was wonderful when some distinguished black Africans, especially Archbishop Desmond Tutu, spoke out in the most constructive, farsighted way. We can do better and we must.

Throughout all of Carnegie's work in and around South Africa, as well as its development of the prevention approach to mass violence, Desmond Tutu has been enormously helpful. Therefore, I was delighted to be asked to write a letter to him that was published in 2006 in a volume edited by one of his friends. The book was titled *We Are Your Beneficiaries.*

WE ARE YOUR BENEFICIARIES

Dear Desmond,

I was thrilled when I heard that your friends were planning to surprise you with some very special letters to celebrate your 75th birthday. I have been very lucky in my 80 years to know and work with people of high ideals, great integrity, dedication, ingenuity and courage. I feel blessed to have had such opportunities. I say with emphasis that no one I've known has had a more profound effect on me than you.

This has been on my mind a lot lately, since I have been working on a book [*Preventing Genocide*] proposing serious methods for the prevention of genocide. In doing so, your ideas and our shared experiences have come back to my mind over and over again. I decided to select for this letter a few of the items (by no means all) that I have put down in this book about you. Their placement is especially significant since the chapter gives my interpretation of how it was that South Africa was able to avoid genocide. This chapter immediately follows a description of several genocides that are horrible beyond belief: the Armenians; the Holocaust; Rwanda; and Darfur. Such horrors could have occurred in South Africa, as if the actual horrors of the apartheid decades were not bad enough. I hope the book makes clear, especially the chapter on South Africa, that your ideas, principles, courage and integrity have much to do with the transition to democracy in your own country and elsewhere.

Knowing you as I do, I realize this may embarrass you, but it is simply the truth. I saw with my own eyes and heard with my own ears and felt with my heart so many occasions in which your deep commitment to non-violent problem-solving, fair negotiations, democratic values and international cooperation came together in a uniquely powerful way to provide all humanity with the benefit of your extraordinary contributions. It is not only South Africa that is much better off as a consequence of your thoughts and actions, but my own country and our common humanity everywhere.

With deepest respect, enduring affection and profound gratitude.

—David

Desmond Tutu's Nobel Lecture, delivered in December 1984, paints a heartrending picture of his homeland:

It is against this system that our people have sought to protest peacefully since 1912 at least, with the founding of the African National Congress. They have used the conventional methods of peaceful protest—petitions, demonstrations, deputations and even a passive resistance campaign.... The response of the authorities has been escalating intransigence and violence. The South African situation is violent already and the primary violence is that of apartheid, the violence of forced population removals, of inferior education, of detention without trial, of the migratory labour system....

There is no peace in Southern Africa. There is no peace because there is no justice. There can be no real peace and security until there be, first, justice enjoyed by all the inhabitants of that beautiful land.

South Africa ... is also a microcosm of the world ... where there is injustice, invariably peace becomes a casualty.... Perhaps oppression dehumanizes the oppressor as much as, if not more than, the oppressed.... We can be human only in fellowship, in community, in peace....

One of the things we did was to get very promising people and try to nurture their careers. We'd bring them to the United States for a time or bring them to Europe for a time, provide research training in South Africa, provide networking in South Africa and outside. And I'm very happy to say that many of those people are leaders in South Africa today, in the government, in universities, and in business. There were a number of blacks who got their first start or their main chance out of some experience with the Carnegie Inquiry.

Transitions to Democracy in Africa

The election of Nelson Mandela as president of South Africa in 1994 ignited transformative thinking around the continent and, indeed, around the world. At the same time, countervailing forces destabilized other African countries, as exemplified by the early 1990s experience in Sierra Leone. Corporation grantees were directly affected by local destructive internal conflicts; institutions of governance were not strong enough to withstand and tame them. The juxtaposition of transitions to democracy in Africa, along with increasing internal conflicts, led Carnegie to establish a new entity—Transitions to Democracy in Africa—to identify and assess evidence-based approaches for maintaining peace, stability, and democracy, and, accordingly, reform development assistance in Africa. These were the themes: advancing knowledge on and strengthening individual and institutional capacity in conflict management and democratic transitions, and experimenting with and building constituencies on behalf of Africa in the United States.

With the primary goal of contributing knowledge on key elements for stable societies in Africa, we sought to promote new approaches to conflict management that reinforce democratic transitions, and also to find ways that outsiders could bolster African-led efforts toward achieving peaceful and sustainable societies, especially identifying promising reforms to development assistance and actions to reinforce constituency building in the United States.

The Southern Africa Security Project, initiated in 1992 and led by Ambassador Joseph Garba, a senior Nigerian diplomat, military leader, and policy scholar, was based at the Institute of International Education and then at the International Peace Academy and initially focused on the reentry of military forces into the newly democratic South Africa. Over the years from 1992 to 1997, Garba and his colleagues brought together generals, military chiefs of staff, researchers in military studies and defense politics, and key political leaders in defense ministries in meetings throughout the continent, leading to recommendations on ways to restructure forces so that they could embark on productive civilian life in South Africa that were applicable in West Africa as well as in the Great Lakes region of east central Africa. This information was widely circulated to the political leaders, military leaders, and scholars.

In 1992, the International Peace Academy, under the leadership of Olara Otunnu, former foreign minister of Uganda and former president of the UN Security Council, proposed a complementary activity to Garba's and Obasanjo's in Nigeria that focused on addressing mechanisms for *conflict resolution and prevention at the highest political levels on the continent*. The academy, the lead nongovernmental organization working on peacekeeping, had organized a meeting with African leaders in Tanzania to consider ways to resolve and prevent internal conflicts in Africa. The report of the meeting urged the Organization of African Unity, the highest-level political body on the continent then, to establish "a mechanism for the *prevention*, management, and resolution of conflict in Africa" (emphasis mine). With Carnegie support, and support from the governments of the Netherlands and Sweden, the academy attempted to win acceptance for the mechanisms at the Organization for African Unity and to work with a wide range of civil society organizations—nongovernmental organizations, universities, business organizations, and the media—to engage them in monitoring the organization's willingness to undertake conflict management for both interstate and intrastate conflicts.

Francis Deng—of the Brookings Institution and then Johns Hopkins University—drawing on his work funded by the Special Projects Committee on Origins of Conflict in Africa and through his appointment as special representative of the UN secretary general for internally displaced persons, embarked with Carnegie support on a new project to illuminate his increasing concern about the responsibility and accountability of national sovereignty in the face of internal conflicts. Deng's work developed the conceptual framework for a new international paradigm. For the first time there were norms for the international community to follow when internal conflicts arise and national sovereignty is no longer responsible and accountable. With the aim of promoting serious scholarship on the subject of democratic transitions and disseminating the results widely not only to scholars but to policymakers, two institutions that represented broad networks of scholars received support. Staff members and African colleagues together explored ways to improve the effectiveness of development and technical assistance. One promising approach considered the design and testing of more collaborative development-assistance models and identified local sources of support.

The Task Force on Development Organizations, chaired by President Jimmy Carter under the auspices of the Carnegie Commission on Science and Technology for Government, led to an innovative approach to development assistance that promoted building country capacity for national development strategies. The Global Development Initiative was developed, piloted, and enacted in Guyana, and then was adapted in Mali, Mozambique, and Albania. From 1993 to 1997, Carnegie contributed to the process of the team's development of the plan, as well as its organization of debates about the plan, from the local villages to ministerial levels. The Guyana National Development Strategy was released in January 1997, and it has been national policy since 2000. Thus, in various ways, Carnegie helped to strengthen both the ingenuity of nongovernmental organizations in development and their collaboration with government. These are paths to democracy: not easy, not quick, but fundamental in the long run.

To David Hamburg:

We owe you and Carnegie an immense debt of gratitude. The study on poverty chaired by Francis Wilson and Mamphela Ramphela has been seminal and your involvement in the nurturing of budding leadership such as that of persons such as Allan Boesak has been critical. Thank you for your penetrating analyses, but much more, your nurturing of emerging leadership, all these have been crucial. I hope the world will listen to the wisdom contained in the reports of your Prevention of Genocide.

—Desmond Tutu

The Origin of the MacArthur Foundation: Personal Cooperative Efforts and Those with Carnegie

I went to the National Academy of Sciences Institute of Medicine in 1975, as the first full-term president. And that's how the John D. and Catherine T. MacArthur Foundation really comes into this story, early in its history, and the psychiatric component is important. The board members were just putting the foundation together operationally, and somebody—I don't know who—told them to come and see me. This was probably in '76. They had a large fund of money but no clear, agreed-upon mission. One thing that made it attractive to come and see me was that the Institute of Medicine had the widest possible window from which to view developments in medicine and the underlying sciences and their extension into public health and public policy, so that if you wanted to know who was doing what and where the frontiers were, the Institute of Medicine was institutionally an excellent place to come. And as the president of it, I was the embodiment of that broad view of the field. And so trustees of the MacArthur Foundation came one by one as they were exploring how to start their new foundation. Most had been business associates of Mr. MacArthur. They thought that *health* might be an important area in which they could reach agreement.

After several trustees came to visit me in Washington, DC, they invited me to come out to Chicago, and I did that. I gave them my perspective of the health field. Roderick MacArthur (Rod) came in very early, and we became good friends right up to the time of his death. He was the son of the founder.

Health was probably the one arena where they might be able to build a consensus and not fight each other. It was a contentious board. Then it turned out that an important part of this was in mental health, so my position as president of the Institute of Medicine, as well as my background before that in psychiatry—and in scientific psychiatry at that—might help to build a consensus, particularly for Rod, but I think for some of the others as well. And I guess I am, by nature, a consensus builder, so I set out to try to help them find some common ground. I wasn't looking for any credit or any axe to grind or any party line, but I did think they had a big opportunity.

They had no initial agreement on what to do, no mandate from Mr. MacArthur, and no history of philanthropy on his part. So the board was searching for a clear vision and access to agreement.

At that time, I knew more about health and mental health than I did about how to put together a foundation. But I learned something from my efforts to seek support for our fieldwork in Africa. Since government funding was not feasible at that time and the major foundations were not interested in the study of human evolution or development of the sciences in East Africa, it was hard to get support. On the other hand, there was a positive experience with smaller foundations. The ingenuity and flexibility of the leadership people at the W. T. Grant and Commonwealth Foundations were impressive. It hinged partly on the fact that in each case, I knew the key people, they knew me, and they trusted me and were willing to take a flier. That taught me something about philanthropy and risk taking. They got a high return on their investment. In the African hostage episode, the W. T. Grant people were wonderful about helping. For example, I wanted to get one member from each of the abducted students' families there. This was, after all, a kind of a kidnap situation. And in a kidnap, you want the parents to be able to say something about the decisions you make. Only one of the families could have been considered high income, so W. T. Grant put up the money to get the parents over there and to meet emergency costs.

At the end, I promised President Julius Nyerere we'd say nothing in detail for ten years, because he, in the end, helped me with the fourth release in a way that he did not want known. So we said nothing, but the W. T. Grant board asked me to meet with them. After all, they'd been supporting it; they'd been wonderful in the crisis. So, "Okay, on a strictly confidential basis, we'll do that." And Betty, my wife, had been handling the American end of it—there was a lot to do on the American end of it—so we came in together. And they were so impressed with her that they asked her to join the board, and she was on that board for many years. In due course, they asked her to become president and she did so valiantly for seven years. Thus, although I had minimal knowledge about foundations, this taught me a lesson about the *scope and flexibility* that are distinctive for foundations.

My first question to the MacArthur people was, "What did Mr. MacArthur want to do?" They all said there wasn't really much guidance. Nevertheless, he had made the money, and his business associates and his son wanted to be faithful to his spirit in some way. It just wasn't obvious how to do that.

Bill Kirby emerged as a leading figure on the health side and then on the communications side. He had a great dedication to Mr. MacArthur and to the foundation. He was willing to give time and energy to it. And I found him to be remarkably open minded, full of enthusiasm. Another key person of the initial board was Rod, the stormy petrel of the group. He continued our contacts for years. He cared deeply about philanthropy and had very humane, democratic values. He was a difficult personality, impetuous and given to severe criticism. But he fundamentally wanted to be a constructive influence in the foundation. It's almost as if he didn't quite know how to be as constructive as he wanted to be. He was devoted to the creativity theme, which he shared with a number of the others. They created a MacArthur "genius" fellowship, and I thought that they were doing well with it. Yet Rod said to me that he considered it a failure. This was after the first year or two. Why? Because it was only a part of the foundation. He really thought it should be virtually the whole foundation. He was also concerned that it wouldn't be sufficiently risk taking, that they would just anoint people who already were going to get a Nobel Prize or something like that. He wanted to use it to confer a stimulus and legitimacy upon a whole set of new creative people beyond the pale. It would somehow break new ground in bringing along very gifted people. Also, he cared a lot about the mental health part, and particularly, within that, about the psychiatric part. He periodically reminded people that it wasn't just mental health; it wasn't just behavioral science; it wasn't just basic science. It was dealing with mental illness—depression and schizophrenia and other serious problems and bringing to bear the knowledge for near-term or at least foreseeable practical benefit. And he would have outbursts about that to influence the mental health program. He did not want anyone to forget the human suffering of mental illness.

When I decided to come to Carnegie, the MacArthur Foundation had formalized my role as the chairman of the Scientific Advisory Committee. In the early years it was very informal. It was, from my point of view, quite fortunate that they added distinguished scientists, such as Jonas Salk, Murray Gell-Mann, and Jerry Wiesner, all of whom I knew pretty well beforehand. They broadened the dimensions of the board and added a degree of professionalism to it. I think Jonas, by the way, was almost saintly in his patient efforts to sort out differences and to work out reasonable procedures so that policy options and grant applications would be considered fairly and thoroughly.

When I came to the Carnegie presidency, I really hit the ground running on the Cold War issues. I was dreadfully concerned about the Cold War, and that was a lot of my motivation to take on the position in the first place. And even though I didn't start until December of '82, by July of '82 I had been talking with scholars around the country and paving the way for these interdisciplinary groups to study avoiding nuclear war. In the summer of '83, my first summer at Carnegie, there was a Ditchley Conference of European and American foundation leaders. Characteristically of MacArthur, it was not the nominal president who came, Jack Corbally, but rather Rod MacArthur. In any event, the Europeans asked me to say something about the program I had just started on avoiding nuclear war. This was in a time of deep Cold War exacerbation. So I gave a kind of thumbnail sketch of what we were doing, and we had a very interesting animated discussion. Other foundations were not active in that field at the time—and indeed, there was considerable pressure not to be for fear of controversy. Rod kept me up about half the night asking me questions about how I had arrived at our formulation.

A few weeks after I got back to Carnegie, I got an urgent call from Jerry Wiesner. Jerry was the person on the board to look after the possibility of a peace and security program. He says, "Just to come straight to the point, Dave, Rod's here. He's just had a tantrum. And he says you've only been there six or eight months, and you've got a terrific program running; and we've been talking for years about doing something, and we don't have anything going. So he says we should just adopt the Carnegie program lock, stock, and barrel, put a lot of money into it and go. It's too dangerous to wait. This is the first day of the board meeting. I've got around me Jonas, Murray, and Rod here. I'm going to put them on in just a minute, but what we want is for you to come out tomorrow, the second day of the board meeting, and tell us what you're doing." He said, "Please tell us realistic things that you're doing, and we'll adopt them."

So I canceled my appointments, and I went that evening to Chicago and met with their board the second day, and I explained it. But on the plane going out, I decided it would not do. Even though obviously they were prepared to adopt the Carnegie program, I thought that wouldn't be a good thing to do for the long term. They needed to have their own distinctive program, and we needed to have some way of dividing up the territory. We had very good communication; we would have informal cooperation. But I knew them well enough to know that it would be a yoke for some, if they were simply going to adopt the Carnegie program. So in Chicago, I sketched out what we were doing, and then I sketched out a number of things that I wished we could do but couldn't—we didn't have enough money—a number of options that seemed to me equally important. We were dealing with urgent policy matters by design. But I thought there was a very important need for more basic scholarship on origins of conflict, conflict resolution, and international relations, and they could do a lot in that.

So they said it was a very good idea, as long as I worked seriously with Rod. "Well, did you think on the plane about who might chair such a group or who might be on it?" I mentioned some outstanding scholars who might be on it, two or three of whom had received these MacArthur so-called genius awards—either they had already or were' about to. I tried to think of people who had both the stature and the recognition factor for them, for example, Alex George and Sid Drell. I suggested McGeorge (Mac) Bundy and explained why I thought he would be so good for it—he was working on his great book about decisions of the nuclear era.

Murray Gell-Mann objected about what he'd done as president of Ford Foundation. It had nothing to with this subject, but about schools. So I could see it was unraveling again, as it had before. Then one of them said, "Well, would you chair it yourself?" And I said, "Well, I could, but then it tends to defeat the purpose, because we're two foundations getting advice for both, not Carnegie telling MacArthur what to do. I'll think of some others. You think of some others."

And then Jerry called me a couple of days later, and he said he withdrew his reservation about Mac, and he was prepared, if I still felt that way, to talk to Murray and see what he could do. Would I talk to Murray? I agreed and eventually they accepted Mac. As the committee evolved, Mac had great patience and insight. He did a draft in six weeks. He met with his committee a couple of times. Altogether, it took about six months.

The joint committee was very influential with both foundations. There were people like Alex George and Sid Drell, who are MacArthur genius people, and John Steinbrunner, who later became a major grantee of theirs and of ours. It was a wonderful group of people. So something really good came out of that. I think they had a fine program over the years. It's a wonderful example of interfoundation cooperation, largely informal, based partly on key personal relationships.

The Foundation Develops

The health program started aiming toward mental health and the notion of networks came in. I was lucky enough to have input on everything related to these developments. That was a point at which, critically, Murray Gell-Mann and I resonated very strongly. We had known each other before that, especially in my year at Caltech in 1974. He was expecting a Nobel Prize in physics (and he got it), and had strong interests in behavioral science, and indeed I had invited him to come and spend a year in our department at Stanford, which he considered seriously. He and I shared an outlook, not only with respect to psychiatry but in general, about the importance of interdisciplinary research, overcoming what were then powerful barriers between disciplines, even in closely related fields.

And so we agreed strongly from the beginning that whatever we did in the mental health field, it ought to be strongly interdisciplinary. The issue here was whether you could pick out certain problem areas, certain lines of inquiry, that were very important, perhaps neglected, that would benefit from interdisciplinary contexts, to get around the contours of the problem by creating networks. Jonas Salk and Jerry Wiesner were quite sympathetic to that approach. I don't think there was any appreciable dissent on the board. Rod found it congenial, as long as we didn't stray too far away from the serious problems of mental illness.

I had much of the intellectual content in selecting consultative groups on different aspects of the mental health field, each one of which was composed in an interdisciplinary way, each one of which considered to some degree a networking possibility. But the main point was to get the board familiar with the different problem areas. And so we did that. Some of the distinguished consultants in this series of meetings were disappointing because they were self-serving, saying essentially, "The only important thing in this field is what I'm doing, and you should put ten times more money into it." But mostly they were empathic with the mission the foundation had and tried to be helpful.

We had a series of consultative meetings in different fields. Some of them fizzled and some didn't. But out of that, we picked some to create networks. There were some differences of opinion about what the scale of each grant ought to be. We could assume that they were going to have substantial research support from NIH, and, therefore, the minimal interpretation was that MacArthur would give them the money for tying them together. A broader interpretation, which I had, was that you should also give them some money for research, per se, that they would be in a stronger position to take advantage of new opportunities if they had a flexible kitty for research—not to replace the NIH, certainly, but some additional flexible research funding. In the beginning, we did do that, and then it faded out, perhaps as I faded from the scene over a few years' time.

In 1980, I completed my term at the IOM and moved on to Carnegie, at the same time leaving my formal position with MacArthur. In my absence, MacArthur took a more centralized administrative structure, that is, not just setting up a network of chairs or co-chairs and then keeping a loose involvement, but rather telling at least some of the chairs and co-chairs what to do. And that led to some resignations and unpleasant situations. It would have been difficult to administer anyhow. They had to learn how to do it. It was quite novel. I feel very good about excellent people that I brought into the MacArthur orbit. At that time I knew the best players and had some persuasive capacity with them.

Generally, we got constructive participation in the sequence of meetings of the consultative groups, then picked the problem areas, then decided on who we wanted to participate.

Jonas Salk was really in an institution-building mode, as he had been with the Salk Institute. He gave a lot of time and energy even when he wasn't well. The last time we met, when he was visiting New York, we had a life-review conversation. This was just a few weeks before he died. We had a long evening, just the two of us. The basic theme of *preventing bad outcomes* in different spheres of life was recurrent. Prevention was basic for both of us, and it was a deeply moving conversation. He was so frail that he needed a taxi to take him back to his apartment from the restaurant two blocks away.

He was not treated well by the scientific community. There was much envy of his public recognition and a tendency to downgrade his contributions. It occurred to me that others were overlooked similarly for various reasons. He was never elected to the National Academy of Sciences. When I was president of the Institute of Medicine, I proposed a new category: to elect some people to membership after age sixty-five. Jonas was past sixty-five. So too were others who deserved proper recognition and could contribute intellectually. So the work on building the MacArthur Foundation provided a stimulus to the Institute of Medicine.

I also had extremely high regard for Jerry Wiesner and great personal fondness for him. I don't remember when I first got to know him, but I may have had a little contact with him during his days as President Kennedy's science adviser. When he was president of MIT, we got to know each other well.

First of all, in that context, I thought he was a wonderfully broadening influence at MIT. I'd spent a very stimulating year at Caltech. They're very similar in their excellence, and also in where their departments overlap, but they have different interpretations of what constitutes an institute of technology. Whereas Caltech felt it should keep it small and narrow—and there are real virtues in that—MIT, particularly in Jerry's time, wanted very much to broaden to include the behavioral and social sciences and humanities in a strong way, including the arts; and also, given Jerry's prior role—and MIT's, for that matter—to keep it actively connected with government, both in their role in public policy through government and independently of government. I also felt he was a very decent, kind, constructive person.

I used to see Jerry sometimes on peace activities during that time. And I very much encouraged, as did he, the then president of the National Academy of Sciences, Philip Handler, to set up some joint study group with Soviet counterparts on arms control. Jerry had far more knowledge and credibility in that field than I did, but I was full time at the Academy, which was helpful in a different way. Handler was concerned about potentially controversial aspects of such initiatives, both within the Academy and with the government. He thought it was a good idea, but whether it was feasible to do anything useful, he was ambivalent. But he did it, to his credit. And he put Jerry and me on CISAC (the Committee on International Security and Arms Control). And we had this pattern of meeting twice a year with our Soviet counterparts, once here and once there. And Jerry and I worked very closely on that—we sometimes traveled together—and I found him deeply informed and thoughtful and constructive. He was able to reach out in a highly respectful way to Soviet counterparts without ever kowtowing to them or giving away any intellectual or moral ground. And I think they very much respected him for it. So I felt that, just as Jonas and I had been kindred spirits in health matters, biology, and human affairs, so, too, were Jerry and I, on the arms control and international relations front. So this was another useful feedback loop on shared, vital interests.

I urged MacArthur to build a staff, which they had been reluctant to do. With some ambivalence, they moved in that direction. One excellent example was a young psychologist, Anne Petersen, who later became the executive vice president of the W. K. Kellogg Foundation after serving as the deputy director of the National Science Foundation. She later was the deputy director of the Center for Advanced Study in the Behavioral Sciences. From a modest start at MacArthur, she has come to have a worldwide reputation for excellence. Betty and I did everything in our power to foster her career at each stage—always impressed with her ability and integrity. I also urged MacArthur to get women of high quality on the board and, after some resistance, that came to pass. I suggested a distinguished judge, Shirley Hufstedler, who later became the first secretary of education when President Carter created that department.

People involved in the foundation community have asked me about the final year of Rod MacArthur. He was sick, troubled, and worried about his foundation legacy. For reasons unclear to me, he was angry with the board and brought a legal suit against them (leaving out one member). I tried to help him with, first of all, arrangements about medical care and helping his wife in her coping with it. My wife was very much involved, was very good with her. Betty remained friendly with her for a number of years after his death. My role with Rod was to help him retain perspective, to see how much they really had accomplished as a foundation. For all the turbulence, I deeply believe that it had come a long way in a short time; that indeed, much of what he'd hoped for had been accomplished. And I just tried to help him see that. On several occasions, I tried to persuade him to withdraw the lawsuit, to make some personal reconciliations with other trustees, and to preserve his life insofar as we could, but to take with him at the end a good feeling about the foundation. I think these efforts were appreciated by his family and the board.

The selection of a new president was crucial and turned out to be valuable. The selection leader was Thornton Bradshaw. He was one of the early businessmen to have a strong interest in education. That linked us. Also, he was friendly with David Rockefeller Sr. I had served for about twenty years on the board of Rockefeller University. In that context I became quite friendly with David Rockefeller, who for half a century was utterly devoted to this great biomedical institution. Bradshaw was going on the MacArthur Board with David Rockefeller's stimulus. He came to see me about how to run a foundation like this and ask me what I knew about MacArthur. When he became chairman of the search committee, then he used to call from time to time and come to visit. We drew up a list of solid candidates. One of them was Adele Simmons.

The idea of an outstanding and relatively young woman who also had roots in Chicago—because it was always part of their notion that they were Chicago-based and should do something special in Chicago—all that made a strong case for Adele. I remember being very supportive of several candidates, with her at the top of the list.

When we zeroed in on her, then he got some last-minute flak. And I don't recall exactly the nature of that, but some of the old guard had a sense of losing too much control. Thornton Bradshaw's concern at the last minute was that they might have a bloody fight, which would get into the press, and yet again the MacArthur Foundation would be discredited. And we talked about ways of working it through. After all, this was going to be one of the most influential foundations.

He admired what Adele was doing at Hampshire College. She also had very active interests in US-Soviet relationships, with specialized knowledge of that and some specialized knowledge about Africa. These interests fit the emerging MacArthur mission. Carnegie had programs in both areas, so we would get together occasionally on those shared substantive interests. I didn't know her well, but well enough to know something about her fine national reputation.

Shortly after her appointment, we gave a reception for her in our offices, for her to meet the New York foundation community. It was a very nice event. Some of the MacArthur trustees came for that event. And then she would visit a couple of times a year in the early years, thereby strengthening the Carnegie-MacArthur cooperation. She was very interested in our programs, how I thought about strategy and some of our operations. We invited her to some of our Aspen congressional meetings. She came to several, particularly during the Cold War, where she had professional interest. And when I finished at Carnegie, she intervened to save the Aspen Congressional Program, and brought in several other foundations to broaden the scope in light of the winding down of the Cold War.

Network with Nodes: A Useful Paradigm

The concept of a network with nodes was stimulating and we adapted it to other situations. For example, the Pritzker family of Chicago, distinguished philanthropists, involved me as a friend and adviser. They put up $15 million for a network that would work for a decade on depression, interestingly enough, with particular focus on adolescent depression.

They had a daughter who committed suicide when she was a Stanford student many years ago. We discussed how this tragedy might be turned into a benefit for humanity by concentrating research in this problem. Over the years, a network or consortium was built involving superb basic and clinical scientists. I suggested that it would be promising to foster cooperative research involving Cornell, Stanford, the University of Michigan, and the University of California, with all the heads of the nodes being people who had worked together and people who to some degree were intellectual progeny of mine. So we met in my office to crystallize the plan with the Pritzkers and the potential heads of these nodes and worked it out. It has become the leader in this important and neglected field. I think the MacArthur-Carnegie experience fostered the network-with-nodes concept across the country and led to larger sustained and systematic communication across disciplinary and university and even national boundaries. It was an important model. Altogether, it was very gratifying to help build what became one of the world's leading foundations.

Helping the MacArthur Foundation to Reduce the Nuclear Danger

Philanthropically, we were largely alone in the field in the dark days of the Cold War, in the early and mid-eighties. But, there were many other influences, to be sure, and it's hard to track those down. It's not like you can put a radioactive label in medicine and follow where the label goes, but you can tell that, for instance, the prevalence of Carnegie-related testimony in congressional hearings is one good measure that it was significant.

When President Reagan announced his Star Wars proposal, we initiated contacts with major scientific organizations in this country to examine it objectively. It was the biggest proposal in history, of vast, enormous complexity, and it needed to be studied from the point of view of technical feasibility, from the point of view of economic costs, and from the point of view of its effect on international relations and on the stability of the delicate balance in the arms race.

So we got many experts, mostly in interdisciplinary groups from major scientific organizations—the American Physical Society, the American Association for the Advancement of Science—and a few of the major universities, to look at that issue. It became very much a part of the currency. These were the independent studies that were largely relied upon to compare with what the government was saying, compare and contrast sometimes, and work out for members of Congress and for the public what this proposal could and couldn't do.

I think the Star Wars initiative was proposed in good faith, with a high aspiration and a high moral commitment to rid the world of the danger of nuclear war, but, unfortunately, it was an awful lot more complicated than it looked at first glance. In some ways it could be very dangerous, in other ways not feasible. In any case, a long way off. So all that needed to be understood. Again, it was public education as well as policymaker education. The independent experts involved in these studies were mainly scientists and scholars, but there also were a number of excellent recently retired military—admirals and generals— who had the expertise, a different kind of expertise, who participated in these studies. The important thing was their independence to look, as objectively as humanly possible, at these issues, whether it be the weapons themselves or defense against the weapons or various notions about military strategies. So I think the contribution to broadening and elevating the discourse was considerable.

Then there were the linkage functions. That is, we know that major leading figures in our Congress regularly participated in these Carnegie-supported linkage meetings. Some were through the Aspen Institute, some were through the American Association for the Advancement of Science, some were through the National Academy of Sciences. There were different sponsoring groups to which we made grants, all of which conducted themselves at a very high caliber of analysis. They typically weren't there to get involved in a debate of the current policy issues, but rather to build a broad and solid factual underpinning. We would say to members of Congress, "The idea is to help you get the facts straight for the long term. You're going to have to make momentous decisions this year, in three years, in ten years, and the more you have a solid factual basis, the better off you'll be." They were usually enthusiastic about that notion.

So what measures can you take of whether it was useful or not? We know that we got, time and again, the most respected people in Congress over a span of more than ten years—from the mid-eighties to the late nineties. They were leading, senior members of the relevant committees, for example, armed services and international relations committees. The other leaders, speaker of the house and so on, people of that kind, came frequently. Some came regularly. So, is that a measure of success? Well, in a way it is. People with highly consequential responsibilities, leaders in the country, were exposed to a wider range and a greater depth of knowledge on the subject from more independent sources than they would otherwise have had, and they often gave fervent testimony to the value of it. We periodically examined the question, should we back off now? Should we fade out of this business? We got the most enthusiastic responses: "David, do not stop this. This is the only time we get this sort of thing." That is one measure of success. It also illustrates the way in which foundations can help each other as well as our government since MacArthur continued these efforts after I left Carnegie to create the Carnegie Commission on Preventing Deadly Conflict.

Project on Ethnic Relations (PER): Achievement and Revival

An important example of conflict-oriented nongovernmental organizations (NGOs) was provided by the Project on Ethnic Relations (PER). It was dedicated to reducing interethnic tensions in a region that has seen some of the most violent, intractable, and destructive conflict since the end of the Cold War. PER's neighborhood encompassed the culturally and politically diverse space of the former Communist bloc—from Russia and the Baltics through Central and Eastern Europe and the Balkans. PER dealt with a universal problem: how to temper the powerful emotions of ethnic identity with the political self-restraint that is essential to democracy. Francis Deng in his work at the UN pursued the same line of innovation.

With the support of Carnegie and our active involvement, PER was founded in 1991 by Allen Kassof, who had a distinguished record as the founding director of International Research and Exchange (IREX), which fostered exchanges of scholars between East and West during the Cold War. His excellent deputy, Livia Plaks, was very helpful with languages, history, culture, and conflict resolution. Her tragic death in 2013 was a terrible loss. PER provided an excellent example of how imaginative, persistent intervention by a small NGO can achieve significant and practical results. PER had the unusual attribute of combining direct involvement as mediators at the highest political level with work in community settings. PER's experience shows that, with insight, patience, and durability, it is sometimes possible to modify the behavior of antagonists even in intense, historically rooted ethnic disputes. Yet the international community is weak in supporting such organizations financially.

PER convened and chaired roundtables for the antagonists, sometimes in their own countries, but sometimes in neutral locations, usually Switzerland but occasionally the United States. Many of the roundtables drew senior participants and observers from the US government, NATO, the European Union, and the Council of Europe. Although such roundtables are informal dialogues, in practice they serve as venues for high-level negotiations.

Although high-level women politicians were always present at the PER roundtables for the entire period of our twenty-plus years of activities, in 2004, with a grant from the US Department of State, PER undertook a special effort to bring to the table a group of women from the Balkans in governments and parliaments to discuss the issue of how to prevent ethnic conflicts and how their role could be made more important in this field. Based on this emerging success, PER invited some of the women to Slovenia to write a short policy analysis from the point of view of women in the specific countries, to discuss how they see the interethnic dialogue and what could be done to improve relations between communities. All of this information is available on the website www.per-usa.org under the label *Women in Governance and Interethnic Relations* (under *PER in the Balkans*).

In recent years, the role of women in development and conflict resolution has grown considerably, largely through the leadership of Hillary Clinton when she became secretary of state, and her right-hand associate, Melanne Verveer. I feel fortunate that in the early phase of this work with women, Carnegie had the opportunity of helping, as I have noted elsewhere.

The resilience of such efforts is now vividly highlighted by a revival of PER, despite the funding problems and tragic loss of Livia Plaks, an authentic leader of great ability and education who will always be sorely missed. On August 25, 2014, I received the following letter from Kassof.

You will be interested, and perhaps amused, to know that the Project on Ethnic Relations, which closed in December 2012—just weeks before Livia died—now has an unexpected afterlife.

In January I travelled to Bucharest at the invitation of the Romanian government to look into some new difficulties in relations with their Hungarian minority in Transylvania, where there is strong nationalist pressure from Budapest's right-wing regime. I travelled there again in March, and in June chaired a renewed PER roundtable to restart the interethnic talks that had been successful in the 1990s. (You'll recall that you participated in the key Swiss meeting.) A new organization, Friends of the Project on Ethnic Relation, has been created by the Romanians to provide funding and auspices for this venture, which I am leading.

I am astonished to be doing any such thing in my 84th year, but of course it is all intensely interesting, and goes back to your original support so many years ago.

—Allen Kassof

This is another example of the permeable membrane between government and nongovernment in conflict resolution and the desire to build the prevention agenda. I only regret that Livia Plaks who was such a splendid pioneer in this field could not have lived to participate in this revival and to go on for years in improving our skills in preventing ethnic conflict.

B. EDUCATION FOR SCIENCE, PROSOCIAL BEHAVIOR, AND PEACE

An Overview of the Carnegie Education Program

During the 1980s, an important consensus began to emerge within the scientific and professional communities about ways of meeting the developmental needs of children and adolescents. Carnegie Corporation sought to clarify this scientific and professional consensus and make it widely understood throughout the nation and beyond, utilizing all the modalities available to the foundation, from community meetings to White House conferences; from research monographs to popular books; from major newspapers to television networks to radio broadcasts; from mayors to governors, to members of Congress, to the president and first lady. Special contributions were made by remarkable corporation staff members Vivien Stewart, Alden Dunham, Michael Levine, Tony Jackson; and excellent board members

Shirley Malcom, Ray Marshall, James Watkins, James Comer, Billie Tisch, Dick Beattie; and Bruce Alberts, then president of the National Academy of Sciences, was especially helpful.

Throughout human history, preparation of children and youth for responsible and productive adult roles has always been a primary task and responsibility of human societies. In this era of drastic change, it is necessary for our society to adapt in order to meet the fundamental needs of child and adolescent development.

The Carnegie approach evolved in distinctive ways that made this work socially useful.

1. The foundation tackled very hard problems that are vitally important for the future of all our children and hence for the future of the nation, including ways of overcoming the adversity of poor, depreciated communities.
2. Those efforts were built on a strong science base, linking biological and behavioral sciences with emerging technologies.
3. This science base was related to real-world problems, translating research into social action as opportunities could be envisioned. To do so, we fostered communication between scientists and practitioners in education and health, supported creative innovations and working models in communities, and put emphasis on evaluative research to assess systematically the upshot of these innovative models—asking what sort of action is useful for whom under what conditions.
4. We used our grant-making, convening, and publishing functions to stimulate and foster a comprehensive, science-based national education reform movement that could be sustained over decades.
5. In doing so, we clarified an array of biological, psychological, social, and technological factors that influence learning, in and out of school. This meant dealing not only with biological and behavioral underpinnings of school readiness, but also with drastic and stressful changes in families and communities—in the powerful context of the transforming global economy.
6. We focused on precollegiate education—from early childhood education through K–12 public schools. This was the arena most urgently in need of long-term upgrading.
7. We put strong emphasis on the preschool years to build motivation and readiness for school and for lifelong learning.
8. For each phase of development, we clarified the essential requirements for development and their implications for lifelong learning, health, and decent human relations. The work linked each phase to the next, constructing a developmental sequence of experiences, opportunities, and interventions that foster constructive, long-term development.
9. The foundation's grantees, staff, and board explored in depth pivotal, frontline institutions that have a daily opportunity to help meet these essential requirements and sought ways to strengthen their capacity to do so under contemporary conditions of world transformation. These frontline institutions are families, schools, health systems, media, and community organizations (including religious ones). And they in turn need support and help, in serious and thoughtful ways, from powerful institutions: government, business, the scientific community, and relevant professions.

10. At the elementary and secondary levels, the foundation used education in mathematics, science, and technology as the entering wedge—both for the intrinsic value of such education in terms of curiosity and problem solving, and for the practical significance of such education in the emerging technical world of the global economy. From the life sciences, there emerged specific education for health; and in due course, education for conflict resolution and violence prevention. Emphasis was placed on equal opportunity for girls and boys, rich and poor, to the maximum extent possible. This work extended to developing countries in Africa.

11. We recognized the centrality of teaching in education and therefore sought, through multiple means, to upgrade teaching as a profession. Several then-governors were especially helpful with this effort, including James Hunt, who has served on the corporation's board, Thomas Kean, who is the foundation's current board chair, and Bill Clinton.

12. In all of this, there was the inextricable linkage of education and health and the effect of the social environment on both. Children impaired by physical or mental health problems tend to do poorly in school. The other side of the coin is that education is a powerful vehicle for shaping health promotion and disease prevention over the entire lifespan. In advancing understanding of these issues, Drs. Julius Richmond, Frederic Robbins, Elena Nightingale, and Betty Hamburg played crucial roles.

In our 2004 book, *Learning to Live Together: Preventing Hatred and Violence in Child and Adolescent Development* (Oxford University Press), Betty Hamburg and I illuminated the major influences that shape the attitudes and beliefs that children and adolescents hold toward other groups. Directing these attitudes and beliefs along a positive path involves a *lifespan* perspective, fostering prosocial influences from infancy to adulthood. It involves an *institutional* perspective, providing developmentally appropriate education that starts in the family and continues from preschool through elementary and secondary schools, and into universities. The book also considers the roles of media, information technology, the Internet, religious institutions, and community organizations in human development today. It is a synthesis that highlights promising lines of inquiry and innovation that can greatly diminish hatred and violence in childhood and adolescence and build a basis for humane relationships.

At the adult level, the book advocates education for political leaders in the prevention of war and genocide as a neglected and potentially valuable contribution to global security. Over the 1980s and 1990s, Carnegie Corporation fostered educational innovations based on independent scholarship that directly involved political and military leaders of the United States, Europe, Russia, and Africa. Experts from various fields brought to bear knowledge and skill in preventing war and genocide. These initiatives showed how scholarship and practice can draw on research-based knowledge to help make education more constructive, conveying both the facts of *human diversity* and our *common humanity*.

Toward Healthy Constructive Child and Adolescent Development

I've long been interested in education for conflict resolution, for mutual accommodation, and for learning to live together. That is, groups have to come to terms with their differences. I think that education is an important part of that—schools, community organizations, religious institutions, military schools. That is a highly significant part of what education has to become in the twenty-first century.

When I came to Carnegie, we tackled the fundamental underpinnings of child and adolescent development. The key structure of it was to make grants to both fill gaps in research and knowledge and to support carefully assessed innovations in education, and to use our convening function to get people together from different sectors of the world of education and child development, to learn from each other, and then from time to time to have high-visibility, high-quality groups from different sectors of American society that would try to make a synthesis. What is known about the zero-to-three age group? What is known about three to ten? What is known about ten to fifteen?

Now, those study and action groups typically were from different sectors. About half the group would be experts on the subject—educators, pediatricians, child psychiatrists, developmental psychologists. And the other half would be leaders in business—for example, Roy Vagelos, CEO of a great pharmaceutical firm; Ted Koppel of ABC; Admiral James D. Watkins, who'd been head of the navy and then secretary of energy—leaders in different sectors, such as distinguished education-oriented governors Dick Riley, Bill Clinton, Tom Kean, Jim Hunt, and Lawton Chiles. The idea of these intersectoral groups was to both seek a broader mix with more stimulation and new ideas, and also to seek more opportunities—when you finished your work, to open the door and get into different sectors, to say, "Look. It's important to reach out a helping hand to our children and here are good ways to do it."

So those groups, I think, were powerful intellectually and perhaps even politically, and they also had a wonderful interplay with the grant program chaired by Alden Dunham and Vivien Stewart, and then later a combined program superbly chaired by Stewart—who later wrote an excellent book on *international education* and made contributions to the educational activities of the UN. Each task force and grant-making effort stimulated and helped the other. It's an art form that I cherish, although it's hard to do, and I certainly don't recommend it as any kind of panacea for the foundation world. I don't even recommend it for the next phase of Carnegie's life. But in this particular phase, it was very useful. We were able to draw on creative prior work such as Betty's adolescent peer counselor program, which caught on in the United States and Europe and stimulated other peer-mediated interventions such as peer mentoring, peer tutoring, and peer mediation to diminish adolescent conflict, as exemplified in the work of Columbia's Morton Deutsch.

Now, the zero-to-three task force was first chaired by Dick Riley, former governor of South Carolina, who had been a wonderful governor on these issues of young children. Then when he became President Clinton's secretary of education, two distinguished scholars took over: Julius Richmond from Harvard, who'd been the father of Head Start, and Eleanor Maccoby, a professor and the dean of Developmental Psychology at Stanford. They took over, co-chaired effectively, and saw it through.

A very touching aspect of that was that my dear friend Jonas Salk served on it. He was ill—it was the last group of that kind that he served on during his life. He was too ill to attend meetings, but we talked on the phone regularly and we corresponded. He sent me a message to be read at the meeting, where we brought out this report, a meeting at which Hillary Clinton was the keynote speaker. That report emphasized the health side of it, primary health care for young children in a broader conception and prenatal care that, for example, included an educational component and a social service component, not just a medical component in a narrow sense. And so, too, with early primary health care.

The second thrust of it was an educational component—not warehousing young children, but providing preschool education essentially on the Head Start model, for poor kids and rich kids alike, some of the attributes of high-quality preschool education, high-quality child care.

Then came various opportunities for *preparing for responsible parenthood*—parent education in different settings, ways of getting the knowledge and skill to be a good parent, especially in this complicated time when both parents are likely to be in the work force outside the home, and a very complicated mix of caretaking by parents and by others, how to strengthen all the relevant institutions.

And, finally, the fourth strand of that report was on community mobilizations, how we can bring together the different sectors on behalf of our young children. If you can't get mobilized over babies, I don't know what could bring us together. So, that zero-to-three was powerful in its public as well as its professional impact—though it did not imply that learning ends at age three.

After early childhood care, there was middle-childhood and mainly elementary-school education, although it had some pre-elementary content in it, and some transition from elementary to junior high (middle school), but it was mainly focused on very important research, particularly coming out of Yale and Johns Hopkins, that could be applied to school systems all over the country. Ways of raising standards, helping kids, especially poor kids, to meet the standards, improving teaching as a profession. So that was an important report, co-chaired by Admiral Watkins and Shirley Malcom, head of educational activities at the American Association for the Advancement of Science. Again, an intersectoral group, high visibility, a coming-out party. We called for national attention each time to get extensive, high-quality coverage. We were extraordinarily lucky in getting very broad and largely accurate, positive media coverage of these reports. And then to have follow-up activities afterward for several years to see what would happen if you implemented the recommendations. But the most ambitious of all these was the Carnegie Council on Adolescent Development.

Meeting the Essential Requirements for Healthy Adolescent Development

In the face of the social and economic transformations of the twenty-first century, all adolescents have enduring human needs that must be met if they are to grow up to be healthy, constructive adults. All must find a valued place in a constructive group; learn how to form close, durable relationships; feel a sense of worth as a person; achieve a reliable basis for making informed choices; know how to use the support systems available to them; express constructive curiosity and exploratory behavior; find ways of being useful to others; and believe in a promising future with real opportunities.

Meeting these requirements has been essential for effective transition into adulthood for millennia. But in a technologically advanced democratic society—one that places an increasingly high premium on competence in many domains—adolescents themselves face a further set of challenges. They must master social as well as technical skills, including the ability to manage conflict peacefully; cultivate the inquiring and problem-solving habits of mind for lifelong learning; acquire the technical and analytic capabilities to participate in a world-class economy; become ethical persons; learn the requirements of responsible citizenship; and respect diversity in our pluralistic society. Adolescence is the last phase of the lifespan in which social institutions have reasonably ready access to the entire population, so the potential for constructive influence and for improving adolescents' life chances for the great transition—the phase during which young people are just beginning to engage in very risky behaviors, but before damaging patterns have become firmly established—offers an excellent opportunity for intervention to *prevent* later casualties and promote successful adult lives. The Carnegie studies and innovations have sought to translate these fundamental needs into actions that will work not only for the students but for their parents and community foci as well. Elena Nightingale played a key role in organizing a high-caliber book on the scientific basis of adolescent development.

We described and illustrated a substantial set of experiences, opportunities, and services that could make a large difference in the lives of today's youth—changing the odds favorably for a healthy and productive adult life. Clearly, the low priority in science policy for research on adolescent development has been a costly mistake. If the nation had given this work a priority commensurate with the gravity of the problems and the scope of the opportunities inherent in adolescent development, we could stand on firmer ground and reach higher in our aspirations. Still, there is no reason to let the perfect become the enemy of the good.

The central question is whether we can do better than we are doing now. The social costs of severely damaging conditions that shatter lives in adolescence are terrible not only in their impact on individuals but also in effects that damage the entire society—the costs of disease and disability, ignorance and incompetence, crime and violence, alienation and hatred. These distorted lives are like a virus that knows no boundaries, that cannot be contained unless prevented in the first place. Looking back over the range of evidence and experience presented in the Carnegie reports, there is abundant reason to believe that we can do better to provide conditions in which adolescents can grow up healthy and vigorous, inquiring and problem solving, decent and constructive. There are worldwide opportunities to make better use of the great developmental transition. But to do so, one must respectfully face the obstacles: religious, ideological, financial, and medical. Thus, we sought to create a long-term interest to link ways of addressing these obstacles effectively. The drumbeat continues now.

The Carnegie Council on Adolescent Development

The Carnegie Council on Adolescent Development was a ten-year effort. We began it as a three-year effort, but it had such a powerful effect in the country that the board felt there was no reason we should wind it down. It was intersectoral, it had leading people, terrific people on it, and they worked very hard. We had a staff in Washington, DC, headed by the very capable Ruby Takanishi, and they interacted with the grant-making staff in New York as well as serious policymakers such as senators Daniel Inouye, Ted Kennedy, and Nancy Kassebaum.

The council was *a stimulating and guiding body*, and we set up, or stimulated others to set up, a number of *convening functions* and *major studies* and *dissemination functions* on various topics of adolescence. Nearly a *million* of our volumes were distributed, and there was a vast amount of *media coverage*, a lot of interaction with *governors* and *presidents* and *cabinet members*. The creation of an Office of Adolescent Health in the Department of Health and Human Services was one ramification of that council.

We put out major reports that focused primarily on *early* adolescence, ages ten through fourteen. We recognized and did some things on middle and later adolescence, but we mainly focused on early adolescence, because it's so neglected. My wife Betty was a pioneer in *formulation, research, education*, and *preventive action* on early adolescence. We both learned a lot from Eric and Peggy, our own children, not only when they were early adolescents, but both before and since, because we were very close. The four of us have been collaborators in almost everything I've done, and they've gone on to wonderful accomplishments in their own right. Eric and Peggy undoubtedly helped Betty and me to make that focus on early adolescence, because it was so neglected and so important. You suddenly go from childhood to something like an adult, and puberty pops up, with its biological and psychological changes. Usually, you go from a little elementary school in the neighborhood to a big junior high school at a distance. You are expected to be something like an adult, but you don't know what. Huge biological, psychological, and social changes converge on this fascinated participant-observer, the young adolescent.

We felt we ought to look at *schools*, we ought to look at the *health system* with respect to those adolescents, we ought to look at *community organizations*, including *religious* ones, we ought to look at the *media*: all the frontline institutions that have an impact on them. We did that with younger children, too, but perhaps we did the most on adolescence. It was a *lifespan development* approach.

This approach began with a major report, called "Turning Points," and what we did there was particularly significant, perhaps as a model for other work. We got together an intersectoral task force again, focused on upgrading school education in early adolescence—junior high or middle schools, what we call generically the middle-grade schools. We looked at the curriculum, the organization of schools, and the surroundings of schools. It was my belief that it's not worth very much to just look in the classroom, important as that is. It's not enough to look just at what happens in the school building, important as that is. We as a society have to consider *all the factors that influence learning in and out of the school*. That means substance abuse and crime television, a whole host of influences—now, of course, the Internet as well.

So that's the approach we took to this "Turning Points" report. One of the leading members of that task force was William Jefferson Clinton, then the governor of Arkansas. We had a set of education governors that we involved from the very beginning in Carnegie activities, some Democrats, some Republicans—Tom Kean, a Republican from New Jersey, is now the chairman of the Carnegie board. We had wonderful governors—Jim Hunt of North Carolina, Lawton Chiles of Florida, Dick Riley of South Carolina, Kit Bond of Missouri, Michael Dukakis of Massachusetts, and so on. The governors really awakened the country to education, and I'm happy to say we had a hand in that. Nevertheless, the political and bureaucratic obstacles mean that it will take a long time to fulfill these evidence-based, farsighted aspirations.

The substance of the report was formulated by *experts on education and child development* and it stimulated an ongoing discussion. We advocated *smaller units*. Break down these factory-like schools into smaller units, a school within a school; organize it in ways that each individual can get *sustained individual attention*. People differ. We advocated having an organizing principle intellectually, which should be the *life sciences*, because the students are experiencing or have recently experienced puberty and their curiosity is enormous, and we want to direct that curiosity at a life sciences curriculum that includes a lot of *health content* in it. High-risk behavior is related to each functional system of the body. We talk about respiration, we talk about smoking. We talk about the brain, we talk about drugs. We talk about reproductive biology, we talk about sexually transmitted diseases. We talk about the cardiovascular system, we talk about diet and exercise and smoking.

So among other things, the grant-making program stimulated a superb new curriculum and multiple practical volumes. It was an interactive, lively curriculum, growing out of Stanford's Human Biology program, of which I was one of the founders thirty years earlier. They have made very creative and sound accomplishments in many fields. Ten years of work were invested in adapting that curriculum from Stanford undergraduates to the middle-grade schools, especially by Stanford faculty Craig Heller and Mary Kiely. So we had, then, this organizing principle for a curriculum that *linked education and health*, and we had the smaller units and ways of getting *sustained individual attention*.

We had life-skills training—to which Betty has been a major contributor since the White House days—including systematic *training in decision making*: rather than making impulsive, uninformed decisions, teaching adolescents how to make informed and deliberate decisions. The life-skills training also dealt with peers learning from slightly older peers about how to *make friendships* and how to *resolve disputes* without violence. Those are practical skills for getting along in the world that have not traditionally been a part of the curriculum. They can be taught in *schools*, they can be taught in *community-based organizations* like the YMCA or Boys and Girls Clubs, with leadership by Jane Quinn, who is distinguished in the constructive use of out-of-school time. They can be taught in *religious* institutions. They're important to *connect with the traditional curricular material*. We also emphasized the value of well-organized *community service* in the middle-grade years.

We worked on *mentoring* and other *social supports*, ways in which particularly lonely or isolated or poor kids, especially in disadvantaged communities, could have some sense of *attachment*, of *reliable human relationships*, with *adult mentors or with slightly older and more fortunate peers*. We also covered the relationship among community organizations, supervised academic community service, and learning to be useful to others beyond yourself.

Then we did a follow-up to that report. Partly thanks to the Clintons and partly to others who participated in the coming-out events for that report, we got a lot of public interest. Then we set up a competition among states—ultimately fifteen states participated—in implementing of the "Turning Points" report. And then we had independent researchers, principally from the University of Illinois and UCLA, assess implementation: (1) the *fidelity of implementation* of recommendations, and (2) *did it make a difference?*

Were academic results better? Were interpersonal results better—for example, less *fighting*, fewer *dropouts*, less *alienation*.

The evidence showed this approach to be helpful. In general, the more faithfully it was implemented, the better the results academically and otherwise. It takes a period of years to do that. This is an illustration of what I mean by an interplay between the grant-making program and a commission or task force that provides an intellectual framework.

The *follow-up to a report is important.* You don't just put it out there and let it sink without a trace. You put it out there, you *disseminate*, you *explain*, you *stimulate interest*, you *stimulate better ideas*, and you also *stimulate studies on how it works.* Can you get it implemented? And if it's implemented, does it work? So "Turning Points" was a good model.

We also had an important report written by Fred Hechinger of the *New York Times*, who came up earlier in this book (in my discussion of Africa). His report, called *Fateful Choices*, was written in a way that would be accessible to the general reader, and it focused on decisions kids make about smoking and weapons and other influences that affect their health and the health of others. So that's an *adolescent-health*, disease-prevention, health-promotion approach, another volume parallel to "Turning Points."

Then there was another report called "A Matter of Time," that examined the time students are out of school and the role of community organizations. Students spend as much time out of school as in school, and a lot of bad things happen in the out-of-school hours these days. So we laid out what the potential is for community organizations, the general notion being to lure kids any way you can make it attractive, with food, with music, with sports, with interested adults, with interested older peers, get them into constructive settings during the after-school hours, and then have educational activities and health-related activities, tutoring, mentoring, nurturing in community activities. The idea is to cover all the waking hours of the kids with an array of constructive activities in school and out of school. If you put "Turning Points" side by side with "Matter of Time," you've got the waking hours covered.

We also stimulated some other organizations to probe more deeply into adolescent health. So, *health* and *education* and the *social environment* of early adolescence were covered pretty comprehensively with these reports, all of which had the aspiration to be intelligible and credible, intelligible because they were translated out of technical jargon into straightforward English, and credible because they were based, to the maximum extent possible, on research and the most carefully evaluated innovations in clinics and schools throughout the country.

That was the approach. It went on for ten years. I think it was probably the most serious sustained effort ever made on issues of adolescence in this country. It was followed up by a forum on adolescence at the National Academy of Sciences, which I chaired for five years and then passed the baton.

But adolescents run up against obstacles in public understanding and policy. We've got to keep relating to adolescents. They tend to be perceived as frightening by many adults—wild animals, raging hormones, dangerous behavior. Young babies have more appeal for most people than adolescents. Adolescence is a fateful time, a crucially formative time, just like infancy, and we've got to pay more sustained attention in this country and all over the world to the fate of our emerging young adults.

Jacobs Foundation: Carnegie Collaboration in Europe's First Foundation on Adolescence

The Swiss Jacobs Foundation was created and endowed by Klaus J. Jacobs with CHF 100 million in cash and kind. This is in the family tree of the Johann Jacobs Foundation, named to recall the memory of Johann Jacobs, who in 1895 started a small business in Bremen (Germany) that, thanks to his nephew, Walther, and then his son, Klaus, was to become one of the world's greatest coffee, chocolate, and confectionery businesses.

The deed of the Jacobs Suchard Foundation defines its purpose as "the encouragement and support of research, programme development and professional activities designed to improve our understanding of human development, particularly that of *adolescents and young people*" (emphasis mine). An important part was *learning conflict resolution.*

The turning point in the charity-oriented philanthropic endeavors of the various foundations supported by the Jacobs family occurred when Klaus J. Jacobs, then chairman and president of the mainly family-owned Jacobs Suchard Company, decided to create a new, modern, research-oriented foundation that would study the problems of young people caught in the whirlwind of the biological, psychological, and social changes of our rapidly transforming world. It would be the *first European foundation based on adolescence.*

The necessity to adapt the foundation's activities to the present pressing needs was motivated and justified by two considerations expressed by Mr. Jacobs in his message published in the first Annual Report of the Johann Jacobs Foundation (1990). It reads as follows: "I am persuaded that the business community should do much more to serve the society in which it lives, in which it makes its money. Nowadays when we, the strong and affluent, help the weak and the needy, it is no longer an act of charity but also justice. It is no longer generosity but wisdom." This thought was translated into practice by the endowment of the Johann Jacobs Foundation with a personal gift worth CHF 100 million. Many noble objectives have failed and worthy causes have been put at a disadvantage because of a lack of professionalism. From this, one may conclude that even in the field of altruism, the instinct of generosity is not enough. To reach goals, to avoid waste, generosity must be channeled in an organized professional way.

Klaus Jacobs heard of the *Carnegie program* and was very interested. He came to visit Carnegie for a couple of days in New York and was strongly impressed. He felt the need to replicate and even extend these functions. He even *suggested that I serve as president of both foundations.* Honored as I was, I did not think this was feasible but *I offered to help him in the first decade to develop his foundation substantively, organizationally, and interpersonally.* This came to pass and joint efforts proved very useful.

Thus, the ground was prepared for a new start. In the summer of 1988, after consulting academics and executives from youth-serving organizations, Klaus Jacobs invited a small group of international experts on youth to a two-day future-oriented seminar to identify problem and opportunity areas as guideposts for future programs of adolescent- and youth-oriented research, action, and social policy.

Six problem and opportunity areas were selected and agreed upon by the experts. The topics and themes identified reflect not only major societal concerns but also major opportunities for human science and social policy. These are the "Six Problem and Opportunity Areas": positive beliefs about self-agency and the future; social relations and generational nexus; life skills and life planning (decision making); cultural and individual diversity; educational values; match between institutions and individual development.

Toward the end of 1988, the founder-chairman of the Jacobs Suchard Foundation invited four respected academics to serve as trustees of the foundation he intended to establish. Alongside myself, these included Paul B. Baltes, director of the Max Planck Institute for Human Development and Education in Berlin; Pierre Ducrey, rector at the University of Lausanne (Switzerland); and Laszlo Nagy, the former secretary general of the World Organization of the Scout Movement. Laszlo Nagy was appointed chief executive officer.

During the autumn of 1988 and the first part of 1989, the chairman and the CEO of the foundation undertook several trips in Europe and in the United States. They contacted foundations, academics, researchers, and educators, with a view to identifying centers of excellence and establishing contacts with prominent institutions in the fields in which the Jacobs Suchard Foundation planned to be active. Permanent contact was established with the scientific members elected to serve as trustees of the board, requesting their intellectual contributions to establish the ideal scope of the foundation. I took considerable *initiative in seeing to it that these aspirations would be fulfilled.*

It was confirmed that the Jacobs Foundation would operate mainly along the lines of the "Six Problem and Opportunity Areas" developed by the Zurich Seminar of September 11–13, 1989. During the discussions two main areas of concern emerged as possible fields of action:

- Support in finding ways to bridge the biological, behavioral, and social gap between young people and social institutions; and
- Support research and program development in organizations serving youth such as the World Organization of the Scout Movement, in particular its R&D committee, and to undertake and finance programs aimed at analyzing adolescent development in the social context of a rapidly changing world and as part of the whole course of life, analyzing the nature of social forces in developing positive and negative adolescent reactions, contributing to the development of new programs of action designed to improve the opportunities of adolescents in life, and promoting the development of respect for the environment and the recognition of widespread problems for future generations that result from the unreasonable exploitation of environmental resources.

It was agreed that the foundation should operate *internationally,* in an *interdisciplinary* way, through communications, by involving *decision makers* and *educators,* by facilitating *research* with people from other sectors, and by promoting research for incentive and *mutual aid.*

In 1989, a further decision was taken, important for the future development of the foundation, that a major annual public conference with lectures should take place on the occasion of each annual board meeting. It was agreed that the first event of this kind could take place in 1991 on the topic of "Youth Unemployment and Lack of Social Role." The fact that a highly qualified scholar, Anne C. Petersen, was involved in this theme supported the choice.

The CEO was instructed to identify further topics and recruit potential organizers and sponsors for similar conferences for the following years under the guidance and with the help of the other members of the board. Finally, and no less importantly, proposals submitted to the board were evaluated and decided upon.

The main efforts were concentrated on the following fields: improve managerial practices, outline the priorities of the foundation within a balanced master plan (matrix), define the grant application procedure and the review process, attract research and program proposals of high quality without geographical restrictions, and organize scientific events on topical subjects with the participation of outstanding invited specialists.

During the summer months of 1990, two further major public conferences were finalized after the one that had been convened by Anne C. Petersen for November 1991.

- It was accepted that the Jacobs Foundation should maintain a balance between *research, education, and service.*
- The *Annual Public Conference* is part of the "Johann Jacobs Conference Series," with the goal to highlight the crucial needs and opportunities of adolescents and to widen the horizons of researchers.
- The *annual conference* series should be completed by a follow-up meeting with the participation of a group to focus on the *practical implementation* of the conferences.

It was also suggested during this important meeting to establish a *Young Scientist Program* for promising scientists under the age of forty-five who already have shown their ability in the field of human development, particularly adolescent development, but who need an impetus enabling them to produce work of exceptional quality. This program was *carried out by the CASBS (Center for Advanced Study in the Behavioral Sciences) at Stanford University* in which Anne Petersen played an important role. It was endowed with SFr. 100'000 per annum during five years. It involved *scholars from developing countries.*

Another important target was to investigate the best ways to encourage research that could have real practical application. An important conference was inaugurated at the Jacobs Foundation Communication Centre at Marbach Castle. It was organized by Anne C. Petersen. This important meeting gathered together forty-five prominent invited scientists and young scholars from Europe and the United States.

The goal of the meeting was to examine the causes and consequences of youth unemployment for both society and the individual. The conference also examined policies and programs intended to contribute to solving these problems. The full text of the proceedings is published by Cambridge University Press in a volume entitled *Youth Unemployment and Society.*

The important groundwork was undertaken to promote the 1994 conference, which was to be *co-organized with the Carnegie Corporation of New York* on the topic of "Frontiers in Education as Health Promoting Environments." This meeting—the biggest ever organized by the foundation—was held in Geneva with a program that placed special emphasis on the practical application of research on the everyday realities of schools. The *Carnegie-Jacobs organizing tandem* also *brought in the World Health Organization in Geneva* for help in preparation of this meeting.

The work of the Jacobs Foundation continues actively in 2015, including annual awards for achievement in research on adolescent development, education, and health.

Education for Refugees

When I left Carnegie, Vivien Stewart's interests changed and I saw an opportunity for her in the UN system. I had served for a decade on the advisory committee of Sadako Ogata, the great leader who was the United Nations High Commissioner for Refugees (UNHCR). So I brought them together in the hope that Vivien could help Sadako in her next venture, and that worked out very well, producing the Refugee Education Trust (RET). Vivien's Carnegie experiences in both educational and violence prevention activities were useful.

Today, there are more refugees than ever before in the world's history. This creates problems not only for the displaced people uprooted by war, civil disturbance, and famine, but for the host countries as well. Although most refugee children have access to primary education, very few get the chance to continue beyond primary level.

With the aid of wise and influential friends, including European philanthropists and Japanese resources, Ogata created a Refugee Education Trust. I suggested that Vivien would be the ideal person to write a paper on this subject, proving the best possible formulation based on evidence of what could be done to provide opportunity for such children. She did an excellent job and the analysis was influential in UN circles. This led naturally into her heading the education program of the Asia Society in New York, a strong organization with worldwide influence.

The Refugee Education Trust was launched by Sadako Ogata, the founding president, on the occasion of the fiftieth anniversary of the United Nations High Commissioner for Refugees, on December 14, 2000. It is an independent foundation based in Geneva, Switzerland, and is governed by an international council of respected individuals, including Mrs. Sadako Ogata (Japan and citizen of the world), Mrs. Francoise Demole (a leading citizen of Geneva and indeed of Europe), Professor Henry Rosovsky (Harvard), and myself.

The RET has been set up to provide postprimary education for the world's refugee children and youth. It seeks funds from donors all over the world in order to make a contribution to global peace through education. The education of refugee children (as with our own) is a vital investment, promoting their self-reliance and employment. Education is probably the best investment donors and governments can make to improve people's lives and to benefit society at large.

The peace and stability of the world are threatened not only by the numbers of refugees and displaced people but also by the injustice and lack of opportunities that accompany forced migration. Unqualified refugee youngsters are at risk of becoming dissidents and dropouts who can easily be manipulated.

The founders sent a questionnaire to twenty-five UNHCR field offices, primarily in those countries with the largest concentrations of refugees. In fact, systematic data on the educational opportunities for refugees are limited.

The RET works with refugees and local communities to find innovative ways of using local skills and resources, such as through distance education and modern technologies, to meet the postprimary educational needs of refugees.

Lessons for the Future

Carnegie Corporation mobilized an excellent staff with full board cooperation and an international network of experts to work on healthy child and adolescent development as well as lifelong learning, linking research, policy, and practice. With focused attention and strategic funding, the corporation made a concerted effort to advance the nation's understanding of child and adolescent development and to foster positive outcomes for children and youth in the face of drastic changes in American families and society. This effort was carried out through many grants for research and innovation, as well as the sponsorship of special study groups making practical recommendations based on solid data and excellent working models.

A recurrent theme for the corporation's work in this area was the prevention of bad outcomes. *Prevention* is based on *anticipation*, even long-range foresight. In this effort, the best available knowledge from research is used to clarify the main paths to a particular kind of adverse outcome—that is, major risk factors. Steps are then taken to counteract or *avoid the risk factors*, especially through appropriate changes in behavior. To do so, attention is given to pivotal institutions that can shape and support behavior positively, away from risk factors and dangerous directions. Thus, in seeking to avoid casualties of childhood and adolescent development—whether in disease and disability, ignorance and incompetence, crime and violence—Carnegie focused on key institutions to shape healthy learning and constructive lifestyles.

Together, these reports covered the entire spectrum of early life, from the prenatal period to age fifteen, and formed the basis of a coherent developmental strategy for all the nation's children and youth. These reports were widely disseminated to the public and have had a stimulating effect on policies and programs throughout the nation. They constitute a valuable resource in this vital field, and their influence is still being felt, but it will take many years to bring them to fruition. We must be persistent and patient.

The work I've pursued in the early twenty-first century flowed from both Carnegie Corporation's efforts to improve child development and its focus on violence prevention. Humanity has reached a situation in which those who retain ancient harsh attitudes and hateful beliefs can acquire destructive powers that dwarf those of our ancestors. Can we raise our children for constructive, prosocial human relations rather than for hatred and violence? This is a central challenge of our time. A fruitful conjunction of developmental and social psychology with educational research can provide the foundation for a humane, democratic, and safe course of child and adolescent development, ultimately helping to protect humanity.

CHAPTER 5

From Local to Global Institutions

Throughout this book, there are many examples of what in biology would be considered a permeable membrane. That is, the opportunity for vital molecules to pass back and forth between different tissues of the body. In the present context, the permeable membrane is the opportunity for nongovernmental organizations, and even for individual people like me, to communicate with governments—mainly democratic of course—and important intergovernmental institutions. My hope is that the experiences I have had in crossing such membranes would be helpful to other individuals and NGOs in contributing to the prevention of human suffering.

THE UNITED NATIONS

In the later years of my career, I have tried to help UN leaders move toward fulfillment of the basic aspirations of the UN as formulated at the end of WWII, especially by Franklin and Eleanor Roosevelt. The Carnegie Commission on Preventing Deadly Conflict put a powerful impetus toward this revival. The UN's preventive efforts in the first decade of the twenty-first century have been vigorously pursued by the current secretary general, Ban Ki-moon. This is reflected in the secretary general's opening remarks at the Inaugural Andrew Carnegie Distinguished Lecture on Conflict Prevention in Honor of David Hamburg (May 1, 2013). I quote his remarks not so much because they honor me as because they show both the *trend toward prevention of catastrophe and opportunities for the interplay between NGOs and intergovernmental organizations.*

It is a great pleasure to welcome you all to the Inaugural Andrew Carnegie Distinguished Lecture on Conflict Prevention in honour of Dr. David Hamburg.

David Hamburg has made truly important intellectual contributions to the world and to the work of the United Nations.

During his 15 years at the head of the Carnegie Corporation, he helped to transform the way the United Nations, governments, NGOs and the broader public look at a range of issues, from public health and education to nuclear non-proliferation to conflict prevention.

His work on conflict prevention has been especially notable.

When I came to office, one of my main priorities was to improve the UN's ability to address brewing tensions before they become bigger and costlier crises. I wanted us to make greater use of the many tools available under Chapter VI of the UN Charter to prevent armed conflict.

In this endeavour, one of our major reference points has been the seminal 1997 report of the Carnegie Commission on Preventing Deadly Conflict. All the key elements of that report resonate and guide us to this very day....

The United Nations and its Member States have much work to do. As we strive to get prevention right, let us continue to be inspired by the contributions of David Hamburg.

His work has enabled us to make quantum leaps in our approach to addressing armed conflict. As the title of his new book puts it, he is helping us all to "Give Peace a Chance."

Thus, the UN (despite all its problems) has steadily been moving toward preventive concepts and techniques. Indeed, consecutive secretary generals have enhanced understanding and initiated innovative actions in prevention of mass violence: Boutros Boutros-Ghali, Kofi Annan, and Ban Ki-moon. They deserve great credit for these efforts and I am deeply grateful for the opportunity of working with each of them on a basis of friendship, mutual understanding, and deep commitment.

During Kofi Annan's term as UN secretary general, I worked for a decade with him in moving toward practical preventive measures in spite of obstacles. I monitored his remarkable speeches carefully and discussed them with his wise principal writer, Edward Mortimer. The Carnegie Commission published a small volume of those focusing on prevention and they had worldwide utility. When he left office, I suggested to him and to my longtime editor, Jennifer Knerr, that we could select other of his speeches of great value and publish them for a wide audience of policy-oriented people who could find inspiration in them for fundamental problem solving. It is gratifying that this collection has now been published and I am singularly grateful for the appreciation expressed to me by Annan, Mortimer, and Knerr.

My work with Kofi Annan during his decade as secretary general was intensive, stimulating, and generated several landmarks. One was the massive attendance at the UN rollout of the Carnegie Commission on Preventing Deadly Conflict in 1997. Another was the first-ever retreat in the half-century history of the UN Security Council that was primarily devoted to prevention, at which Annan and I gave major presentations. He was trying hard to stimulate senior staff to find ways to implement recommendations emerging from the Carnegie Commission.

I also played an active role in the drafting, launching, and implementation of Annan's landmark report on the prevention of armed conflict in 2001 and his related call to the UN's departments and agencies to pursue the issue on that priority and explore new initiatives.

In 2001, he invited me to join the Strategic Planning Meeting with a panel of his closest advisers and other experts to shape the priorities of his second term as secretary general. My particular role was to see to it that the previously neglected prevention approach should be an important part of his second term.

Between 2001 and 2004, Annan sought special input from the best advisers he could get, both within the UN and outside it, to make prevention a reality. When he encountered undue delay in overcoming barriers to establish a formal advisery committee he asked me to organize an informal "core" group of individuals to focus on implementation of his recommendations outlined in his major report on prevention of armed conflict. This group met informally in my office and included Ragnar Angeby of Sweden, Melanie Greenberg, Jane Holl, Tom Leney, and Connie Peck. All of them were major contributors to the work of the Carnegie Commission as well as other UN activities related to the prevention agenda. In due course, he was able to establish a formal advisery committee on prevention of genocide and asked me to chair it. I had the privilege of working in this committee with such deeply thoughtful, ingenious, and courageous people as Desmond Tutu and Sadako Ogata.

Mediation became an important subject, intellectually and operationally, in the UN. Stimulation was provided by Nita Yawanarajah, who helped to create a Mediation Support Unit and won a UN worldwide award for documenting UN mediating efforts in conflicts of the past several decades. Jan Eliasson, now the deputy secretary general of the UN, was supportive.

UNITAR, the United Nations Institute for Training and Research, is an important component of the UN that deserves more recognition. It has played a major role in linking theory and resolution in conflict resolution.

A leader in UNITAR for years was Dr. Connie Peck. Shortly after she had finished her graduate work in psychology at the University of Wisconsin, she undertook a period of work in the Australian Foreign Ministry and then came to the UN, where she settled in for a long and creative period of work based in Geneva, which has resources second only to New York in the UN system. She and I collaborated and I served on the UNITAR board.

She took a great interest in the work of the Carnegie Commission on Preventing Deadly Conflict, especially our distinction between structural prevention (building long-term preventive pillars) and *operational prevention* (*preventive diplomacy*), which deals with rapid action in the face of moving danger to reach an early settlement with good prospects for turning it into an enduring one.

She and I explored what turned out to be a rather extensive set of efforts in this field being encouraged by each secretary general who came to power shortly after the end of the Cold War. We felt that these UN peacemaking representatives (like Cyrus Vance) could learn a great deal from each other if there was a systematic process for sharing information, ideas, and techniques. In a way, it was another form of my long preoccupation with *peer learning*, which Betty originally developed in the context of adolescent tensions and which over the years has become increasingly useful in a wide variety of intergroup and international differences. Therefore, I offered support for Connie Peck to convene people with relevant experience and build strength in the whole field by the sharing of their experiences.

In late November 2014, just as we were about to go to press with the present book, I received from Connie Peck a recently published multiauthor book masterminded by her over the preceding year that showed great progress from this sort of cooperative procedure. Indeed, this was the publication celebrating the twentieth anniversary of the Fellowship Program in Peacemaking and Preventive Diplomacy. The volume is entitled *Strengthening the Practice of Peacemaking and Preventive Diplomacy in the United Nations: The UNITAR Approach*, and it is now being distributed to all alumni from that twenty-year period, as well as all of the permanent missions of the UN in New York and Geneva, all of the relevant UN departments, and a variety of regional organizations and nongovernmental organizations. Connie says, "Given that you were so helpful in the early days in terms of supporting the program (intellectually and financially through Carnegie) I thought you would be happy to see that this important initiative continues." She writes in her inscription, "With great admiration for your splendid and amazing work and with much gratitude for your support for the Fellowship Programme and my other initiatives over so many years."

Peck points out that over these twenty years, the program has gained a reputation for excellence and has elicited strong interests throughout much of the UN system and other international organizations. It has provided training for 700 participants who have conveyed the deepening of their knowledge and skill. Many of the participants have been promoted through the ranks of the UN Secretariat as well as ministries of foreign affairs of individual democracies and some regional organizations. In short, this important experience has facilitated the advancement of the fellows in a variety of ways and locations. It has been the springboard for other initiatives as well.

Going back to our work together, Peck says the following: "In 1996, Dr. David Hamburg of the Carnegie Commission on Preventing Deadly Conflict commissioned a book on conflict prevention mechanisms of the United Nations and regional organizations." The book (Peck, *Sustainable Peace: The Role of the UN and Regional Organizations in Preventing Conflict*) had various follow-on effects, the most striking being a major conference organized in Ottawa, Canada, entitled Strengthening Cooperative Approaches to Conflict Prevention: The Role of Regional Organizations and the United Nations.

When Peck's book was originally presented to the Carnegie Commission, there was a surprising amount of opposition, chiefly on the grounds of its novelty. I strongly defended her approach in the meeting and the commission decided to back her further work in this field. Over the twenty years of the program, the participants have given their assessment in some detail of the effects on practices of the UNITAR program in peacemaking and conflict prevention. The results are highly positive and well documented.

One of the lessons drawn from this experience is summarized in the new book in relation to preparing for negotiation and mediation using conflict analysis. Connie Peck has a chapter on interest-based, problem-solving approaches to UN mediation, emphasizing early dispute resolution and the value of skilled third-party mediation. From these experiences, the participants generated several procedures for generating useful diplomatic options: (1) identify general principles, in a mutually acceptable negotiation framework or a range of objective standards; (2) break a problem into smaller parts or "fractionate" it; (3) brainstorm potential options; (4) use model agreements; (5) identify issues that might be linked and traded; (6) help parties identify or create spheres of influence; (7) create a "single-text" negotiating document; and (8) build a positive future vision.

Peck summarizes lessons for mediation for UN envoys: (1) helping to ripen a situation; (2) deciding on a most appropriate mediator; (3) choosing whom to include in the process; (4) building a good working relationship with the parties; (5) listening to understand parties' interests; (6) being an honest broker and providing honest feedback; (7) maintaining impartiality; (8) agreeing on a venue; (9) establishing a framework for mediation; (10) identifying issues and ordering an agenda; (11) finding the best balance between direct and indirect talks; (12) unraveling the linkage between issues; (13) balancing asymmetrical power; (14) introducing new ideas; (15) introducing international norms, standards, and models; (16) finding solutions that satisfy interests; (17) using friends of the secretary general; (18) avoiding artificial deadlines; (19) using influence and leverage wisely; (20) dealing with "spoilers"; (21) the special issue of accommodating peace and justice; (22) settling for a less-than-perfect deal; (23) achieving peace agreements that facilitate implementation; (24) establishing public commitment; and (25) maintaining patience and persistence.

In describing support for this work over the past twenty years, Peck notes that Carnegie provided the first and the largest number of foundation grants. The feedback from this support was useful for Carnegie in the grant-making program.

Several secretary generals have become increasingly interested in this approach. A statement by the current secretary general, Ban Ki-moon, in 2013 illustrates this point. "Recently the United Nations has become more active in not only promoting a culture of prevention, but also in beginning to operationalize its practice. The UN Department of Political Affairs ... has a mandate for preventive diplomacy, and has begun to increase its activities in this realm. The creation of the Mediation Support Unit and the popularity of its Standby Team ... have also contributed to more preventive diplomacy efforts."

WEILL CORNELL MEDICAL COLLEGE

The Weill Cornell Psychiatry Program (in Collaboration with Columbia-Presbyterian Psychiatry)

During the first decade of the twenty-first century, I worked at the Cornell Medical Center and was given maximal freedom to work on preventing mass violence in cooperation with people at the UN and the EU, as well as the medical, scientific, and public health community. This was made possible by my half-century friend and collaborator, Jack Barchas, now chairman of the department.

The program at Weill Cornell was centered by five underlying goals that are similar to those Jack Barchas and I envisioned in the 1960s when we were building the novel Stanford Department of Psychiatry:

- To maintain and extend the recognized excellence and uniqueness of the department in its missions of clinical care, research, scholarship, education, and public service—missions that can interact with immense benefit for all.
- To further psychiatry as a behavioral science open to the full range of knowledge that can inform mental illness with basic, translational, and clinical data—leading to new hypotheses, improved specific diagnoses, and more specific treatments.
- To facilitate an open attitude and willingness for dialogue between different approaches—such interactions and collaborations may lead to a science base for a truly integrated new developmental-biopsychosocial psychiatry, including human conflict.

- To incorporate the multiple forms of the sciences and disciplines in an atmosphere that fosters the spirit of inquiry and creativity—and reaches beyond medicine.
- To obtain the resources necessary to permit the program to thrive long term with appropriate opportunities for trainees, faculty at all levels, and staff.

A unique clinical environment

The department is responsible for 300 inpatient beds in what is believed to be the largest private university hospital service in the world. The department has over 150 full-time faculty and 500 voluntary faculty representing all areas of mental health. As a consequence of its size, most of the inpatient clinical program is divided into highly specialized units with full-time faculty who are expert in the specific areas. Examples include geriatrics, eating disorders, child disorders, adolescent disorders, women's problems, mood disorders, and psychotic disorders.

The program includes a variety of outpatient activities, including a new one on autism spectrum disorders. A new partial hospitalization program has also been developed for children and adolescents in addition to those for adults. The result of this large clinical program is that there is almost no condition that is not represented, which is important for training and for research as well as for clinical and public service missions.

The founding chair of the department in its current form, Dr. Robert Michels, later served as dean. For fifteen years the dean of the Medical College, Antonio Gotto Jr., and his key deputy, Dr. David Hajjar, were extremely supportive, a tradition continued in the past two and a half years by Dean Laurie Glimcher, who has provided direct help and encouragement in recruitment of outstanding junior faculty and in the retention of superstar senior faculty. In terms of the hospital, Dr. Herbert Pardes, a psychiatrist and former head of the National Institute of Mental Health, was the CEO and president over a ten-year period and was key to the success of the merger of the Columbia and Cornell hospitals that had occurred earlier. The scope and flexibility of these activities well accommodates a program of prevention of mass violence—that is, suffering beyond the transitional tasks of medicine.

A set of major educational programs with unique goals exists at every level

Dr. Elizabeth Auchincloss is vice chair for education. She is responsible for overseeing all training efforts in an attempt to enhance collaboration. Dr. Auchincloss is a gifted clinician who is outstanding in psychodynamic medicine, an award-winning teacher, and a thoughtful mentor. The activities of the educational program fit with the departmental goals in terms of recognizing many different approaches and pursuing them in collaborative ways.

The department is very broad in its activities, including predoctoral training programs in neuroscience, and in collaborative work involving postdoctoral trainees within our own department, as well as collaborative work with other departments such as pharmacology, pediatrics, medicine, biochemistry, and physiology. There are also collaborations with components of the Ithaca campus. Individuals who are particularly active in such broad efforts are Francis Lee, vice chair for research, and B. J. Casey, director of the Sackler

Institute. Dr. Casey is also the highly regarded director of a summer institute that attracts individuals from many countries for a program in cognitive neuroscience.

A central theme of the department is a developmental biopsychosocial framework. The approach is also being applied in other areas and in collaborations with persons from other departments and institutions, including Bruce McEwen at the Rockefeller University, with whom there is a close collaboration. Some of the approaches are also being used in our work with the Pritzker Consortium (which, in addition to Weill Cornell, involves Drs. Akil and Watson at the University of Michigan; Dr. Schatzberg at Stanford; Dr. Bunney at Irvine; and Dr. Myers at Hudson Alpha). I took the initiative years ago with Jack Barchas to launch the Pritzker Consortium and continue as an adviser.

Part of the scholarship of the department relies upon the study of history, social process, and intellectual development. Those have all come into play in the studies of Dr. George Makari, highlighted in his highly acclaimed book examining Freud in the perspective of intellectual history. Dr. Rosemary Stevens has studied the development of the early history of the VA system and lessons that can be extracted from that development. The department has a library in the history of psychiatry of approximately 40,000 volumes that is considered to be one of the best in the world and has been used by many scholars at Cornell and elsewhere in the preparation of scholarly volumes and papers.

Jack Barchas emphasizes, "There are other important broad questions which are critical for our field and for the future. Perhaps nothing better illustrates that possibility than the work of Drs. David and Betty Hamburg in establishing a program in Social Medicine and Public Policy. Their broad efforts dealing with teaching children not to hate led to a major volume. Their work on methods of prevention of genocide has become a modern classic. Remarkably, part of the power of their work has come from its cross disciplinary orientation. Fields such as history, sociology, psychology, anthropology, politics, and public health use similar approaches in dealing with disease—connecting what has happened in the past with what needs to happen in the future to prevent recurrence."

DEVELOPMENT OF THE CARTER CENTER

Although I did not know President Carter before he was elected, nor did I ever have an official capacity in his administration, I did form a relationship with him from an early time in his presidency based on shared interests and values. One example is his commission on mental health, which to a considerable extent had been substantively planned at the Institute of Medicine early in my presidency. Both he and Rosalynn Carter had strong interest in improving the mental health field. So I offered ideas, people, and organizational suggestions about the commission.

As it turned out, Betty Hamburg became director of studies for the commission and worked closely with Mrs. Carter in a very effective way. The work of that commission and its excellent staff had a very stimulating influence on the field, even though the next president had little interest in mental health policy. It became clear that whatever President and Mrs. Carter would do after leaving the White House, there would be a strong mental health component, and that has proved to be the case.

Similarly, I brought my Tanzanian experiences with me to the Institute of Medicine (enlightened by the hostage episode) and then used my influence in the Academy as a whole to strengthen scientific interests in the problems of developing countries. Peter Bourne, a member of President Carter's staff and later his biographer, had been a resident of mine and had worked on similar stress research. From his White House vantage point, he kept the president informed about our international activities, and, on leaving office, the president decided this was a field he would wish to pursue, that is, how to improve the health of poor people in the developing world.

I also helped President Carter pick the key people for his "health cabinet" and they served him well. Throughout his term, I worked closely with his dynamic, farsighted secretary of health, education, and welfare, Joseph Califano; with Julius Richmond, his surgeon general, who had been the "father" of Head Start; and Don Kennedy, my colleague from Stanford who became the first non-MD to head the Food and Drug Administration and later served creatively as president of Stanford and one of the "founding fathers" of the program on human biology. President Carter was very appreciative and all of us were stimulated to envision future possibilities.

Shortly after President Carter left office he came to see me for advice on the possibility of developing a Carter Center of the highest quality that could continue some of his earlier work during the White House years. I offered him the best help I could on substantive, organizational, and financial matters, also making efforts to involve other foundations. Immediately after I completed my term at Carnegie, President Carter asked me to join the Carter Center board and I was an active member for many years.

Over the intervening decades, now in 2015, President and Mrs. Carter held a serious annual meeting in mental health and extended their range of contacts to other first ladies, to the World Health Organization, and to his own staff. Thus, mental health has become an integral part of the long-term Carter Center, as have tropical diseases.

The other main focus of the Center is of course peace, the president's passion. He asked me to help him locate a suitable full-time director who could address the problems of developing countries through advanced technology. I recommended that he appoint John Stremlau, who had played a key role in the Carnegie Commission on Preventing Deadly Conflict, to take over the peace program. So in recent years, the two main programs of the Carter Center have been focused on peace and health in developing countries. In 2015, Stremlau completed an eight-year highly successful stint and returned to South Africa, where he and his family have deep commitments going back to the struggle for democracy and especially his initial role in the Carnegie Commission on Preventing Deadly Conflict.

When I was chairman of an advisery group for a foundation underlying the European Union's work in this field, I selected John Stremlau to serve on this committee. He had a distinguished record in the Rockefeller Foundation, the World Bank, and the State Department. He also devoted a decade, together with his wife, to building an international peace program in the well-respected University of Witwatersrand. Moreover, he continued active involvement in Carnegie, particularly with working with me and Jane Holl (now Lute), and was in an excellent position to provide leadership for these activities in the Carter Center. So I recommended him to President Carter to run the peace program and this worked out very well.

On one occasion, President Carter asked me to develop a distinguished advisery group for the long-term future of the Carter Center. This group included several people who served well in his presidency, including Don Kennedy, Bill Perry, Warren Christopher, Jim Laney (former president of Emory University), and some leading political figures. Our task was to think through options for the longer term so that these issues could have a continuing life for years to come, maintaining the central values of the Carter Center.

We considered as carefully as we could how such an institution could sustain basic values: peace, health, and human rights. One aspect that became increasingly clear was the necessity of a strong, enduring symbolism as well as substantive agenda on these core values. For that, it would be valuable to strengthen relationships with Emory University, which was moving closer to the Carter Center. Among other things, we recommended a shared board between the two institutions with President Carter and the president of Emory University jointly providing key leadership. This came to pass and is working effectively at the present time.

The Carter Center played a role of high initiative in making possible the monitoring of elections and establishing standards for authentic democracy. It was important as a practical matter to draw on President Carter's unique experience in building democracy while at the same time building a network of staff, collaborators, and consultants who could pursue the basic requirements of a strong democracy program without requiring more time than President Carter could possibly give. So this is another instance of institution strengthening for effective action in humane, democratic values in which I had the privilege of active participation.

When I was chairing a group of leadership people in and around the European Union on prevention of genocide, they requested that the final meeting be held at the Carter Center with Carter's influence. He generously agreed to my request and the meeting was well received in both Europe and the United States. It also fostered continuing contact on modes of building democracy between the two institutions.

Altogether, the Carter Center is a unique institution that has worldwide significance.

PRESIDENT'S COUNCIL OF ADVISORS ON SCIENCE AND TECHNOLOGY (PCAST)

Since I had worked on educational and research matters with both president-elect Clinton and Hillary, it made sense that I should be a member of PCAST and indeed help them select some of the other members. It was a privilege to do so, especially since I felt strongly about both the quality and the scope of talent on the president's science advisery committee. In the course of the eight years of Clinton's term, I served several years as chairman of the education committee, a most interesting experience including such people as Shirley Malcom from AAAS and Sally Ride, who was a pioneer in space and a very good scientist. I also was active in fostering arms control summits and other ways in which the scientific community could help to wind down the Cold War. Vice President Gore, who chaired many of the PCAST meetings, had a prior interest in science and had been associated with Carnegie's work in that area. We all sought to stimulate President

Clinton's interest in science, too, and this clearly evolved over the years. I was asked early to chair a committee on the scientific community and conflict resolution. I did this with pleasure and with strong support from the entire PCAST group.

My initial suggestion, just before Bill Clinton's inauguration as president, that *Hillary should have an international agenda of her own*, proved to be very stimulating for her and she made the most of the opportunity, giving special emphasis to the human rights of women and children. Indeed, this initial suggestion, which surprised her, proved to have a lasting effect on her career and public service. As her international contacts spread, she sought ways to improve the health, education, economic, and political opportunities of women in developing countries, including her famous speech in Beijing, which constructively called attention to the neglect of rights for women in all too many countries, including China. Melanne Verveer, her chief of staff during much of the White House time, proved to have excellent knowledge and skills in this sphere and together they planned a strong nongovernmental organization called Vital Voices to carry forward this agenda after leaving the White House. I had the privilege of serving on the board of Vital Voices and tried to be helpful in any way I could.

When Hillary became secretary of state, she created a new entity in the department to foster the well-being of women around the world along the same lines of her work in the White House and then in Vital Voices. Verveer was properly appointed to direct this operation and did so with great distinction. I keep in touch with them and take much satisfaction in the stimulating role I was able to play in Hillary's worldwide agenda, cul-minating late in her term as secretary of state.

ROCKEFELLER UNIVERSITY

Rockefeller University was created early in the twentieth century as a major center for medical research, even though this part of science was mainly in its infancy. The Rock-efeller family, and particularly David Rockefeller, made major philanthropic contributions to the institution on various occasions, made outstanding leadership appointments, and broadened the scope so it became legitimate to call it Rockefeller University. It had a very unusual pattern of organization, with no departments or deans, highly decentralized laboratories, and little scientific representation on the board. This meant there had to be a strong president's office, guiding faculty appointments very carefully.

Deep searches were conducted by a president who was not only greatly distinguished but extremely careful. That made Joshua Lederberg an extremely appropriate choice. Dur-ing the 1980s and '90s, he appointed highly respected faculty members such as Torsten Wiesel (a Nobelist who succeeded Josh as president after some years); Bruce McEwen, a pioneer in the linkage of biochemistry and behavior; and Jan Breslow in the genetics of atherosclerosis. A particularly appropriate appointment was that of Paul Greengard, a neurobiologist and friend of mine from Yale and joint activities of NIH. To have so many appointments of such high caliber gave the institution a unique aura. Shortly after his appointment, Greengard received the Nobel Prize in medicine. He is also a person of broad interests and humane values. My daughter Peggy was lucky enough to do some research with him while she was in medical residency next door at Cornell Medical School.

With a strong sense of responsibility, Josh turned to people he had worked with before in a trustworthy way, and that included Rod Nichols, who had been at Rockefeller for some years, and me. We would counsel on all serious problems, usually conferring after each meeting of the committee on scientific affairs, which for some years I chaired.

There were of course problems to be overcome, and one was whether RU needed a hospital. The upshot was creating a small but excellent hospital with first-rate leadership. The quality of the faculty was such that people throughout the biomedical research field often made remarks about the likelihood that RU had "more Nobel Prize winners per square foot" than any other place in history. That was an exaggeration, but it did certainly reflect the striving for very high quality. My only disappointment was that the faculty leaders for some years felt they could not find an appropriate female faculty member. I took on that chore and eventually had some positive influence, at least marginally so. In this respect, I was less successful than in similar roles at the American Museum of Natural History and the New York Academy of Medicine, but over a period of years the problem was solved.

My role at this great institution was primarily to work toward a mutual understanding of philanthropic board members and faculty. Lederberg played a similar role on the Carnegie board and this is another example of mutual aid in the scientific community. David Rockefeller kindly asked me to be a sort of troubleshooter for problems within the faculty or between faculty and board. I did so and we remain good friends to this day.

MOUNT SINAI MEDICAL CENTER, NEW YORK

Mount Sinai Medical Center is a great medical institution that has given extraordinary devotion, service, and skill to patient care for over 150 years. I served on its board of trustees for several decades. In recent years, with the appointment of Jack Rowe as leader and more recently Ken Davis (who was a research fellow with me at Stanford), the Mount Sinai leaders have made great progress in the research and educational aspects of their programs. It has an extremely strong philanthropic base involving people who are not only charitable in their inclinations but seriously interested in the work of the institution and continually offering ideas and time as well as money to build the institution. In my personal experience, this remarkable philanthropic group is very similar to the one I served with at Stanford for a quarter of a century—for example, Peter Bing, Bill Hewlett, and David Packard—people who care deeply about the nature of the institution, its quality of service, its openness to innovation, and the connection of various centers of excellence within the institution. They are well exemplified at Mount Sinai by Frederick Klingenstein and Carl Icahn.

One of Mount Sinai's extraordinary characteristics is the quality of its medical staff, drawing on the inflow of new research and setting high standards for devoted attention to patient care. Two examples from my own experience are Dr. Valentin Fuster, a great cardiologist—I had the privilege of working with Jack Rowe to recruit him from Harvard, and he has built a superb multifaceted cardiovascular center—and Dr. David Thomas, who has been a shining example of excellence in primary care, which has for so long been a shortcoming in American medicine, as we noted in the work of the Institute of Medicine. Mount Sinai responded by constructing a new building, with additional staff and special education for primary care. Recent appointments have greatly strengthened what we now call translational medicine, linking basic science with clinical research. This is especially true in neurobiology of mental illness. Dr. Davis and his wife Bonnie were pioneers in this area and Mount Sinai has been one of the world leaders in tackling the enormously important and profoundly difficult problem of Alzheimer's disease. I have done what I could to stimulate research on this disease, starting at the Institute of Medicine, and continuing at Harvard and Mount Sinai.

One of the newest and most striking developments in the great cardiovascular field that has been developed at Mount Sinai is teaching heart-healthy habits to high-risk children and families. The American Heart Association has made a large grant to promote this through early education, targeting high-risk children and their parents in Harlem and the Bronx. This research will study the genes and lifestyles of 600 preschoolers and their parents in these communities that have high rates of cardiovascular-related disease. Ever since Dr. Jack Rowe and I recruited Dr. Fuster from Harvard, the institution has backed his ingenious efforts to strengthen the understanding, prevention, and treatment of cardiovascular disease, from the molecular and cellular level to population-based medicine. Dr. Fuster is widely recognized as one of the world's great leaders in the cardiovascular field.

AMERICAN MUSEUM OF NATURAL HISTORY (AND THE NEW YORK ACADEMY OF MEDICINE)

Many New Yorkers speak about "growing up" in this great museum. It has a long history of accomplishment and innovation. But the time came for the selection of a new president and because of my forward perspective I was asked to chair the search committee. I identified a group of distinguished scientists and national leaders and we met with them. As it turned out, one was a woman and there was a vaguely formulated assumption that this would probably not be appropriate. But I was deeply impressed with Ellen Futter, then president of Barnard College, and felt that her particular strengths suited the needs of the museum extremely well. There was considerable surprise in the board and beyond when our search committee recommended her as our choice and she has done a phenomenal job. After she was in office a few years, I was asked to review her performance and there was overwhelming approval from the board, staff, and public officials about what she had done. She and I spent considerable time in working on ways to further strengthen the education program of the museum, both reaching out to young people through the New York public school system and also reaching to a higher level of education through the creation of a graduate school in cooperation with Columbia University. Ellen Futter accomplished much else and is still providing extraordinary leadership, including wonderful new facilities, well over a decade after her appointment. So the world is ready to have women in roles of leadership, and indeed this is vitally necessary.

Similarly, I played an active part in recruiting a distinguished physician, health policymaker and world health scholar Jo Ivey Boufford, to be president of the distinguished New York Academy of Medicine (built over a century ago by Andrew Carnegie). In the recent years of her leadership, the Academy is doing exceedingly well. It is today one of the world's leading institutions focusing on urban health. She also serves effectively as foreign secretary of the Institute of Medicine. So women have come a long way, and it is indeed overdue.

UNIVERSITY OF CALIFORNIA SYSTEM

When the Carnegie Commission on Preventing Deadly Conflict (with Vance and myself as co-chairs) was completed in its core form (with many other special studies still to come), there were three major rollout events in the United States: (1) at the White House with Hillary Clinton in the chair; (2) at the UN with Kofi Annan, Vance, and me sharing the chairs; and (3) a West Coast rollout at the University of California, Los Angeles (UCLA), with Chancellor Albert Carnesale in the chair. He presented a special medal to Kofi Annan for all of his contributions at the UN, not least his turning the institution toward preventive measures. This event, taken together with preexisting interest in our work in the University of California system, led to a considerable amount of time, energy, and gratification in much of the "thousand-mile campus." Stretching from the far north to far south of the state, one finds a number of excellent universities with a strong inclination toward issues of war and peace. I was drawn into a pattern of spending the better part of a week at each of almost all the campuses: University of California, Berkeley (twice); University of California, San Francisco; University of California, Santa Cruz; University of California, Irvine; and University of California, San Diego. These were extremely stimulating occasions and illustrated for me the depth of interest and the range of ideas emerging in excellent universities, not only on the West Coast but across the country and throughout the world. The capacity of universities in many countries is growing in respect to linking science and scholarship with policy analysis and education of the general public on critical issues.

EUROPEAN UNION

My activities in the European Union in recent years also pivoted around the prevention of deadly conflict and genocide, and the records at Cornell Medical Library cover 2003–2010. Parallel to the Advisory Committee at the UN, I also chaired an advisery committee to the secretary general of the council of the European Union, Javier Solana, with special attention to an international center on the prevention of mass atrocities based out of the EU. Between 2007 and 2010, I also became involved with the European Union Institute for Security Studies (EUISS), both as an adviser and as an active participant in meetings and conferences. Solana was a powerful stimulus for building a prevention agenda.

My work with Solana and Enrique Mora (his excellent chief of staff) with respect to prevention of deadly conflict and other mass violence was marked by several key landmarks. The primary theme of our work together was the intention to establish an EU Center for the Prevention of Genocide. I met Solana in 2005, where we discussed the Carnegie Commission on Preventing Deadly Conflict and especially the prevention of genocide. I facilitated a connection between Solana and President Jimmy Carter in establishing the "steering committee regarding the feasibility of the EU Center for Genocide Prevention," in which key staff from the Carter Center participated.

In July of 2007, I participated in a meeting of the EUISS in Paris in which Solana played a key role and the prevention of genocide was discussed. Following that meeting, my relationship with the EUISS continued and I was in regular contact with Solana and Mora regarding EUISS meetings and the potential there for implementing the prevention agenda.

In early 2006, I was appointed as chairman of a steering committee of the Madriaga Foundation reporting to the secretary general to discuss the feasibility of creating an International Center on the Prevention of Genocide. According to the group's 2006 proposal,

> Members of the Steering Committee included Ragnar Ängeby of the Folke Bernadotte Academy, Raymond Georis of the Madariaga European Foundation, Enrique Mora as Personal Representative of Javier Solana, and John Stremlau of the Carter Center. Beatrix A. Hamburg of the Social Medicine and Public Policy Program at Cornell University was a constant collaborator throughout this initiative. At its third and final meeting in Atlanta on 11–12 July 2006, the Committee benefited from the supportive presence of President Jimmy Carter.

After completion of his term of office at the EU, I had a wonderful reunion with Solana in Washington, DC, in October 2014 and was deeply impressed with his grasp of world problems and options for coping with them.

AMERICAN ASSOCIATION FOR THE
ADVANCEMENT OF SCIENCE (AAAS)

During several phases of my career, the AAAS has meant a great deal to me. During the past several years, the AAAS has been my second home and provided the opportunity to push on with several books—*Preventing Genocide*, *Give Peace a Chance*, and the current memoir. Colleagues here, as is typical of the institution, have given me much stimulation, encouragement, and insight.

In the 1980s, during the several years when I served on the board and particularly the year I was president, I did everything in my power to stimulate the vast capacity of the scientific community, particularly to strengthen its programs in education and arms control, including the original SDI ("Star Wars"), heightening the interest of members, statesmen, and journalists.

The AAAS and the National Academy of Sciences have the powerful advantage of serving as "umbrella organizations" for the scientific community. They cover the entire span of the sciences and have legitimacy with respect to linking science and policy. Taken together, they have been for some time unique in the world, and I have done everything in my power to strengthen these institutions.

In its long history, AAAS developed the unique capacity to publish the journal *Science*, which has been and probably still is the most widely read scientific journal in the world. During my presidency, I did whatever I could to help the journal fulfill its potential. One odd but fruitful episode occurred when Phil Abelson, the superb long-term editor of the journal, decided to retire and the board had to pick a successor. We were hung up for a while by focusing only on persons living in Washington, DC, since in earlier times that convenience offered practical advantages. Then it occurred to me that in the era of new technology, we could reach beyond Washington and indeed take advantage of the entire country. The board agreed and by an odd twist of fate, we followed Abelson with four superb editors, all from California: first, Daniel Koshland from the University of California, Berkeley, then Don Kennedy from Stanford, then Floyd Bloom from Scripps, and most recently Bruce Alberts from the University of California, San Francisco. Although I was a fond ex-Californian I had no idea that we would end up with this West Coast series but the important point was the way in which the AAAS broadened its horizons and made fuller use of the entire membership than ever before.

During my presidency of the Carnegie Corporation of New York, being well aware of the capacities of AAAS (as well as of the National Academy of Sciences), I made every effort to look for distinctive contributions the AAAS could make. For instance, there had been considerable ferment in the AAAS board during my time about the need to strengthen the capacity of the State Department to make use of science and technology for diplomacy and other purposes. So when the opportunity arose, Carnegie sponsored a Ditchley conference in England to convene a wide range of science advisers to high government officials, building on the pattern of interaction between the president of the United States and the scientific community during and shortly after World War II, but broadening the range far beyond weapons and military issues. This led to a continuing series over some years, each government supporting its own meeting. William Golden, longtime treasurer of AAAS, gave strong impetus to these efforts.

During my time on the AAAS board and particularly as president, I was more and more impressed by the potential of the AAAS to "mobilize" the scientific community to strengthen science education over the full range of the sciences. In this process, I first observed a very gifted and dedicated member of the AAAS staff, Shirley Malcom, and I encouraged the extremely able Bill Carey, our executive officer, to give her additional opportunities.

When I completed my AAAS stint, I focused on what Carnegie could do to help AAAS (and other institutions) to improve both the content and process of American education. One part of these efforts was to facilitate and enhance the educational program under Shirley Malcom and others. AAAS responded with enthusiasm and made use of the entire scientific community. These efforts continued throughout my term as president of Carnegie, and AAAS became a bulwark of American education. Later, I made Shirley Malcom a member of the Carnegie board. She not only helped us with the Carnegie program but became very interested in Carnegie's international program and has extended her reach over the years. I also encouraged the Clinton planning group to make her a member of PCAST (President's Committee of Advisors on Science and Technology) and we worked together in that context. Fostering Shirley's contributions has given me great satisfaction. AAAS now constitutes a bulwark of ongoing education, both in the United States and elsewhere. I am pleased that my leadership of Carnegie gave me the opportunity to facilitate this program.

With Carnegie's initiative and support, the AAAS issued two groundbreaking reports, "Science for All Americans" (1989) and "Benchmark for Science Literacy" (1993). These reports were put together by innovative leaders who recognized the valuable "umbrella" function of the AAAS. They spelled out basic concepts of learning in science, mathematics, and technology for all citizens and helped set national standards of achievement, explaining the rationale for the fundamental value of such knowledge for working toward shared prosperity and developing new opportunities for the entire population. Their basic ideas and suggestions are very much a part of today's ferment in educational reform.

In the depth of the Cold War, especially from my Carnegie vantage point, we encouraged and supported studies and meetings in arms control, especially to get the facts straight for members of Congress, science writers, and, especially during the big annual meeting, the general public. Elsewhere in this book, I have referred to Gorbachev's interest in AAAS reaching out to us for help in relation to the Soviet scientific community, especially improving the Soviet capacities for rational, peace-oriented policymaking. Altogether, I feel a deep indebtedness to the AAAS and wish it well for many years to come.

PRESIDENTIAL MEDAL OF FREEDOM (AND NATIONAL ACADEMY OF SCIENCES PUBLIC WELFARE MEDAL)

In the 1990s, President Clinton gave me the Medal of Freedom, which is meant to be the highest civilian honor of the United States, and I must say I was very deeply moved. In the citation, they dealt with my whole career, both the domestic and the international side of it. I was touched, on the morning of the event. President Clinton, looking at the citation, told some of his colleagues that he felt there was not enough said about the international and peace side of things and the African accomplishments. There was a lot about the domestic side, education, child development, and behavioral science, but he wanted a more balanced statement. So they scurried around to make the final formulation. In 2014, President Obama invited the medalists to an event honoring us and above all President Kennedy, who created the idea of the Presidential Medal of Freedom fifty years earlier.

A few years ago, the National Academy of Sciences (NAS) gave me its highest award, the Public Welfare Medal. Since the Academy has been so important in my life, that was very, very meaningful. All of these awards were total out-of-the-blue surprises, and they cited both domestic and international activities. The Public Welfare Medal is symbolic of the Academy, that is, the Academy not only recognizes great achievement in science, but it also recognizes the uses of science for the benefit of society. In that, it differs considerably from many other academies in the world. So those awards were enormously meaningful to me, and I cherish them.

Moreover, I have worked with others in the NAS to encourage other academics throughout the world to link their scientific strengths in cooperative ventures to address policy problems of worldwide significance—for example, Bruce Alberts during his NAS presidency joined with Kofi Annan and me to organize with great care a worldwide Inter-Academy Council to foster excellent research on problems of developing countries, especially in Africa. Annan continues this work to the present day and Bruce Alberts is a world leader in scientific cooperation.

CHAPTER 6

Conclusion

OVERVIEW: WHERE CAN WE GO FROM HERE?

The Foreign Policy Association, in a quarterly book review during 2014, said the following that bears on the conclusions of this memoir.

The publication of *Give Peace a Chance: Preventing Mass Violence* coincided with the Foreign Policy Association's newest endowed lecture: the Andrew Carnegie Distinguished Lecture on Conflict Prevention in Honor of David Hamburg. In the presence of Secretary-General Ban Ki-moon, David Hamburg delivered the inaugural lecture in the newly renovated ECOSOC Chamber of the United Nations. The lecture was a tour de force and the distillation of his latest book the core ideas of which remain consistent with earlier works: Conflict resolution is best achieved through mediation; nuclear disarmament is essential; community is the best route toward a world without mass violence; and the key to these lofty goals is the protection and healthy development of the world's children.

The most unique feature of *Give Peace a Chance* is David Hamburg's scientific approach to problem solving and his strong sense of optimism in regard to the scientific community as a whole: "The scientific community, by increasing its attention to development, can provide a model for decent human relations and mutually beneficial cooperation that can help to transcend the biases, dogmas, and hatreds that have torn our species apart throughout history and have recently become so much more dangerous than ever before."

In 2015, in a time of widespread turmoil in the Middle East, with extraordinary violence, it is a profound and pervasive challenge to people everywhere. Can our common humanity learn to live in paths leading to peace and prosperity, to equitable socioeconomic development? In some parts of the world, some international organizations, some NGOs, there is a conjunction of new moral commitments, new ideas, new organizations, and new initiatives for existing institutions. Tools and strategies are being developed beyond prior experience and tried out in highly innovative ways across some nations and sectors. No one can be sure how far and how fast this movement will go, especially in the face of the current turbulence. The long-term prognosis has great potential for a healthy humanity. Persistence, ingenuity, and dedication to humane values will be essential and probably feasible. My strongest wish is that this book will stimulate serious interest and better ideas in the years ahead.

A determined commitment to *nonviolent conflict resolution* is essential. As a practical matter, the *international community must cooperate for its own survival.* Ignorance is no longer a viable excuse for inaction. The years required to go from any initial jeopardy to destruction in whatever form offer an interval for the international community—if it is *alert, well informed, morally committed, and organizationally prepared*—to take preventive actions, the *earlier* and more *cooperative* the better. The urgency and gravity of human problems, currently evident in one way or another on every continent, cry out for a fundamental upgrading of education at all levels on matters of conflict resolution—especially mechanisms for early, ongoing mutual accommodation. We need prompt and just ways of dealing with grievances and learning how to construct solidly an evidence-based set of attitudes, policies, and practices that truly permit us to live together constructively.

We must clarify superordinate goals and show how highly desired aims (e.g., avoidance of nuclear war, very lethal terrorism, infectious pandemics, or drastic climate change) can be achieved only by cooperation. This becomes feasible if we can mobilize the intellectual, technical, and moral strength over sufficient time to bring it about. We must formulate well-analyzed attitudes, norms, and patterns of behavior that bring us together in our *common humanity.* There is need for global understanding of the paradox that, while advances in technology are beneficial through both education and innovation, they are also exceedingly dangerous through fostering hatred, striving for the deadliest weapons, and the encouragement of unbridled egocentric behavior. We must clarify the *pillars of prevention,* make them *widely understood,* and strengthen institutional/policy/practice paths to their *implementation.*

These pillars of prevention, as we have highlighted, are education for peace and justice, indeed for survival; *early, proactive* help to countries in trouble with *intergroup* relations; the building of *equitable socioeconomic democratic* development; the *protection and promotion of human rights; serious constraints on weaponry; and alertness to new dangers such as drastic climate change and cybersecurity.* In short, these issues are so important for humanity that they must be clarified on an interdisciplinary and international basis involving all sectors of society and broad public understanding. In the remainder of the twenty-first century, these problems are likely to be too severe for any one nation or any single organization. Well-organized, deeply committed cooperation will be essential.

PUTTING THE PREVENTION AGENDA INTO PRACTICE

Cooperative Help in Early Conflict Resolution: A Lifespan Approach

A peaceful world, free from mass atrocities, war, and terrorism, will depend on an international community, and especially the established democracies (a long-term growing community), ready and willing to be on the alert for sister countries in trouble, and to apply skills, attitudes, and external help to prevent bad outcomes. Troubles that must be addressed include intergroup hostility, governmental repression of vulnerable groups subject to prejudicial stereotypes, rising hate speech, systematic violation of human rights, ignoring jeopardy such as drastic climate change, and the inclination to deal with problems by violence. The conundrum is that no favorable outcome can occur without substantial changes, and these are unlikely to happen without outside help. Yet those countries most in need, and especially those with repressive leaders, are most likely to be suspicious of, and resistant to, outside help. Often these negative manifestations are detectable at an early stage, well short of mass violence. There are many countries, and sizeable groups within almost every country, who find hatred and violence *unwelcome*, especially as reality impinges upon them through observations of harm like Syria in the early twenty-first century. But how to help soon enough?

What are some examples of *points of entry for proactive help*?

1. Provide tangible *economic development*, including *public and private investment*, linked with *internal conflict resolution mechanisms throughout the development process.*

2. Help to *build national capacity for early, ongoing conflict resolution*—with *empathic international outreach.*

3. Cultivate relations with *moderate, pragmatic, emerging leaders*—*democratically inclined and supported vigorously.*

4. *Foster peer learning* between similar groups, similar nations that have overcome the ingroup/outgroup hostilities—including *content and process of education for peace.* Why not learn from each other before it is too late?

5. *Foster relations with the incumbent regime showing that the development of a constructive, problem-solving civil society is in its own interest.*

6. *Mediate*, preferably at an *early* stage before revenge motives become severe. Offer such mediation with explanation of its *benefits for the nation itself,* and press with international cooperation to make clear the *incentives for accepting such mediation.* Encourage units, such as those of the United Nations Development Program, in a troubled country to build strength in mediation, illuminating the *prospect of economic benefits* and the *major gains* from *following a peaceful path.*

7. Strengthen organizations such as UNICEF in their valuable activities for *healthy child and adolescent development* as well as *education.* Extra support for such constructive units can be very effective, especially in light of the almost *universal human attraction to the well-being of our own children.*

8. *Strengthen health units in each region,* through the World Health Organization, public health agencies, and nongovernmental organizations that are health-oriented. They can offer immediate relief of suffering along with a vision of long-term health improvements. Given the virtually universal yearning for good health, and especially the health of children, *health can be a bridge to peace.*

9. Mobilize the world's universities for cooperative efforts to help prevent harm, whether in conflict, disease, or whatever.

International Centers for the Prevention of Mass Violence

I had the privilege of working with the UN (especially Kofi Annan), the EU (especially Javier Solana), and some individual democracies (especially Sweden) in serious efforts, however difficult, to build pillars of prevention of mass violence. Together with *an international coalition of democracies,* a broad-based network *intensely focused on preventing damage* could create a *critical mass of knowledge and skill* by assembling a permanent core of professional staff drawn from scientists, scholars, diplomats, lawyers, political and military leaders, and specialists in the fields of early conflict resolution and violence prevention. It could collect and constantly update reliable information from all sources about circumstances in troubled countries or regions that would predispose them to violence. It could monitor these potential conflict situations, where threats of mass violence are emerging. It could also establish an integrated warning-response system in which experts would analyze and evaluate early warning indicators of severe human rights violations. It would then link them to a *full array of constructive responsive options,* based on its *reservoir of knowledge and skill in prevention.* This approach fosters a network of cooperating organizations, including those concerned with climate change and environmental deterioration.

We made Carnegie grants and *Cornell Medical Center initiatives* to foster such institutions (from 1982 to 2012). Key friendships in these organizations stimulated interest and generated new ideas as well as *institutional innovations.* I tried in various ways to stimulate this early prevention approach based on my career-long emphasis on interdisciplinary international efforts to *address problems of human suffering by linking the scientific and policy communities*—and to do this *through international cooperation.* This is a long, hard road but an *essential direction for human decency and well-being.* I believe it is most likely to be useful in the context of authentic *friendships* and *sharing of credit* for whatever progress may be made.

As a practical matter, international cooperation is essential to be sure that the *pooling of strengths* can provide adequate *financial, technical, and human resources* to help the process of *socioeconomic development over decades,* working toward a responsibly regulated market economy and *fully open society.* The metric may be *decades or generations,* but this after all is only a moment in human history and evolution. The democracies working together can build capacity for *nonviolent conflict resolution in economic matters* and in *relations between ethnic and religious groups.* This is feasible when most people in a society feel that they have *decent life chances;* when they are *not oppressed,* have their *basic needs met for child and adolescent development,* and live in a *social environment conducive to hope, physical security, and a reliable standard of living.*

Early Prevention of Violence: Basic Concepts

As the years have passed, and remarkable personal experiences have accumulated, I have become deeply convinced that the crucial need and opportunity for decent human life is in *preventing* bad outcomes, whether it is in individual development, the well-being of populations, or the avoidance of mass violence. To do this, I reiterate that we must accumulate knowledge and start early, building institutions that foster the prevention of human suffering.

What is distinctive about the *early prevention* approach to mass violence? It clarifies a *lifespan* approach to healthy practices, starting in early childhood. It emphasizes *proactive help* to groups or countries getting into trouble—if possible, *prior to any serious damage.* Since danger signals are typically evident years before carnage, there is *ample warning time* to act constructively. It recommends the formulation and dissemination of *specific response options* and *contingency* plans to deal with early warning signals. It draws together *many tools, strategies, and practices* to prevent mass violence—drawn from diverse intellectual, technical, and geographical sources. It clarifies how various *international organizations* can use those tools, strategies, and practices most effectively, and emphasizes the *role of the established democracies* in organized, collaborative, respectful analysis and action. It establishes firm units consisting of informed, caring, empathetic people who cooperate steadily over time. Indeed, the decency of human life depends on *empathy* at every level of the *lifespan*, starting in early childhood.

Education, Health, and Peace: The Struggle for Democracy in Overcoming Prejudice and Wishful Thinking

Fundamental in the long run is work with children and youth to build a solid foundation through education so they can shape a peaceful life that embodies mutual understanding and cooperation among human groups throughout the world. They can grow up to develop a strong *constituency for prevention* of mass violence, supporting leaders who are peacefully inclined, and fostering leaders in various sectors who are informed and skillful in minimizing disputes.

A few years ago, my wife Betty and I published a book titled *Learning to Live Together: Preventing Hatred and Violence in Child and Adolescent Development* (Oxford University Press, 2004). We emphasize that humanity is now a single, interdependent, crowded, worldwide, weaponized species—vulnerable to pervasive stress from severe poverty, harsh disparities, drastic climate events, cyberattacks, and much more. So we humans must *cooperate in our own self-interest*. This should be *crucial in modern education and policy*. If we want to survive and enjoy and learn and help and feel a sense of worth, we must *cooperate on a lifespan basis*.

The strengthening of education includes many elements, for example, understanding *how democracy actually works*; *educating girls* and *women*; teaching *science and technology* for *shared prosperity*; gaining practical *understanding of nonviolent conflict resolution*; and helping leaders understand different cultures and local communities.

Democracy is not an American or Western monopoly. Rather, democratic variations share the common themes of seeking *fairness, widespread participation*, and *broad involvement in decisions* important to the lives of the population and cooperation with people from different groups. They keep ubiquitous human conflict below the threshold of mass violence. Thus, substantial grasp of democratic concepts, aspirations, norms, and practice should be a key component of contemporary education. In the long run, the prevention of mass violence depends heavily on *broad public education* and commitment to these assets. The human and financial costs of this approach are much less than traditional struggles. Preserve Humpty Dumpty, do not smash him.

Problem solving involves a shared effort to *find a mutually acceptable solution*. The parties to a dispute learn to talk freely to one another about their interests and priorities, work together to identify the core differences dividing them, open their minds creatively in search of alternatives that bridge their opposing interests, and jointly assess these alternatives in seeking circumstances of mutual benefit. It is particularly helpful if *friendly neighbors* who have gone through *similar experiences* can be engaged. Benign international organizations, global or regional, can help to identify and encourage such neighbors.

THE SCIENTIFIC COMMUNITY: PROBLEM SOLVING, PUBLIC UNDERSTANDING, AND PATHWAYS TO PEACE

From my own experience over several decades, I am convinced that the scientific community provides understanding, insight, and novel ways of viewing important problems—not least the prevention of deadly conflict. Through their institutions and organizations, scientists and educators can *strengthen research and education* in areas pertinent to *mass violence*: the biology and psychology of aggressive behavior; prosocial child development; peaceful intergroup relations; diminishing prejudice and ethnocentrism; the origins of wars, genocide, and other mass atrocities; and mutual accommodation and early conflict resolution. Science can generate new knowledge and explore the application of such knowledge to urgent problems in contemporary society. Here as elsewhere, *personal friendships* based on *open sharing* of information and trustworthy relationships can be crucial.

The relevant knowledge and skills cover the sciences broadly: physical, biological, behavioral, social. In the world of the twenty-first century, it is crucial to understand incentives and obstacles for cooperation, and strategies that mobilize useful and effective cooperation. We need pervasive insight into the reality of *mutual accommodation for mutual aid.*

No group can justifiably demand that all its interests be fully implemented; but every group should be heard, with full access and input to legislative bodies. Democracy requires a modicum of political equality among citizens. To move in this direction, especially in poor countries, requires civic education, incentives from established democracies, and serious *worldwide commitment to humane and compassionate values.*

The community of established democracies could promote explicitly sustained antidotes to hatred and violence by

1. setting standards for fair, free elections, monitoring their conduct, and following up to assure that the results are correctly implemented;
2. providing education at all levels—from children and youth to political and business leaders as well as scholars in institutions of higher learning—on specific paths to decent interpersonal and intergroup relations, conflict resolution, violence prevention, and enduring peace; and
3. mobilizing intellectual and moral leadership in the universities, democratic entities, religious institutions, and other powerful sectors to focus on these crucial issues—above all on prevention of hatred and violence—and bringing diverse groups together gradually on the basis that *both have to gain from empathetic cooperation.*

Altogether, such activities provide an authentic basis for hope in intergroup relations, regional cooperation, building capacity for internal conflict resolution, and, in the long run, *building capacity through international cooperation for democratic socioeconomic development.*

Indeed, it is often crucial for the parties to come to see that the violent path they are on can only lead to *mutual suicide*. Somehow, they must be helped to move past the wishful thinking of winner-takes-all. Rather they must learn give and take, compromise for the sake of all, and mutual accommodation to foster peace and prosperity—and, indeed, to preserve their own lives. We depend on one another everywhere, whether we are aware of it or not. In every sphere, we must come to educate ourselves on the *pervasive and profound benefits that come from mutual aid* and the enduring benefit of decent human relations in the context of our *common humanity*.

BUILDING CONSTITUENCY
FOR PREVENTING HUMAN SUFFERING

We need constant vigilance to mobilize human capacities for fully learning to live together in personal dignity and shared humanity. We can do a lot to stimulate interest in this great mission, to disseminate the best ideas we can find, and generate better ideas so that our children and grandchildren will be able to move us into a world of decent human relations in spite of all the obstacles.

I reiterate the importance of human intellect, problem-solving ability, fundamental decency, shared aspiration, and common humanity. Yet the tasks are exceedingly difficult and the events of 2014 show no utopia on the horizon. We must learn from the slippages from earlier advances and apply our full capacities in the context of our best values to prevent a great deal of human suffering. This book strives to clarify the dangers, and above all to suggest from research and personal experiences how we can at last learn to live together amicably and fruitfully. Eventually, we can build a *worldwide constituency for prevention* of human suffering. In essence, this would be a global cooperative venture for the shared, enduring mutual benefits that are inherent in the approach that has guided my life.

Afterword

In our later years, Betty and I have been reminded vividly of our early work on social support systems, as we have now benefited from support, encouragement, and care in Washington, DC, getting us through the illnesses and injuries that all too often go with advanced age. In sixty-five years of married life, we have helped each other in every possible way. We especially want to thank the Pascual family (Minda, Greg, Sherry, Rita, and Grace), Susan Smith and David Santini, Elena and Stuart Nightingale, Lee Schorr, Delores Parron and Sherman, Ginger Anthony, Mia Papa, Florita Nicolas, Jack Barchas and Rosemary Stevens, Rick English, Vivien Stewart, David Robinson, Carrie Hunter, Melanne Verveer, Jane and Doug Lute, Melanie Greenberg, Bill Perry, Sam Nunn, Alan Leshner, Biff Bunney, Sid Drell, Kofi and Nane Annan, Noel Lateef, Francis Deng, Laurie and Doug Hofstadter, Richard Wrangham, David and Emilie Riss, Barbara Smuts, Steve Smith, Anne Petersen, Michelle Trudeau, Bruce and Betty Alberts, David Speedie, Nita Yawanarajah, Karen Sklar, Martha and Newton Minow, Graham Allison, Al Carnesale, John Kerry, Dick Lugar, Julie George, Shirley Malcom, Emily Benedetto, Rod Nichols, Sarah Brown, Nancy Merrick, Jack Rowe, Don Kennedy, Deborah Phillips, Marsha Renwanz, and Ruby Takanishi.

For medical care in our later years, we are deeply indebted to Valentin Fuster, David Thomas, again Jack Rowe, Elizabeth Cobbs, Brian Choi, William Dement, Herant Katchadourian, Jeff Bronstein, David Hansen, Craig Faulks, Mark DeAntonio, Jim Mark, Steve Potkin, and Deb Marin. These people extended our lives and the quality of our lives—making it possible to complete this book with the invaluable help of Jennifer Knerr and Sherry Pascual.

I close with a deep tribute to our immediate family. With great foresight and generosity, our daughter Peggy and her husband Peter built an apartment for us into their beautiful home and have seen to it we get any care we need. So too, our son Eric has commuted between Los Angeles and Washington to help us in every way he can. We are so lucky to have three remarkable grandchildren, Rachel, Evan, and David, who give us great stimulation and joy. They and their generation may well be the essential beneficiaries of the messages in this book.

Oddly but happily, in the past month I had four significant honors. These came from the UN, the State Department, Columbia University, and a marvelous reunion of Carnegie people here in Washington. For some reason, people I have had the privilege of working with came together in the fall of 2014 to say how much it meant to them; but I pointed out that the shoe is really on the other foot—their wonderful ingenuity, cooperation, and dedicated efforts made it possible for me to accomplish whatever I did. A singularly vivid example is provided by Jack Barchas, who has collaborated with me for half a century—before, during, and after the Stanford and Cornell years. His personal, scientific, and institutional support has made possible much of this work.

An additional cluster of family has also been exceedingly helpful: Roger Hamburg, Nancy and Richard Walch, Debbie Stein, and Shirley Ward. Bless them all.

So our common human capacities for insight, friendship, empathy, cooperation, and generosity can take us a long way beyond the troubles of our history as a species. I fervently hope that our children and grandchildren—and millions like them around the world—will benefit from the approach expressed in this book.

APPENDIX

Members of the Carnegie Commission on Preventing Deadly Conflict

David A. Hamburg, co-chair
Cyrus Vance, co-chair
Gro Harlem Brundtland
Virendra Dayal
Gareth Evans
Alexander L. George
Flora MacDonald
Donald F. McHenry

Olara A. Otunnu
David Owen
Shridath Ramphal
Roald Z. Sagdeev
John D. Steinbruner
Brian Urquhart
John C. Whitehead
Sahabzada Yaqub-Khan

SPECIAL ADVISERS TO THE COMMISSION

Arne Olav Brundtland

Herbert S. Okun

MEMBERS OF THE ADVISORY COUNCIL

Morton Abramowitz
Ali Abdullah Alatas
Graham T. Allison
Robert Badinter
Carol Bellamy
Harold Brown
McGeorge Bundy
Jimmy Carter
Lori Damrosch
Francis M. Deng
Sidney D. Drell
Lawrence S. Eagleburger
Leslie H. Gelb

David Gompert
Andrew J. Goodpaster
Mikhail Gorbachev
James P. Grant
Lee H. Hamilton
Theodore M. Hesburgh
Donald L. Horowitz
Michael Howard
Karl Kaiser
Nancy Kassebaum Baker
Sol M. Linowitz
Richard G. Lugar
Michael Mandelbaum

Robert S. McNamara
William H. McNeill
Sam Nunn
General Olusegun Obasanjo
Sadako Ogata
Javier Pérez de Cuéllar
Condoleezza Rice
Eliot L. Richardson

Harold H. Saunders
George P. Shultz
Richard H. Solomon
James Gustave Speth
Desmond Tutu
Admiral James D. Watkins, USN
Elie Wiesel
I. William Zartman

COMMISSION STAFF

Jane E. Holl
John Stremlau
Esther Brimmer
Thomas J. Leney
Robert E. Lande
Cornella Carter-Taylor
Katherine Veit

Gabrielle Bowdoin
Marilyn Butler-Norris
Wanda Ellison
Jeffrey R. Pass
Heather Podlich
Traci Swanson
Nancy Ward

Recommended Readings

CHAPTER 1: EARLY INFLUENCES

Bowlby, John. *A Secure Base: Parent-Child Attachment and Healthy Human Development*. New York: Basic Books, 1988.

Brewer, Marilyn, and Norman Miller. *Intergroup Relations*. Pacific Grove: Brooks/Cole Publishing Company, 1996.

Deutsch, Morton, and Peter Coleman, eds. *The Handbook of Conflict Resolution: Theory and Practice*. San Francisco: Jossey-Bass, 2000.

Hamburg, David. *Today's Children: Creating a Future for a Generation in Crisis*. New York: Times Books/Random House, 1992.

Hamburg, David, and Beatrix Hamburg. *Learning to Live Together: Preventing Hatred and Violence in Child and Adolescent Development*. New York: Oxford University Press, 2004.

Schlesinger, Arthur M., Jr., *The Coming of the New Deal, 1933–1935*. Vol. 2, *The Age of Roosevelt*. Boston: Houghton Mifflin Company, 1965.

Wistrich, Robert S. *Antisemitism: The Longest Hatred*. New York: Pantheon Books, 1991.

CHAPTER 2: THE WIDER WORLD AND WARTIME EXPERIENCES

Deutsch, Karl W. *The Analysis of International Relations*. 3rd ed. Englewood Cliffs, NJ: Prentice Hall, 1988.

Hamburg, David, and J. Adams. "A Perspective on Coping Behavior: Seeking and Utilizing Information in Major Transitions." *Archives of General Psychiatry* 17 (1967): 277–284.

Howard, Michael. *War in European History*. Oxford: Oxford University Press, 1976.

Kennedy, David M. *Freedom from Fear: The American People in Depression and War, 1929–1945*. New York: Oxford University Press, 1999.

Redlich, Fritz. *Hitler: Diagnosis of a Destructive Prophet*. New York: Oxford University Press, 1999.

Roll, David L. *The Hopkins Touch: Harry Hopkins and the Forging of the Alliance to Defeat Hitler*. Oxford: Oxford University Press, 2013.

Stern, Fritz. *Five Germanys I Have Known*. New York: Farrar, Straus and Giroux, 2006.

Weitz, Eric D. *Weimar Germany: Promise and Tragedy*. Princeton, NJ: Princeton University Press, 2007.

CHAPTER 3: INSTITUTION BUILDING

America's Vital Interest in Global Health: Protecting Our People, Enhancing Our Economy, and Advancing Our International Interests. Washington, DC: National Academy Press, 1997.

Berkowitz, Edward D. *To Improve Human Health: A History of the Institute of Medicine.* Washington, DC: National Academy Press, 1998.

Cavalli-Sforza, Luigi Luca. *Genes, Peoples, and Languages.* New York: North Point Press, 2000.

Cohen, Jon. "Chimpanzee Research Today." *Science.* April 2, 2010: 30–43.

Collier, Paul. *The Bottom Billion: Why the Poorest Countries Are Failing and What Can Be Done About It.* New York: Oxford University Press, 2007.

Dahl, Robert. *On Democracy.* New Haven, CT: Oxford University Press, 1998.

DeVore, Irven, ed. *Primate Behavior: Field Studies of Monkeys and Apes.* New York: Holt, Rinehart and Winston, 1965.

Gertner, Jon. *The Idea Factory: Bell Labs and the Great Age of American Innovation.* New York: The Penguin Press, 2012.

Goodall, Jane, and David A. Hamburg. "Chimpanzee Behavior as a Model for the Behavior of Early Man: New Evidence on Possible Origins of Human Behavior." In Vol. 6, *American Handbook of Psychiatry,* edited by David A. Hamburg and H. Brodie, 14–43. New York: Basic Books, 1975.

Hamburg, David. "An Evolutionary Perspective on Human Aggression." In *The Development and Integration of Behavior: Essays in Honour of Robert Hinde,* edited by Patrick Bateson, 419–457. Cambridge, UK: Cambridge University Press, 1991.

———. "Conflict Prevention and Health: An Array of Opportunities." In *Anna Lindh Programme on Conflict Prevention,* edited by Anders Mellbourn, 33–34. Brussels: Madariaga Foundation, 2006.

———. "Human Aggressiveness and Conflict Resolution." In *World Change and World Security,* edited by Norman Dahl and Jerome Wiesner, 39–60. Cambridge, MA: MIT Press, 1978.

———, ed. *Psychiatry as a Behavioral Science.* Behavioral and Social Sciences Survey Monograph Series. Englewood Cliffs, NJ: Prentice Hall, 1970.

Hamburg, David, Glen Elliott, and Delores Parron, eds. *Health and Behavior: Frontiers of Research in Biobehavioral Sciences.* Washington, DC: National Academy Press, 1982.

Hamburg, David, and Jane Goodall. "Factors Facilitating Development of Aggressive Behavior in Chimpanzees and Humans." In *Determinants and Origins of Aggressive Behavior,* edited by J. de Wit and W. Hartup, 59–85. The Hague: Mouton Publishers, 1974.

Hamburg, David A., and Elizabeth R. McCown, eds. *The Great Apes.* Menlo Park, CA: Benjamin/Cummings, 1997.

Hamburg, David A., and Michelle Trudeau, eds. *Biobehavioral Aspects of Aggression.* New York: Alan R. Liss, 1981.

Haq, Mahbub ul. *Reflections on Human Development.* New York: Oxford University Press, 1995.

Hare, Brian, Victoria Wobber, and Richard Wrangham. "The Self-Domestication Hypothesis: Evolution of Bonobo Psychology Is Due to Selection against Aggression." *Animal Behaviour* 83 (2012): 573–585.

Katchadourian, Herant. *The Way It Turned Out.* Singapore: Pan Stanford Publishing, 2012.

McGrew, William C., Linda F. Marchant, and Toshisada Nishida, eds. *Great Ape Societies.* Cambridge, UK: Cambridge University Press, 1996.

Merrick, Nancy J. *Among Chimpanzees: Field Notes from the Race to Save Our Endangered Relatives.* Boston: Beacon Press, 2014.

Mitani, John C., Josep Call, Peter M. Kappeler, Ryne A. Palombit, and Joan B. Silk, eds. *The Evolution of Primate Societies.* Chicago: University of Chicago Press, 2012.

Power, Samantha, and Graham Allison, eds. *Realizing Human Rights: Moving from Inspiration to Impact.* New York: St. Martin's Press, 2000.

Sherif, Muzafer, and Carolyn Sherif. *Groups in Harmony and Tension: An Integration of Studies on Intergroup Relations.* New York: Octagon Books, 1966.

Shultz, George S., Sidney D. Drell, Henry A. Kissinger, and Sam Nunn. *Nuclear Security: The Problems and the Road Ahead*. Stanford, CA: Hoover Institution Press, 2014.

Solana, Javier. "The Health Dimension to Security." In *Anna Lindh Programme on Conflict Prevention*, 2006 ed. Health and Conflict Prevention, edited by Anders Mellbourne, 9–14. Brussels: Madariaga Foundation, 2006.

Smuts, Barbara, B. Dorothy, L. Cheney, Robert M. Seyfarth, Richard W. Wrangham, and Thomas T. Struhsaker, eds. *Primate Societies*. Chicago: University of Chicago Press, 1986.

Stanford Historical Society. Oral History Program. Interview with David Hamburg, conducted by Christy Wise. Available at https://stanford.app.box.com/s/lnwnds4ug85snrwso2b3.

Wrangham, Richard. *Catching Fire: How Cooking Made Us Human*. New York: Basic Books, 2009.

——. "Why Apes and Humans Kill." In *Conflict: The 2005 Darwin College Lecture Series*, edited by Martin Jones and Andy Fabian, 43–62. Cambridge, UK: Cambridge University Press, 2006.

Wrangham, Richard, and Luke Glowacki. "Intergroup Aggression in Chimpanzees and War." *Human Nature* 23, no. 1 (March 2012): 5–29. Available at www.ncbi.nlm.nih.gov/pubmed/22388773.

CHAPTER 4: THE CARNEGIE YEARS

A. War and Peace: Prevention of Mass Violence

Allen, John. *Desmond Tutu: The Rainbow People of God: The Making of a Peaceful Revolution*. Foreword by Nelson Mandela. New York: Doubleday, 1994.

Allison, Graham T. *Nuclear Terrorism: The Ultimate Preventable Catastrophe*. New York: Henry Holt/Times Books, 2004.

Allison, Graham, and Philip Zelikow. *Essence of Decision: Explaining the Cuban Missile Crisis*. 2nd ed. New York: Addison Wesley Longman, Inc., 1999.

Benesch, Susan. "Inciting Genocide, Pleading Free Speech." *World Policy Journal* 21, no. 2 (Summer 2004): 62–69.

Boutwell, Jeffrey, Michael T. Klare, and Laura W. Reed, eds. *Lethal Commerce: The Global Trade in Small Arms and Light Weapons*. Cambridge, MA: Committee on International Security Studies, 1995.

Brewer, M. B. "The Psychology of Prejudice: Ingroup Love or Outgroup Hate." *Journal of Social Issues* 55, no. 3. (1999): 429–444.

Brown, Archie. *The Gorbachev Factor*. New York: Oxford University Press, 1997.

Brown, Archie, and Lilia Shevtsova, eds. *Gorbachev, Yeltsin and Putin: Political Leadership in Russia's Transition*. Washington, DC: Carnegie Endowment for International Peace, 2001.

Brown, Michael, and Richard N. Rosecrance. *The Costs of Conflict: Prevention and Cure in the Global Arena*. Lanham, MD: Rowman and Littlefield, 1999.

Bundy, McGeorge, William J. Crowe, and Sidney D. Drell. *Reducing Nuclear Danger: The Road Away from the Brink*. New York: Council on Foreign Relations Press, 1993.

Carnegie Commission on Preventing Deadly Conflict. *Preventing Deadly Conflict, Final Report*. Washington, DC: Carnegie Commission on Preventing Deadly Conflict, 1997.

——. *Preventive Diplomacy, Preventive Defense, and Conflict Resolution: A Report of Two Conferences at Stanford University and the Ditchley Foundation*. Perspectives on Prevention. New York: Carnegie Corporation of New York, October 1999.

Chayes, Abram, and Antonia Handler Chayes, eds. *Preventing Conflict in the Post-Communist World: Mobilizing International and Regional Organization*. Washington, DC: The Brookings Institution, 1996.

Cirincione, Joseph. *Bomb Scare: The History and Future of Nuclear Weapons.* New York: Columbia University Press, 2007.

Cortright, David, ed. *The Price of Peace: Incentives and International Conflict Prevention.* Foreword by David A. Hamburg and Cyrus R. Vance. Carnegie Commission on Preventing Deadly Conflict, Carnegie Corporation of New York. Lanham, MD: Rowman and Littlefield, 1997.

Craig, Gordon A., and Alexander L. George. *Force and Statecraft: Diplomatic Problems of Our Time.* 3rd ed. New York: Oxford University Press, 1995.

Drell, Sidney. *Facing the Threat of Nuclear Weapons.* Seattle: University of Washington Press, 1983.

Drell, Sidney, and James Goodby. *The Gravest Danger: Nuclear Weapons.* Stanford, CA: Hoover Institution Press, 2003.

Fisher, Roger, and William Ury. *Getting to Yes: Negotiating Agreement without Giving In.* New York: Penguin, 1983.

Garwin, Richard L., and Georges Charpak. *Megawatts and Megatons: The Future of Nuclear Power and Nuclear Weapons.* Chicago: University of Chicago Press, 2001.

Genocide Prevention Task Force. *Preventing Genocide: A Blueprint for U.S. Policymakers.* Washington, DC: United States Holocaust Memorial Museum, the American Academy of Diplomacy, and the Endowment of the United States Institute of Peace, 2008.

George, Alexander, ed. *Avoiding War: Problems of Crisis Management.* Boulder, CO: Westview Press, 1991.

Goodpaster, Andrew J. "When Diplomacy Is Not Enough: Managing Multinational Military Intervention." A Report to the Carnegie Commission on Preventing Deadly Conflict. New York: Carnegie Corporation of New York, 1996.

Greenberg, Melanie C., John H. Barton, and Margaret E. McGuinness. *Words over War: Mediation and Arbitration to Prevent Deadly Conflict.* Carnegie Commission Series. Lanham, MD: Rowman and Littlefield, 2000.

Hamburg, David A. *No More Killing Fields: Preventing Deadly Conflict.* Lanham, MD: Rowman and Littlefield, 2002.

Hayner, Priscilla B. *Unspeakable Truths: Transitional Justice and the Challenge of Truth Commissions.* 2nd ed. New York: Routledge, 2011.

Jentleson, Bruce W., ed. *Opportunities Missed, Opportunities Seized: Preventive Diplomacy in the Post–Cold War World.* Carnegie Commission on Preventing Deadly Conflict Series. Lanham, MD: Rowman and Littlefield, 1999.

Kennedy, Donald, David Holloway, Erika Weinthal, Walter Falcon, Paul Ehrlich, Roz Naylor, Michael May, Steven Schneider, Stephen Fetter, and Jor-San Choi. *Environmental Quality and Regional Conflict: A Report to the Carnegie Commission on Preventing Deadly Conflict.* New York: Carnegie Corporation of New York, 1998. Available at www.amherst.edu/media/view/100916 /original/EnvironmentalQualityAndRegionalConflict.pdf.

Lucas, Adetokunbo O. *It Was the Best of Times: From Local to Global Health: The Autobiography of Adetokunbo Olumide Lucas.* Ibadan, Nigeria: Bookbuilders, Editions Africa, 2010.

Lute, Douglas E. "Improving National Capacities for Response to Complex Emergencies." A Report to the Carnegie Commission on Preventing Deadly Conflict. New York: Carnegie Corporation of New York, 1997.

Mandela, Nelson. *Long Walk to Freedom: The Autobiography of Nelson Mandela.* Boston: Little Brown, 1994.

Matlock, Jack F., Jr. *Autopsy on an Empire: The American Ambassador's Account of the Collapse of the Soviet Union.* New York: Random House, 1995.

Minow, Martha. *Between Vengeance and Forgiveness: Facing History after Genocide and Mass Violence.* Boston: Beacon Press, 1998.

Naimark, Norman M. *Fires of Hatred: Ethnic Cleansing in Twentieth-Century Europe.* London: Harvard University Press, 2001.

National Research Council of the National Academies. *The Unique U.S.-Russian Relationship in Biological Science and Biotechnology: Recent Experience and Future Directions.* In cooperation with the Russian Academy of Sciences. Washington, DC: National Academy Press, 2013.

Peck, Connie. *Sustainable Peace: The Role of the UN and Regional Organizations in Preventing Conflict.* Carnegie Commission Series. Lanham, MD: Rowman and Littlefield, 1998.

Rubin, Barnett L. *Blood on the Doorstep: The Politics of Preventive Action.* New York: Century Foundation Press, 2002.

Sen, Amartya. *Identity and Violence: The Illusion of Destiny.* New York: Norton, 2006.

Snyder, Jack. *From Voting to Violence: Democratization and Nationalist Conflict.* New York: W. W. Norton and Company, 2000.

Solomon, Frederic, and Robert Marston, eds. *The Medical Implications of Nuclear War.* Foreword by Lewis Thomas. Washington, DC: Institute of Medicine, National Academy of Sciences, National Academy Press, 1986.

Stares, Paul B., and Micah Zenko. "Partners in Preventive Action: The United States and International Institutions." *Council Special Report*, no. 62 (September 2011). Council on Foreign Relations: Center for Preventive Action.

Stern, Jessica. *Terror in the Name of God: Why Religious Militants Kill.* New York: HarperCollins, 2003.

Taubman, Philip. *The Partnership: Five Cold Warriors and Their Quest to Ban the Bomb.* New York: HarperCollins, 2012.

Zartman, I. William, ed. *Preventive Negotiation: Avoiding Conflict Escalation.* Carnegie Commission on Preventing Deadly Conflict Series. Lanham, MD: Rowman and Littlefield, 2000.

B. Education for Science, Prosocial Behavior, and Peace

Aronson, Elliot. *Nobody Left to Hate: Teaching Compassion after Columbine.* New York: W. H. Freeman, 2000.

Bandura, Albert. *Aggression: A Social Learning Analysis.* Englewood Cliffs, NJ: Prentice Hall, 1973.

Brooks-Gunn, Jeanne, and Anne C. Petersen. *Girls at Puberty: Biological and Psychological Perspectives.* New York: Plenum Press, 1983.

Carnegie Council on Adolescent Development. *Great Transitions: Preparing Adolescents for a New Century.* Concluding Report. New York: Carnegie Corporation of New York, 1995.

Casper, Gerhard. *The Winds of Freedom: Addressing Challenges to the University.* New Haven, CT: Yale University Press, 2014.

Clark, Margaret S., ed. *Prosocial Behavior.* Newbury Park, CA: Sage Publications, 1991.

Cousens, Elizabeth M. "Conflict Prevention." In *The UN Security Council from the Cold War to the 21st Century*, edited by David M. Malone, 108–115. Boulder, CO: Lynne Rienner Publishers, 2004.

Deutsch, Morton. "Educating for a Peaceful World." *American Psychologist*, May 1993.

Diamond, Larry. *Developing Democracy: Toward Consolidation.* Baltimore: Johns Hopkins University Press, 2005.

———. *The Spirit of Democracy: The Struggle to Build Free Societies throughout the World.* New York: Times Books, 2008.

Ekbladh, David. *Education for Peace in the Twenty-First Century: A Report on the Advisory Meeting on the Academic Program of the University for Peace.* University for Peace, United Nations, New York, March 23–24, 2001.

Hamburg, Beatrix A., Delbert Elliott, and Kirk R. Williams, eds. *Violence in American Schools: A New Perspective.* New York: Cambridge University Press, 1998.

Hamburg, David. "Understanding and Preventing Nuclear War: The Expanding Role of the Scientific Community." In *The Medical Implications of Nuclear War*, edited by Frederic Solomon and Robert Martson, 1–11. Washington, DC: National Academy Press, 1986.

Hamburg, David, Beatrix Hamburg, and Jack Barchas. "Anger and Depression in Perspective of Behavioral Biology." In *Emotions: Their Parameters and Measurement*, edited by L. Levi, 235–278. New York: Raven Press, 1975.

Hoffman, David E. *The Dead Hand: The Untold Story of the Cold War Arms Race and Its Dangerous Legacy*. New York: Doubleday, 2009.

Lerner, Richard M., Anne C. Petersen, Rainer K. Silbereisen, and Jeanne Brooks-Gunn, eds. *The Developmental Science of Adolescence: History through Autobiography*. New York: Psychology Press, 2013.

Rosenfield, Patricia L. *A World of Giving: Carnegie Corporation of New York—A Century of International Philanthropy*. New York: Public Affairs, 2014.

Sen, Amartya. "Democracy as a Universal Value." In *The Global Divergence of Democracies*, edited by Larry Diamond and Marc F. Plattner, 3–18. Baltimore: Johns Hopkins University Press, 2001.

Skolnikoff, Eugene B. *The Elusive Transformation: Science, Technology, and the Evolution of International Politics*. Princeton, NJ: Princeton University Press, 1993.

Slavin, Robert E. *Cooperative Learning: Theory Research and Practice*. 2nd ed. Boston: Allyn and Bacon, 1995.

Smiley, Tavis, with David Ritz. *Death of a King: The Real Story of Dr. Martin Luther King Jr.'s Final Year*. New York: Little, Brown and Company, 2014.

Stewart, Vivien. *A World-Class Education: Learning from International Models of Excellence and Innovation*. Alexandria, VA: ASCD Member Books, 2012.

Zartman, I. William, Mark Anstey, and Paul Meerts, eds. *The Slippery Slope to Genocide: Reducing Identity Conflicts and Preventing Mass Murder*. New York: Oxford University Press, 2012.

CHAPTER 5: FROM LOCAL TO GLOBAL INSTITUTIONS

Annan, Kofi. *Interventions: A Life in War and Peace*. New York: The Penguin Press, 2012.

———. *Towards a Culture of Prevention: Statements by the Secretary-General of the United Nations*. New York: Carnegie Commission on Preventing Deadly Conflict, 1999.

———. *We the Peoples: A UN for the 21st Century*. Edited by Edward Mortimer. Boulder, CO: Paradigm Publishers, 2014.

Barchas, Jack, and JoAnn Difede, eds. "Psychiatric and Neurologic Aspects of War." Vol. 1208, *Annals of the New York Academy of Sciences*. Boston: Blackwell Publishing, 2010.

Boutros-Ghali, Boutros. *An Agenda for Peace: Preventive Diplomacy, Peacemaking and Peace-Keeping: Report of the Secretary-General Pursuant to the Statement Adopted by the Summit Meeting of the Security Council on 31 January 1992*, A/47/277–S/24111. June 17, 1992. Available at http://unrol.org/files/A_47_277.pdf.

Brinkley, Douglas. *The Unfinished Presidency: Jimmy Carter's Journey beyond the White House*. New York: Viking, 1998.

Carnegie Commission on Preventing Deadly Conflict. *Preventing Deadly Conflict: Final Report*. Washington, DC: Carnegie Commission on Preventing Deadly Conflict, 1997.

George, Alexander, and David A. Hamburg. "Toward an International Center for Prevention of Genocide." *Foreign Policy Forum* 15/16 (2005): 85–89.

Hamburg, D. A., and K. Ballentine. "Boutros Boutros-Ghali's Agenda for Peace: The Foundation for a Renewed United Nations." In *Boutros Boutros-Ghali: Amicorum discipulorumque liber* 1 (1998): 489–509.

Kennedy, Paul. *The Parliament of Man: The Past, Present, and Future of the United Nations*. New York: Random House, 2006.

Office of the AU Panel of Eminent African Personalities. *Back from the Brink: The 2008 Mediation Process and Reforms in Kenya*. African Union Commission, 2014.

Peck, Connie. "Special Representatives of the Secretary-General." In *The UN Security Council: From the Cold War to the 21st Century*, edited by David M. Malone, 325–339. Boulder, CO: Lynne Rienner Publishers, 2004.

Peck, Connie, and Eleanor Wertheim, eds. *Strengthening the Practice of Peacemaking and Preventive Diplomacy in the United Nations: The UNITAR Approach*. Geneva: United Nations Institute for Training and Research, 2014.

CHAPTER 6: CONCLUSION

Ackerman, Peter, and Christopher Krueger. *Strategic Nonviolent Conflict: The Dynamics of People Power in the Twentieth Century*. Westport, CT: Praeger, 1994.

Armstrong, Karen. *Fields of Blood: Religion and the History of Violence*. New York: Random House, 2014.

Barraclough, Geoffrey. *Main Trends in History*. New York: Holmes and Meier, 1991.

Behrman, Greg. *The Most Noble Adventure: The Marshall Plan and the Time When America Helped Save Europe*. New York: Free Press, 2007.

Bok, Sissela. *Mayhem: Violence as Public Entertainment*. Reading, MA: Perseus, 1998.

Boutros-Ghali, Boutros. *Egypt's Road to Jerusalem: A Diplomat's Story of the Struggle for Peace in the Middle East*. New York: Random House, 1997.

Bredeson, Carmen. *Presidential Medal of Freedom Winners: Collective Biographies*. Springfield, NJ: Enslow Publishers, Inc., 1996.

Christopher, Warren. *Chances of a Lifetime: A Memoir*. New York: Scribner, 2001.

Coelho, George V., David A. Hamburg, and John E. Adams, eds. *Coping and Adaptation*. New York: Basic Books, 1974.

Commonwealth Commission on Respect and Understanding. *Civil Paths to Peace: Report of the Commonwealth Commission on Respect and Understanding*. London: Commonwealth Secretariat, August 2007.

Davis, David Brion. *Inhuman Bondage: The Rise and Fall of Slavery in the New World*. New York: Oxford University Press, 2006.

De Cerreno, Allison L. C., and Alexander Keynan. *Scientific Cooperation, State Conflict: The Roles of Scientists in Mitigating International Discord*. New York: New York Academy of Sciences, 1998.

Deng, Francis. *Talking It Out: Stories in Negotiating Human Relations*. New York: Columbia University Press, 2006.

Deutsch, Morton. *The Resolution of Conflict: Constructive and Destructive Processes*. New Haven, CT: Yale University Press, 1973.

European Centre for Conflict Prevention and Swedish Peace Team Forum. *Preventing Violent Conflict and Building Peace: On Interaction between State Actors and Voluntary Organizations*. Stockholm: XBS Grafisk Service, 2002.

George, Alexander L. *On Foreign Policy: Unfinished Business*. Boulder, CO: Paradigm Publishers, 2006.

Glover, Jonathan. *Humanity: A Moral History of the Twentieth Century*. New Haven, CT: Yale University Press, 2000.

Goldschmidt, Walter. *Man's Way: A Preface to the Understanding of Human Society*. New York: Holt, Rinehart and Winston, 1959.

Goldstein, Joshua S. *Winning the War on War: The Decline of Armed Conflict Worldwide*. New York: Dutton, 2011.

Gorbachev, Mikhail. "On Nonviolent Leadership." In *Essays on Leadership*, edited by David A. Hamburg and Cyrus R. Vance, 67–70. New York: Carnegie Commission on Preventing Deadly Conflict, 1998.

Greenblatt, Stephen. *The Swerve: How the World Became Modern*. New York: W. W. Norton and Company, 2011.

Hamburg, David A. *Give Peace a Chance: Preventing Mass Violence*. Boulder, CO: Paradigm Publishers, 2013.

————. *Preventing Genocide: Practical Steps Toward Early Detection and Effective Action*. Rev. and updated ed. Boulder, CO: Paradigm Publishers, 2010.

Hamburg, David A., Alexander George, and Karen Ballentine. "Preventing Deadly Conflict: The Critical Role of Leadership." *Archives of General Psychiatry* 56 (November 1999): 971–976.

Hamburg, David A., and Cyrus R. Vance. *Essays on Leadership*. New York: Carnegie Commission on Preventing Deadly Conflict, 1998.

Hinde, Robert. *Changing How We Live: Society from the Bottom Up*. Nottingham, UK: Spokesman, 2011.

Howard, Michael. *The Invention of Peace: Reflections on War and International Order*. New Haven, CT: Yale University Press, 2000.

Human Security Now. New York: Commission on Human Security, 2003.

InterAcademy Council. *Inventing a Better Future: A Strategy for Building Worldwide Capacities in Science and Technology*. Study Panel on Promoting Worldwide Science and Technology. Jacob Palis and Ismail Serageldin, co-chairs. Amsterdam: InterAcademy Council, 2005. Available at www.interacademycouncil.net/24026/25995.aspx.

————. *Realizing the Promise and Potential of African Agriculture*. Study Panel on Agricultural Productivity in Africa. Speciosa Kazibwe, Rudy Rabbinge, and M. S. Swaninathan, co-chairs. Amsterdam: InterAcademy Council, 2004. Available at www.interacademycouncil.net/24026/AfricanAgriculture.aspx.

Isaacson, Walter. *The Innovators: How a Group of Hackers, Geniuses, and Geeks Created the Digital Revolution*. New York: Simon and Schuster, 2014.

Jentleson, Bruce W. *American Foreign Policy: The Dynamics of Choice in the 21st Century*. 3rd ed. New York: W. W. Norton and Company, 2007.

Kupchan, Charles A. *How Enemies Become Friends: The Sources of Stable Peace*. Princeton, NJ: Princeton University Press, 2010.

Lenski, Gerhard, Patrick Nolan, and Jean Lenski. *Human Societies: An Introduction to Macrosociology*. 7th ed. New York: McGraw-Hill, Inc., 1995.

Mandelbaum, Michael. *The Ideas That Conquered the World: Peace, Democracy, and Free Markets in the Twenty-First Century*. New York: Public Affairs, 2002.

McNeill, William H. *The Pursuit of Power: Technology, Armed Force and Society since AD 1000*. Chicago: University of Chicago Press, 1982.

Nye, Joseph S., Jr. *Understanding International Conflicts: An Introduction to Theory and History*. 2nd ed. New York: Longman, 1997.

Ogata, Sadako. *The Turbulent Decade: Confronting the Refugee Crises of the 1990s*. New York: W. W. Norton, 2005.

Pinker, Steven. *The Better Angels of Our Nature: Why Violence Has Declined*. New York: Viking, 2011.

Roberts, Adam, and Timothy Garton Ash. *Civil Resistance and Power Politics: The Experience of Non-Violent Action from Gandhi to the Present*. New York: Oxford University Press, 2009.

Rock, Stephen R. *Why Peace Breaks Out: Great Power Rapprochement in Historical Perspective*. Chapel Hill: University of North Carolina Press, 1989.

Sandel, Michael. *What Money Can't Buy: The Moral Limits of Markets*. New York: Farrar, Straus and Giroux, 2012.

Sen, Amartya. *Development and Freedom*. New York: Knopf, 1999.

———. *The Idea of Justice*. Cambridge, MA: Belknap/Harvard University Press, 2009.

Sennett, Richard. *Together: The Rituals, Pleasures and Politics of Cooperation*. New Haven, CT: Yale University Press, 2012.

Staub, Ervin. *Overcoming Evil: Genocide, Violent Conflict, and Terrorism*. New York: Oxford University Press, 2011.

———. *The Roots of Evil: The Origins of Genocide and Other Group Violence*. Cambridge: Cambridge University Press, 1989.

Stiglitz, Joseph. *Making Globalization Work*. New York: W. W. Norton, 2006.

———. *The Price of Inequality: How Today's Divided Society Endangers Our Future*. New York: W. W. Norton, 2010.

Taylor, Donald M., and Fathali M. Moghaddam. *Theories of Intergroup Relations: International Social Psychological Perspectives*. 2nd ed. London: Praeger Publishers, 1994.

Ury, William. *Getting to Peace: Transforming Conflict at Home, at Work, and in the World*. New York: Viking, 1999.

World Bank. *World Development Report: Conflict, Security, and Development*. Overview by President Robert Zoellick. Washington, DC: World Bank, 2011.

About the Author

David A. Hamburg, MD, is Visiting Scholar at the American Association for the Advancement of Science and DeWitt Wallace Distinguished Scholar at Weill Cornell Medical College. He is President Emeritus of the Carnegie Corporation of New York, where he served as president from 1982 to 1997. Hamburg has a long history of leadership in research and innovation in biological and behavioral sciences. He has been a pioneer in prevention of mass violence. He has been a professor at Stanford University and Harvard University, President of the Institute of Medicine, National Academy of Sciences, and President of the American Association for the Advancement of Science as well as a member of the American Philanthropic Society and American Academy of Arts and Sciences. Among many honors, Dr. Hamburg has been awarded the Public Welfare Medal of the National Academy of Sciences and the Presidential Medal of Freedom (the highest civilian award of the United States).